A COMPENDIUM OF PETERS PARTICULAR PALATABLES

and

Family Recollections

Happy Cooking Kathy

by
MARY PETERS
1990

Mary Peters

Copyright 1990 by Mary Peters
All rights reserved including the right to
reproduce this book or parts thereof in any form
Library of Congress Catalogue Card Number 68-13245
Printed in the United States of America

TABLE OF CONTENTS

- APPETIZERS .... pages 1 - 18
- BEVERAGES & DRINKS .... pages 19 - 32
- BREADS .... pages 33 - 56
- CAKES AND FROSTINGS .... pages 57 - 78
- CANDY .... pages 79 - 86
- CASSEROLES, QUICHES, CREPES .... pages 87 - 106
- COOKIES .... pages 107 - 128
- DESSERTS .... pages 129 - 154
- MEATS .... pages 155 - 174
- PIES .... pages 175 - 186
- POTATOES, PASTA, RICE .... pages 187 - 198
- POTPOURRI .... pages 199 - 216
- POULTRY & GAME .... pages 217 - 236
- PRESERVES, JELLIES, PICKLES .... pages 237 - 242
- SALADS .... pages 243 - 258
- SALAD DRESSINGS .... pages 259 - 266
- SAUCES .... pages 267 - 276
- SEAFOOD & FISH .... pages 277 - 288
- SOUPS .... pages 289 - 300
- VEGETABLES .... pages 301 - 315

Douglas Peters has taken me to most of the great restaurants in the United States and Europe and some in the Far East. There is hardly a place that I cannot recollect and remember with happiness either for the cuisine or the very special ambiance. The adventure of eating is a great pleasure; but, as with all pleasure, there is a price to pay. But it is an imposition whose importance is constantly denied when one considers the returns rendered. I really did not presume that I would be as impressed by the art of gastronomy as I have been. Surely one needs to cook in order to appreciate the art. But a good deal of my personal bliss has been measured by sharing fine times at an excellent table with wonderful people. How can one improve on that combination. It is making love.

Thankyou to all you dear people who have so generously shared your special recipes. If I didn't love you, I wouldn't have asked you to participate.

No one will be happier than my husband and children and relatives when these recipes get under cover. They have long endured harassment and entreaty as time has marched on to produce this small volume. Even childbirth seems a bit less bleak to a 60-year old after going through book-pains to deliver this tome. I salute the artistry of authorship.

I
dedicate
this
COOKBOOK
to
my dear husband and traveling companion
DOUGLAS E. PETERS
who
kindly kept his nose out of it.

This book is for all these zany children shown above and quite a few more. The most fun the Peters family has is "Calling the Clan" and setting a festive board. At full strength, we are lucky to number around 35 and there never seems to be a shortage of food. We are so blessed by the Lord and this little book is a testimonial to His first premise

L O V E and a lot of it

In answer to the cry - "Mom, how do you make - - - - - ?" a cookbook was born incorporating recipes from many family members and friends. But as the recipes increased, stories of people and lovely recollections came creeping in that needed to be recalled. And, all of a sudden, the stories became as important to me as the recitation of food preparation and ingredients.

So the book is really a documentation of the life and times of a family and, I hope, will recall some stories that the children might have forgotten and that will give them again, warmth around the heart.

BROTHER DOUG   BROTHER JOHN

Lawyers
Hunters
Raconteurs
Gourmets
Barbershoppers
All 'Round Good Fellows

BROTHER PETE

THREE PETERS BROTHERS
FAMILIES

Mary Dunnell married Douglas Peters, Jr.
  Douglas III married Mary Wilcox
    Matthew
    Billy
    Kathleen
    Brian
  Gere married Steve Simmons
    Kate
  Malcolm married Maggie Moore
    Alex

Irene Dunnell married John M. Peters
  Scott married Jane Tarson
    Claire
  John, Jr. married Sue McElderry
  Jim married Brigitte Faulant
  Cory

Jane Savidge married Peter J. Peters
  Jeffrey
  Andrew
  Mark
  Jake married Lisa Sawin

Grandmother Jerry Peters Dodson
Grandmother Irene Stickney Dunnell
Aunt Daphne Peters
Aunt Gladys Peters
Grandmother Irene Savidge

CORY PETERS
ARTIST EXTRAORDINAIRE

Cory Peters' bright humor and considerable artistic talent needs to be especially noted as she is responsible for the artwork of the section dividers and the covers of the Cookbook.
But more importantly, she grabbed the baton as I was wavering near the finish line and pulled this book together. Were it not for her printing expertise and unlimited help, I am sure we would not have gone to press. Thankyou, dearest niece, for your enormous knowledge, your tenacity to the job, and always your lovely positive attitude that makes me your most ardent fan. Thankyou from ALL of us.

TABLE GRACES

(Hold Hands)

        God is great
        God is good
        And we thank Him for our food.
        By His hand
        We all are fed
        Give us, Lord, our daily bread.
        HALLELUJAH!

Bless, O Lord, these gifts of food to our use
And bless us to Thy everlasting service,
In Jesus' name we ask it - Amen

Give us grateful hearts, Our Father,
For all Thy mercies;
And make us mindful
Of the needs of others,
Through Jesus Christ our Lord - Amen

Give food to the hungry, we pray you, Father;
And may those of us who have plenty to eat,
hunger for You!
Through Christ Our Lord, we pray. Amen

-----O Heavenly Father-----

We thank Thee for food
And remember the hungry.
We thank Thee for Health
And remember the sick.
We thank Thee for friends
And remember the friendless.
We thank Thee for freedom
And remember the enslaved.
May these remembrances stir us to service
That Thy gifts to us may be used for others – Amen

Appetizers

Finger Sandwiches

APPETIZERS

Beranek/Whitmer Hot Canapés	15
Boursin Au Poivre	6
Boursin Cheese Appetizers	7
Chafing Dish Hot Crabmeat Dip	16
Cheese Ball	13
Cheese Cookies	9
Cheese Puffs	8
Chicken Liver Spread	7
Chopped Chicken Liver Pate	11
Christmas Cereal Mix	14
Cocktail Dip	8
Crab Meat Canapés	12
Crab Puff	15
Curried Chicken Balls	12
Duck Breast Broil – 4 Star Appetizers	15
Easy and Tasty Guacamole Dip	10
Hot Artichoke Dip	5
Hot Chipped Beef Dip	10
Hot Crab Spread	11
Layered Mexican Dip	11
Pate Normandy	3
Philo-Tri Curry/Walnut chicken	4
Pickled Watermelon and Bacon Appetizers	9
Salmon Party Ball	13
Sardine Pate	16
Shrimp Spread	14
Spinach Balls	5
Spinach Dip in Bucket Bread	5
Tomato Sauce for Cocktail Hamburger Balls	9
Veggie Squares	4
Zucchini Appetizers	10

PATE NORMANDY   Jane S. Peters

2 Tblsp vegetable oil
2 Tblsp butter
1 onion, coarsely chopped
4 Tblsp Calvados (French apple brandy)
1 Granny Smith (tart) apple, peeled, cored and chopped
salt and pepper to taste
1/2 tsp thyme
1 lb chicken livers
1/4 lb sweet butter

Heat vegetable oil and butter in a heavy saucepan, add the onions, apples, salt and pepper and thyme and sauté them until they are lightly brown; cover the pan and simmer until the apples are soft (about 3 min.). Then remove this mixture from the pan, and put aside. In the same pan, saute the chicken livers, adding a little more butter if necessary. Make sure not to overcook them. The liver should still be pink inside. Heat the Calvados, put aflame and pour over the chicken livers; when the flame has died out, add the onions and apples, mix well and let cool. Put mixture through food processor, add 1/4 lb of butter, a Tblsp at a time and puree til smooth. Place in dish and refrigerate for several hours before serving.

Maggie Peters is an example for us all. She uses time so beautifully that in 6 years she has moved and decorated a house, helped produce an Appetizer Cook Book, been Club and City golf champion, taught school full time, gotten her Master's Degree, works at her Dad's Bank in "spare" moments, takes on huge Christmas sewing projects and always seems to be there for her family and friends and party times. Now, she and Malcolm have presented us with wonderful Alex. If Maggie didn't bring the hors d'oeuvres, we'd all go into a decline.

PHILO - TRI CURRY/WALNUT CHICKEN   Maggie Peters

1 pound Philo pastry
2 chicken breasts, cooked & cubed
1/2 cup chopped walnuts   1/2 tsp salt
2 Tblsp butter   1/8 tsp salt
2 1/2 Tblsp flour   1 tsp curry powder
1 cup milk   1 pound butter, melted & cooled

1. Thaw dough as directed on package
2. Put 2 Tblsp butter in sauce pan, add curry and flour and cook 2 minutes. Add milk and stir until thick. Add chicken cubes & walnuts, season with salt, pepper and cool.
3. Take one sheet of Philo dough and brush with butter, repeat a second time and a third time. Cut sheets that are 9 x 13 in half horizontally and then cut 3 times vertically making 6 sections of dough. Place a spoonful of chicken mixture on each square and fold as you would a flag into triangles. Now pay attention:
As the rectangle faces you on your working table,
   A. Take the LEFT lower corner and fold over the chicken to the center of the dough.
   B. Take the RIGHT lower corner and fold to the RIGHT top corner.
   C. Then take the RIGHT lower corner and fold to the LEFT top corner. Voila! a flag fold!
   D. Ask your resident Boy Scout if all else fails. Believe me, these are worth it - people just scream and yell for more.

Put triangles on a cookie sheet, brush with melted butter and bake 10 minutes at 400°. Serve with Sweet-Sour sauce and Hot Mustard Sauce purchased in any grocery Oriental section.

VEGGIE SQUARES
Another famous Peters Putt and Pork sensation

Flatten a **package of refrigerated Crescent Roll dough** in the bottom of a jelly roll pan. Stretch the edges of the dough to fit. Bake til light brown, about 8 minutes. Mix an **8 oz. pkg. of cream cheese** with **1 cup of mayonnaise** and **1 package of Knorr's Vegetable Soup Mix** and spread over cooled crescent roll mix. Cut up veggies including **broccoli, radishes, carrots, cauliflower, green pepper and celery** in SMALL pieces and spread a layer over cream cheese and roll mix. Press down vegetables with spatula and cut into squares.

> The greatest thing about senility is that you can hide your own Easter eggs   -- Fanny Jones

SPINACH DIP IN BUCKET BREAD — Maggie Peters

1 round loaf of bucket bread, dark rye
Cut center from rye bucket bread, cube into bite size pieces as you will use them to eat the dip.
1 10 oz. pkg frozen chopped spinach
1 cup sour cream
1 cup Hellman's mayonnaise
1 pkg. Knorr's Vegetable Soup Mix (dry)
1 8 oz. can water chestnuts, chopped
Thaw spinach and squeeze dry. Combine spinach with remaining ingredients and chill 3 hours or more. Fill center of bucket bread with dip and serve with reserved bread cubes.

SPINACH BALLS

10 oz. pkg. frozen chopped spinach, cooked and well drained
2 cups herb seasoned crumb stuffing
1 cup chopped onion   **3 eggs, slightly beaten**
6 Tblsp melted margarine
6 Tblsp grated Parmesan cheese
3/4 tsp garlic salt   **1/4 tsp pepper**

Mix all ingredients in a bowl. Shape into two-inch balls. Bake at 350° for 20 minutes.

HOT ARTICHOKE DIP — Maggie Peters

1 12 oz. can artichoke hearts
1 cup mayonnaise
1 cup chopped green chilis
8 oz. Parmesan cheese

Drain artichokes and chop into pieces. Mix with rest of ingredients and put in 9" pie plate. Bake at 375° for 35 to 40 minutes. Serve with Triscuits.

PRIDE GOETH BEFORE A FALL
AND A HAUGHTY SPIRIT BEFORE DESTRUCTION
(ISD)

BOURSIN AU POIVRE _____ Irene Peters

1 8 oz. package cream cheese or Neufchatel
1 clove garlic, crushed
1 tsp caraway seed
1 tsp basil
1 tsp dill weed
1 tsp chopped chives

Blend cheese with seasonings, mold into a round flat shape and sprinkle with lemon pepper on all sides. Refrigerate for several days, before using.

BOURSIN CHEESE APPETIZERS

1 8 oz. package cream cheese
1/4 cup sweet butter, softened
1 Tblsp chives
1/2 pound of snow peas
1/3 cup sour cream
1 small clove garlic, pressed
1 Tblsp chopped parsley
1/4 tsp thyme
salt to taste and ground pepper (1 tsp) coarse

Wash, drain, remove stems and dry snow peas; split open. Put soft cheese in pastry tube and fill pea pods with cheese using a decorative tip. Delicious!

CHICKEN LIVER SPREAD   Mom Schenck

Simmer **2 lbs. chicken livers** in a little chicken stock til they are just cooked through. Grind them with **4 hard cooked eggs** in a food processor - not too fine. Chop **2 medium onions** and brown them in **1/4 cup rendered chicken fat.** Combine all ingredients and salt and pepper to taste. Serve with freshly made thin toast points.

Thank heavens for people like Jerry Peters Dodson who made life such a pleasure for so many people. How she did love a party; birthdays, anniversaries, and Holidays were all reason for the Clan gathering, usually with Helga Petersen in the kitchen tending the Leg of Lamb and the Eggplant casserole. Jerry's parties were legion - luncheons, bridge parties, dinners. And she had a knack for selecting the proper gifts for people that was uncanny. The presents were always wrapped elegantly and presented with elaborately inscribed cards that made the recipients' ego soar with happiness.

COCKTAIL DIP _____ Jerry Dodson

This is Jerry Dodson's famous potato chip dip written in her own handwriting. This can be thinned out for salad dressing or used as a fresh vegetable dip . . .

Cocktail Dip

2/3 c Mayonnaise
1/3 c Sour Cream
1 TS chopped parsley   (TABLESPOON)
1 TS chopped onion   (TABLESPOON)
1 tsp Beau Monde   (TEASPOON)
1 Tsp Dill Weed   (TEASPOON)

CHEESE PUFFS _____ Helga Petersen

1 egg white, beaten stiff   **1 pinch of salt**
1/4 tsp baking powder   **2 tsp Worcestershire sauce**
2 tsp prepared mustard
1/2 lb American "nippy" cheese or use New York sharp cheddar

Have cheese rather dry and grate it fine. Cut 1 1/2" bread rounds with a canape cutter from white store bread. Toast these rounds on **one side** til tan. Mix together cheese, mustard, Worcestershire sauce, baking powder and salt. Gently stir in egg white, beaten stiff. Mound filling on the UNTOASTED side of the bread rounds and put under the broiler until cheese puffs up and begins to tan. Serve hot.

Cory sez: I don't remember a whole lot about my parents' dinner parties other than being patted on the head and pinched on the cheek and trying to stay out of sight. BUT I DO REMEMBER pilfering these cheese puffs from the kitchen when Helga wasn't looking, and they are so good you can eat them until you get really sick.

> Let every man, if possible, gather some good books under his roof, and obtain access for himself and family to some social library. Almost any luxury should be sacrificed to this.
> -- W.E. Channing

CHEESE COOKIES — Jerry Dodson

1/2 pound Nucoa (margarine)	1/2 pound snappy cheese
1 tsp salt	1 tsp boiling water
1 Tblsp baking powder	1 cup flour

Grate cheese, and blend with softened margarine. Add water, then rest of ingredients. Make a roll and refrigerate. Slice thin and sprinkle with paprika. Bake at 400° around 5 minutes.

PICKLED WATERMELON AND BACON APPETIZERS

One pound of lean bacon
One jar of pickled watermelon rind

Wrap 1/2 slice of bacon around bite size pieces of watermelon pickle rind and fasten with toothpicks. Put on cookie sheet and bake at 350° for at least 1/2 hour til bacon looks cooked - serve warm. YUM!

TOMATO SAUCE FOR COCKTAIL HAMBURGER BALLS
Eva Deane

1 cup catsup	1 Tbsp onion, fine mince
1/2 tsp salt	1 Tbsp celery, fine mince
3 Tblsp brown sugar	1 tsp chili powder
2 Tblsp vinegar	1/4 tsp paprika
1 tsp Worcestershire sauce	1/4 tsp cayenne
1 tsp prepared mustard	1/4 cup boiling water

Cook slowly for 1/2 hour. Pour over tiny cooked hamburger balls in chafing dish & serve with toothpicks. To make Barbecue sauce, just add green pepper & soy sauce.

ZUCCHINI APPETIZERS — Ruth Larsen

3 cups shredded zucchini
1 medium clove garlic, chopped fine
1 cup Bisquick mix
1/2 cup onion, chopped fine
1/2 cup grated Parmesan cheese
2 Tblsp finely chopped parsley
1/2 tsp basil
salt and pepper
4 eggs, slightly beaten
2 Tblsp green pepper
1/2 tsp marjoram
1/2 cup vegetable oil

Mix all ingredients and spread in a 9 x 13 baking pan. Bake 25 minutes at 350° til set. Cool slightly and cut in squares.

EASY & TASTY GUACAMOLE DIP — Cory Peters

2 to 3 avocados, peeled and mashed
3 to 5 big glops of sour cream (this is a precise measurement...)
Hot or medium picante sauce, to taste
Coarsely chopped tomatoes and onions

Serve with lots of taco chips. Even better if it sits overnight in the fridge.

HOT CHIPPED BEEF DIP — Martha Walsh

8 oz. cream cheese
1 pkg dried chipped beef, cut up
1/2 cup green pepper, diced small
1/4 tsp pepper
1/2 cup broken pecan meats
1/2 tsp salt
2 Tblsp milk
2 Tblsp finely chopped onion
1/2 tsp garlic salt
1/2 cup sour cream
2 Tblsp melted butter

Mix first 8 ingredients together and put in a baking dish that you will serve the dip in. Sauté the pecans in the melted butter until brown but not burned. Watch carefully and keep stirring. Salt the nuts and spread over the top of the dip. Bake dip for 20 minutes in 350° oven until hot and serve with rounds of ice box rye bread thinly sliced.

CHOPPED CHICKEN LIVER PATE´   Momo

1 lb. chicken livers washed and drained on towels
4 Tblsp rendered fresh chicken fat
2 onions, diced   3 hard cooked egg yolks
1 tsp salt   1/4 tsp freshly ground black pepper
1 oz. very good cognac

Heat 2 tblsp of chicken fat in a skillet and cook the onions until they are brown. Remove from pan.
Cook livers in same pan for 10 minutes in the remaining oil from the onions. Grind onions, liver and egg yolks in a food processor until you have a smooth mixture.
Add salt, pepper, cognac and remaining fat.
Mix and taste for seasoning.
Chicken liver pate will firm up as it cools.
This must be refrigerated, as it is very perishable.

LAYERED MEXICAN DIP   Maggie Peters

Layer I: On round pan or plate
   1 can refried beans softened with 1/2 cup sour cream
Layer II: **Guacamole dip - one carton**
   Rest of the one pint of sour cream
Layer III: **Shredded mozzarella and cheddar cheese**
Layer IV: **Chopped tomatoes and black olives**
Chill dip and serve with tortilla chips.

HOT CRAB SPREAD

2 packages of GOOD mock crabmeat, frozen
1 pound of cream cheese
1/2 cup mayonnaise
1 bunch green onions, chopped
2 dashes hot red pepper sauce
1 tsp Worcestershire sauce
A handful of slivered almonds

Defrost and chop crab meat coarsely and mix all ingredients together after softening cream cheese. Put in bake-and-serve dish and bake at 350° for 20 minutes. Serve with crackers.

CURRIED CHICKEN BALLS

**Cream 1 8 oz. package cream cheese with
4 Tblsp mayonnaise.
Sauté 1 1/2 cups chopped almonds in
1 Tblsp butter until just lightly browned.
Add 2 cups cooked chicken finely chopped
3 Tblsp chopped chutney
1 tsp salt
2 tsp curry powder**
Combine all ingredients with cream cheese and roll in hands into walnut size balls.
1 cup grated coconut
Roll each ball in coconut and chill in fridge. Makes about four dozen.

CRAB MEAT CANAPES   Helga Petersen

**1 can of very good crabmeat - can substitute mock crab
Cut 1 1/2" rounds of white store-bought bread** with canapé cutter. Throw crusts to birds. Chop **1 tsp of capers,** add to crab meat that has been drained and broken up. Add **2 dashes of Worcestershire sauce, a little salt and pepper and 2 tablespoons of mayonnaise.** Mound crabmeat mixture on rounds of white bread circles and top with paprika. Refrigerate till served.

COLLEGE BUDDIES

Nancy Jenkins lived a few blocks from us in Fremont, and she and Gordie recalled an extraordinary Saturday evening when they were dinner guests along with 6 other lovable people at our house. Our son, Malcolm, was a sophomore in Highschool, really needed extra cash and agreed to police the kitchen and dishes while his Father and I held forth at the dining room table.

As dessert finished, Mac appeared in the dining room in a chef's toque, a chef's apron and hip waders. The dishwasher had overflowed.

So the gentlemen guests phoned a sainted plumber who declared he would come at 10 o'clock of a Saturday evening to put us to rights and everyone was so grateful for his supereminence that we insisted he join us at the dinner table for a nightcap. A most entertaining evening!

❖ ❖ ❖ ❖ ❖ ❖ ❖ ❖ ❖

CHEESE BALL_____Lou Filbert

1 8 oz. package Philadelphia Cream Cheese
1/4 lb. grated sharp cheddar cheese
1 3 oz. piece of Roquefort cheese or Blue cheese
Mix above cheeses with
1/3 cup mayonnaise
1/2 tsp curry   **1 1/2 Tblsp Worcestershire sauce**
1 tsp lemon juice   **garlic salt to taste**
Form into a ball when mixed and roll in chopped parsley or chopped nuts.

❖ ❖ ❖ ❖ ❖ ❖ ❖ ❖ ❖

SALMON PARTY BALLPhyllis Weinberg

1 lb. can red salmon   **1 tsp horseradish**
1 8 oz. pkg cream cheese   **1/4 tsp salt**
1 Tblsp lemon juice   **1/4 tsp liquid smoke**
2 tsp grated onion   **1/2 cup chopped pecans**
3 Tblsp chopped parsley

Drain salmon well, remove skin and bones. Combine all ingredients but nuts and parsley. Form into ball and roll in chopped nuts and parsley.

SHRIMP SPREAD _____ Joyce Pogge

1 lb. or 1 1/2 cups chopped shrimp or crab
3/4 cup chopped celery
1/2 tsp salt
1/2 cup Miracle Whip salad dressing
1/4 tsp curry powder
1 Tblsp lemon juice
2 tsp chopped onion
1/2 tsp Worcestershire sauce

Mix together, chill well and serve with sippets or crackers.

CHRISTMAS CEREAL MIX _____ Maggie

In a big roaster or foil pan
1 pkg Rice Chex   1 pkg Wheat Chex
1 pkg Cheerios   1 1/2 pkg Pretzels (knots or sticks)
1 lb mixed nuts   1 can cocktail peanuts
1 box Cheez-its   Melt 3/4 lb butter and add
1 1/2 Tblsp Worcestershire sauce

Put cereal in roaster pan and heat for 15 minutes at 250°. Then add butter and Worcestershire and stir every 15 minutes for 45 minutes.

Add 1 1/2 Tblsp celery salt
1 Tblsp garlic salt
Stir into cereal mix and stir every 30 minutes for 1 1/2 hours. Cool and put into baggies or gift cans. Can be frozen.

HOW'S THIS FOR A MENU ON A PICNIC TABLE?
BRISKET B B Q
HARVEST POTATOES
PEAS AND CHEESE SALAD
BUTTERMILK CAKE & STRAWBERRY ICE CREAM
or
SOUR CREAM RAISIN PIE

The recipes are all in this book waiting for you . . . !

BERANEK/WHITMER HOT CANAPES

Divide CLUB CRACKERS into as many sections as you care to prepare. Mound freshly grated Parmesan cheese on each cracker and top with a strip, cut to fit, of very lean bacon. Place sections on cooling racks over cookie sheets to bake at 200° for 2 hours. Serve warm and fresh.

❖ ❖ ❖ ❖ ❖ ❖ ❖ ❖ ❖

DUCK BREAST BROIL - 4 STAR APPETIZERS
Malcolm Peters

4 Mallard breasts are marinated overnight in a plastic baggie, in:
2 Tblsp bourbon
2 Tblsp Soy sauce
1 Tblsp cooking oil   Hard to believe, isn't it?

Following day, remove breasts from bag, put under hot broiler for 3 to 5 minutes per side depending on breast thickness. Remove from broiler and slice into bite size pieces. Pieces should be medium rare. Serve pieces with toothpicks and a small bowl of Durkees dressing for optional dipping. A Fremont favorite and served throughout the Mallard season when birds are plentiful.

CRAB PUFFS  Joyce Pogge

1/2 pound crab meat or shrimp
1/4 cup chopped olives either green or black
2 Tblsp finely chopped onion
2 Tblsp finely chopped green pepper
2 Tblsp finely chopped celery
3 drops Tabasco sauce
1/2 to 3/4 cups Hellman's mayonnaise
24 baked miniature cream puffs cut in half (Cream puff recipe in Dessert section)

Combine all ingredients with enough mayonnaise to make a smooth filling. Fill shells and heat uncovered on a paper plate in a moderate oven for two minutes or so. Serve immediately. Makes 24.

CHAFING DISH HOT CRABMEAT DIP — Joani Mitten

Joani and David Mitten used to have EVERYBODY over at any time on Christmas Day when they lived on Nye Avenue and then at Lake Ventura. I always thought it an act of courage to assemble the multitudes; but Heavens, everyone was so grateful to get out of the house on that day and show off the children, that they made a bee-line for cocktails and fun and usually this dip, which was a great favorite of us all.

Cook together:

4 1/2 Tblsp butter
4 1/2 Tblsp flour
3/4 cup milk
dash of nutmeg

3/4 cup whipping cream
1 Tblsp Worcestershire sauce
1/2 cup dry sherry
salt and pepper

Into this fold **1 pound of good crabmeat** cut in bite size pieces and place over hot water in a chafing dish accompanied with crackers for dipping.

SARDINE PATE — Mom Schenck

3 cans sardines in oil
6 hard cooked eggs chopped very fine
2 small onions minced
1 Tblsp chopped parsley
Salt and pepper to taste

Mix all ingredients until smooth and stir in enough **mayonnaise** to make a spreadable pate.
Add **1 Tblsp brandy**
A bit of lemon juice to taste
Cool the pate and serve with Melba Toast.

NEW YEAR'S EVE
at Momo & Poppo's

Katie & Bear
discussing
PICNIC MENU:

**1 jar of honey
2 Tootsie Pops**

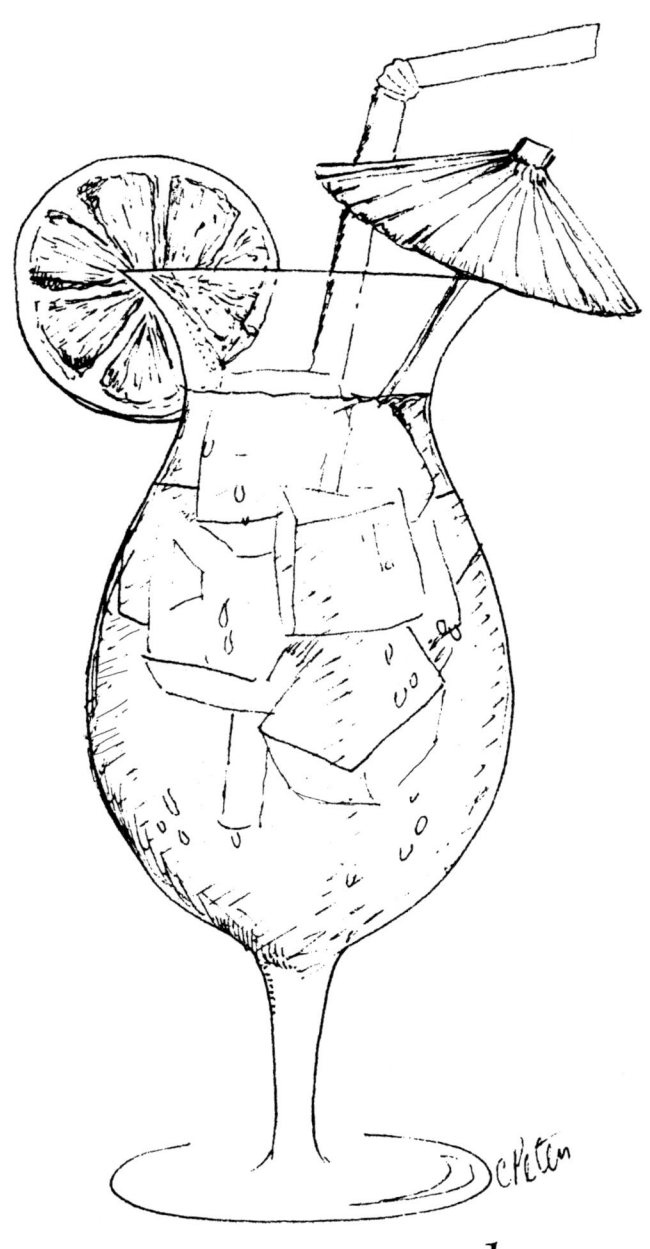

Beverages & Drinks

BEVERAGES

Bailey's Irish Cream	22•
Bengal Lancer Punch	30•
Bloody Bull	28 •
Bloody Mary	28 •
Bronx Cocktail	25•
Brown Jersey	28•
Cappuccino	30•
Cider Punch	25•
Cocoa from Scratch	27•
Egg Nogg	21•
Egg Nogg for Thousands	21 •
Fish House Punch	26•
Fresh Peach Daiquiri	29•
Gin Twist	22•
Governor's Coupe	25 •
Harry's Mimosa	28•
Horses Neck	28•
Junior League Mint Ice Tea	30•
P.E.O. Wassail	26•
Pina Colada	22•
Raffles – Singapore Sling	29•
Red Velvet Punch	29•
Sangria	25•
Sazerac Cocktail	21•
Scorpion Punch	22•
Screwdriver	28•
Spring Fever	29•

SAZERAC COCKTAIL   New Orleans •

1 jigger Old Overholt Rye whiskey
6 shakes Peychaud bitters
3 shakes Angostora bitters
1 splash simple syrup
1 splash of Pernod
Add ice and a lemon twist

EGG NOGG

1 pint Four Roses bourbon whiskey
1 jigger Jamaica rum
1 pint milk
1 pint cream
6 eggs, separated
Add 1 cup sugar to the egg yolks and beat well.
In another bowl add 1 Tblsp sugar to egg whites and beat til medium stiff.

Mix all the ingredients, except the egg whites which you may fold in last, just before serving. Put nogg in punch bowl and float a **quart square of vanilla ice cream** in the bowl. Sprinkle with nutmeg when serving the cups.

EGG NOGG for thousands

1 gallon of 1/2 and 1/2 cream
1/2 tsp salt
2 quarts bourbon (Four Roses)
1 pint Jamaica rum
3 cups sugar
24 eggs

Beat 24 egg YOLKS with 2 cups sugar until thick. Add salt to the egg WHITES and beat until thick. Add 1 cup of sugar and beat until stiff. Fold the yolks into the 1/2 and 1/2 and combine all the ingredients. Put in punch bowl and float a **1/2 gallon of vanilla ice cream.** Serve in punch cups and dust with nutmeg.

SCORPION PUNCH

1 1/2 Fifths of golden rum
2 oz. gin
1/2 Fifth of sweet White Wine
2 oz. brandy
1 1/2 pints of Orgeat syrup (almond flavor)
1 pint of lemon juice
1/2 pint of orange juice

Pour over cracked ice in a punch bowl and garnish with gardenias. Serves 12. *Just be sure they're REAL good friends.*

BAILEY'S IRISH CREAM — Maggie Peters•

1 1/2 cup Scotch whiskey
3 eggs
1 can Eagle Brand Condensed Milk (14 oz.)
1 pint Half and Half cream
1 tsp coconut extract
1 Tblsp canned Hershey's chocolate syrup

Put all ingredients in blender and blend for 60 seconds. Serve over the rocks or in hot coffee. Will keep in refrigerator for weeks.

PINA COLADA

5 oz. pineapple juice
4 oz. golden Rum
2 oz. coconut syrup
2 oz. fresh lime juice
Shake with 3 or 4 ice cubes and serve.

GIN TWIST

2 oz. gin
1 1/2 oz. grapefruit juice
1/2 tsp Creme de Menthe
A twist of mint, add ice and a little soda water.
Pretty and cool for summer or a loud ladies' luncheon.

Serving gourmet dinners at one another's homes was a very frequent treat between the Peters and the Dr. Harveys. Setting a fine table and serving a wonderfully prepared meal for adulation by the guests was tantamount to batting .450 . . . .
Then, it started. Whimsical references were made to small failures which ultimately turned into waggish jesting. Finally, the Doctor and the Lawyer went to the mattresses and letters of pungent criticism were sent through the mails. I herewith include a letter from each of the
GREAT CRITICIZERS

Mr. and Mrs. Douglas E. Peters
The Olde Haslam House
Fremont, Nebraska

            Re: Dinner, October 21
Dear Mr. and Mrs. Peters:
  We wish to thank you for a very enjoyable evening, however, we feel that constructive criticism is valuable for neophytes in their culinary endeavors.
  The menu, which was ostentatious, was confusing to the epicure with two languages included. Lack of foresight was evident when the wine list was omitted, and lack of preparation was obvious when the guests arrived to find the host and hostess busily preparing the basics of dinner.
  The Crepes Homard rated very good, and it is only with sadness that this critique must include the rest of the meal. Leftover hors d'oeuvres in no way enhance canned soup. The capon breasts were AMAZINGLY large, explaining the paucity of the sauce (which the host stated was good!) We agree with you that the spinach was excellent, and do thank you for bringing this to our attention. The wild rice was a little bland and overcooked. The pumpkin bread was good, but we question the propriety of a sweet bread with this meal. We found the salad refreshing and tasty. The soufflé rated superb. Wines accompanying dinner were cold, and merit no other comment. After dinner liqueurs were limited, and the Absinthe was poisoned.
       Sincerely, Dr. and Mrs. Alexander Thom Harvey

Dr. and Mrs. Alexander T. Harvey
2049 North I Street
Fremont, Nebraska

Re: Dinner, July 9

Dear Dr. and Mrs. Harvey:
    It goes without saying that Mrs. Peters and I always accept an invitation to dine at your manse with some trepidation as we have had some rather unsettling experiences in the past which are so familiar to all of us as to not bear repeating. Keeping the past separate from the present is sometimes difficult, but I believe the following critique will be free of prejudice occasioned by previous incidents.
    Vichyssoise has long been thought of as a culinary experience with a cold, finely mashed or ground potato base which has been mixed with a generous and tastefully contrived portion of rich cream and other ingredients to make a smooth, palatable, well-chilled pre-entree delight. Unfortunately, the vichyssoise served the other evening was somewhat lumpy, somewhat thin, lacked the usual wedge of lemon and, while artfully served, on a scale of one to ten would be apt to rate about a three. As usual, the toast served with the soup was delicious, and for that matter, is without peer in Dodge County, nay, in the state of Nebraska.
    The veal roast was, to say the least, filled with gristle, but the sauce was delicious. The canned carrots were an interesting addition to the evening's repast, and the string beans would rate a nine. It was good to note the absence of flies in the butter. In general, the entire dining room and silver were much improved over our last visit, as was the service. The Mouton Cadet was of no note, but the Bordeaux was first rate. While not the best red wine to pass my lips in recent months, it certainly was excellent, although it must have cost a pretty penny.
    The dessert is better left unmentioned as I have seen finer soufflés prepared by the Freshman students in the Home Economics class at the Junior High level.
    Both Mrs. Peters and myself have put aside this painful summary for some days, but hope it will serve more as a guide for future endeavors on the part of the culinary experts in the Harvey household than as a criticism of the insufficiencies of the chef and his helper.

                                Bon appetite
                                Henri Soufflé and wife

SANGRIA
Marilyn Diers

1 bottle Zinfandel wine   1 cup strawberries, sliced thin
1 cup fresh pineapple chunks   1 lemon, sliced thin
Sprinkle **sugar** over the fruit and combine well. •
Add wine, cover and chill overnight. •
Strain into a pitcher next day and add **1 pint soda water and ice.** Place•
in glasses with fresh berries or a pineapple stick and serve with a thin •
slice of lemon.•

CIDER PUNCH

8 cups apple cider   1 cup sugar
3 sticks cinnamon   2 cups orange juice
2 tsp whole cloves   1/2 cup lemon juice
1 whole nutmeg   1/2 cup apple brandy
dash of Grand Marnier

Simmer cider 15 minutes with spices and sugar. Add juices and brandy. Without the liquor, this is very nice served to ladies for a Winter evening Meeting with mixed doughnuts.

GOVERNOR'S COUPE
Blackstone Hotel

1 scoop coffee ice cream   1/2 oz. light cream
1 oz. Kahlua   1/4 oz. vodka

Whirl in blender til smooth, pour in Champagne glass and dust with grated nutmeg.

BRONX COCKTAIL
Very popular at grand dinner parties during the turn of the Century.

1 part Gin
1 part French vermouth (dry)
1 part Italian vermouth (sweet)
1 part orange juice

Plenty of ice, shake well, and serve in 3 oz. glass with a slice of orange.

P.E.O. WASSAIL
From Cottey College at the Hanging of the Greens
Serves 100

1 1/4 gallons Apple cider
2 pints Grapefruit juice
1 1/2 pints Spiced tea
Claret wine, as desired

1 1/2 pints Orange juice
1 cup Cranberry juice
Simple syrup

To make simple syrup: Mix **1 pint of water** with **2 pints of sugar** and bring to a boil.•
To make spiced tea: Tie **1 tsp of whole cloves with 1 whole cinnamon stick** in a cloth bag and simmer 10 minutes with **1 1/2 pints of tea.**
Heat all ingredients together and add more sugar if needed. Let wassail stand overnight or longer.

FISH HOUSE PUNCH

Fish House Punch should be approached with reverence and deep respect for its noble history. George Washington and Lafayette drank it and it has been handed down to us intact. Bob Weinberg served a large bowl of this at Christmastime at his elegant Men's Haberdashery store in Fremont, Nebraska for many years. Friends would remember very little of the rest of the evening. Except for the time that an abused Christmas tree was dragged one snowy winter's eve into the store, carols were sung and Judeo-Christian relations were at an all-time high. There must be something patriotic about this punch as the Weinbergs and the Peters always flew flags at their homes and were faithful about seeing them raised.

Over a large block of ice in a 1 gallon punch bowl place:
Juice of 6 lemons
1/2 pound of powdered sugar
1/2 pint of Brandy
1/4 pint Peach Brandy
1/4 pint Jamaica rum 151 proof
3 quarts of sparkling water

Serve cool.

"BREAKFAST IN BED, PLEASE"

COCOA FROM SCRATCH_____*(Like Mother used to make)*

1 heaping tsp of cocoa   **1 heaping tsp of sugar**
Mix together with a little water **Add 2 cups whole milk**
1/2 tsp vanilla   **Pinch of salt**

Stir and cook til hot and pour in large cups.
Add marshmallows - sip slowly

HORSES NECK

1 jigger Bourbon
Fill glass with Ginger ale & a loooong spiraling twist of lemon zest.

SCREWDRIVER

1 jigger of Vodka
Fill glass with fresh orange juice
Squeeze in a section of fresh lime

HARRY'S MIMOSA

Fill a chilled glass 2/3 full of Champagne and top off with fresh orange
juice and 1 Tblsp of Curacao.

BLOODY BULL

1 jigger of Vodka
Fill glass half full of tomato juice and half full of canned bouillon.
Add a twist of lemon.

BLOODY MARY

1 jigger of Vodka
Fill glass with: **tomato juice, lemon juice, celery salt, Worcestershire sauce, pepper, a shot of Tabasco,** and add a stalk of celery or cucumber as a swizzle stick.

BROWN JERSEY

In a Waring Blender place
1 egg
4 jiggers of **Creme de Cocoa**
3 jiggers good **Bourbon**
1 heaping tsp brown sugar
1 jigger Brandy

Blend briefly and add **Milk** to the above mixture to 1" from the top of the blender. Blend briefly again. Pour over cracked ice.

In the morning, this drink is better than an Alka Seltzer; but you cannot go through life depending on B. J.'s.

RAFFLES - SINGAPORE SLING

1 ounce Gin
3/4 ounce Cherry Brandy
few drops of Cointreau
few drops of Benedictine
juice of 1/2 lemon medium size
2 ounces of pineapple juice, fresh if possible
1 to 2 drops Bitters
1 dash Grenadine, for color

Cover the shaker and shake hard for about 10 seconds with 4 ice cubes. Pour the foaming liquid in a 10 ounce glass with 2 ice cubes. Garnish with a pineapple wedge and a cherry.

FRESH PEACH DAIQUIRI

Into a blender:
1/2 medium UNPEELED peach, chunk cut
1 1/2 oz. good Rum
Juice of half a lime
At least 3 tsp of sugar - taste to be sure
1 cup or less crushed ice

Process in blender for about 10 seconds at high speed. Very good for a ladies luncheon.

RED VELVET PUNCH

8 cups cranberry juice cocktail
6 oz. can frozen orange juice concentrate
6 oz. can frozen pineapple juice concentrate
6 oz. can frozen lemonade concentrate
2 cups Brandy
2 fifths chilled Champagne

Combine all fruit juices and chill. Pour into punch bowl over ice. Add champagne, stir and garnish with slices of lemon and lime. Add the Brandy only if you want a powerful punch.

SPRING FEVER   Bill Schenck •

1 jigger Rum
1 jigger Rose's lime juice
Fill with Schweppe's tonic water
Decorate with a slice of lime

JUNIOR LEAGUE ICE TEA

If there is anything in this family that is universally made, it is the following recipe. It is lovely when served at a luncheon, but the family loves to lace it with Rum or Vodka for a summer cooler. We all make ice tea in gallon containers, but this is the basic recipe.

1/2 cup lemon juice
1 1/4 cup sugar
Steep the above in 2 cups of boiling water
3 small tea bags
6 sprigs fresh mint
Steep the above in 2 cups of boiling water also.

Strain together after steeping 20 minutes into a pitcher and add 4 cups of cold water. Chill and serve over ice.

CAPPUCCINO — from the Tosca Cafe in San Francisco

1 tsp grated Hershey sweet chocolate
1 oz. hot water
3 oz. hot milk
1 oz. brandy

BENGAL LANCER PUNCH

1 cup sugar
1/2 cup orange juice
1/2 cup fresh pineapple juice
1/2 cup lemon juice
3 oz. Barbados Rum
3 oz. Curacao
1 qt. of Claret
1 pint sparkling water
1 qt. Champagne

CHARRRRRRRRGE!!!

HOW TO FRY YOUR HAND AND LEAVE A BIG SCAR THOUGH OVER SIXTY

1. ☐ Fill the kitchen up with lots of people who are drinking and talking and standing in front of the hot pad drawer.

2. ☐ Get grease so hot it smokes. Be sure someone asks you, at that moment, to retrace your genealogy starting just before the Revolutionary War.

3. Allow a guest to scream as she is jostled and spills her drink.

4. ☐ Be sure the phone is ringing and that no one answers it. Also, more guests should be arriving at the front door and the doorbell is ringing.

5. Is your dog underfoot and wants to be picked up?

6. Who brought all those children?

7. ☐ Someone has asked for a towel to get the Dip off the davenport and carpet.

8. ☐ Is your husband doing anything or is he just going to stand there forever talking and laughing. Mr. Personality! Whose idea was it to have this party, anyway?

9. "You did what?" "Boy, that looks nasty."

10. ☐ "No, I don't know where the Unguentine is. Let's see, the last time I saw it, Billy had lit a match and dropped it on his toe, and that was April or May, I think."

11. ☐ "Does it hurt? You want a drink? Oh, hi Al, did you see the Raiders last week? Some game, huh?"

"What do you mean, you don't like it?"

Packing for a weekend •
at•
Momo & Poppo's•
• • • • • •
Leave room for the dogs!•

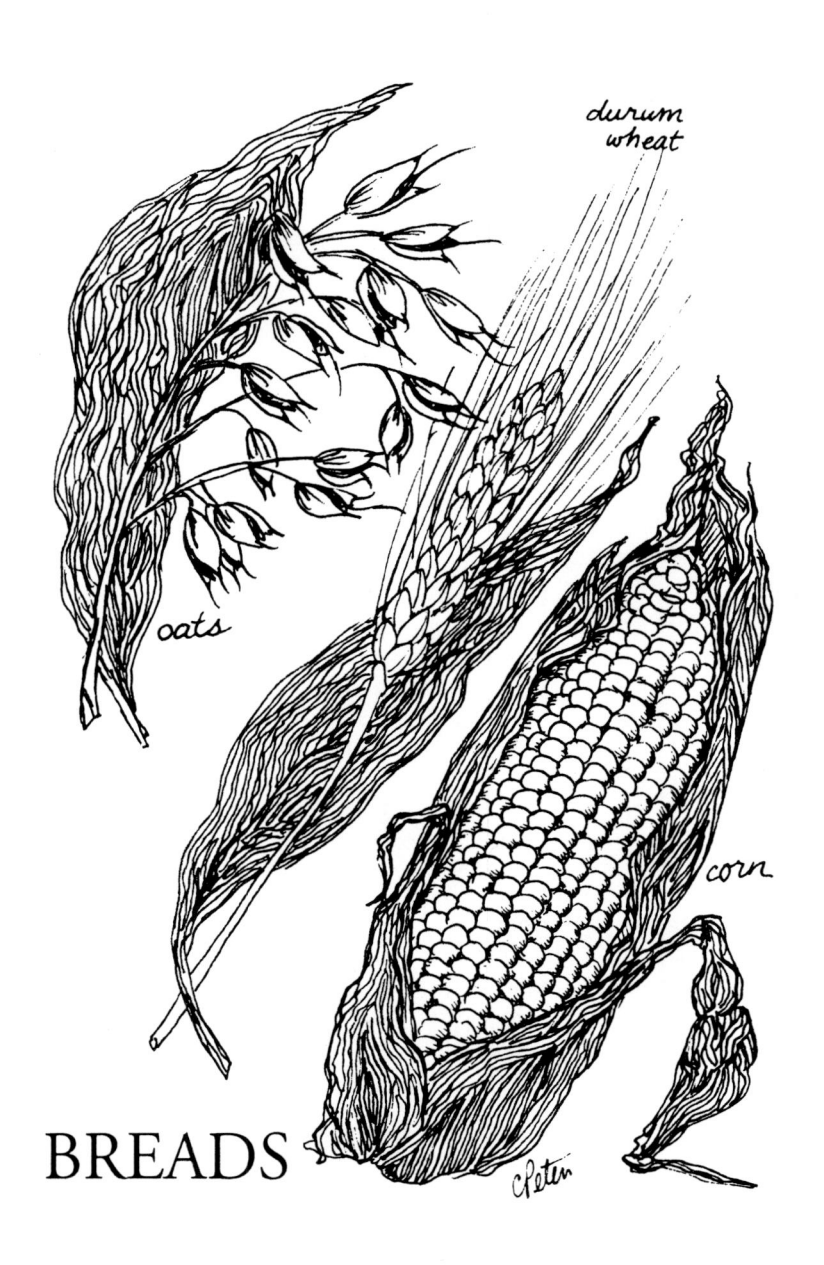

BREADS

BREADS

3-2-1 Bread	48•
17 Mile House Cornbread	53•
Angel Biscuits	38•
Aunt Daphne's Soft Cornbread	54•
Banana Bread	36•
Biscuit Mix	47•
Biscuits	40•
Buttermilk Scones	52•
Can Can Bread	50•
Cheezy Tomato Garlic Loaf	45•
Cinnamon Bow Knots	37•
Croissants	45•
Dumplings	38•
Famous Sour Dough Bread	43•
Greeley Herb Bread	52•
Hushpuppies	50 •
Melba Toast Baskets	38•
New England Blueberry Muffins	39•
Orange Sweetie Rolls	48•
Penny Rolls	56•
Pumpkin Bread	51•
Rich Plain Roll Dough	37•
Sippets	36•
Sour Cream Coffee Cake	47•
Standard Rolls	35•
Starter for Sour Dough Bread	43•
Sweet Bran Muffins	55•
Sweet Rye Bread	51•
Whole Wheat Bread – Organic	42•
Yorkshire Pudding	55 •
Zucchini Bread	49•

STANDARD ROLLS _____ Mary W. Peters•

4 Tblsp butter
1/3 cup sugar
2 tsp salt
1 3/4 cup warm milk

1 pkg dry yeast
6 cups exactly of white flour
2 eggs

Mix the butter, sugar, salt and milk in a large bowl and let cool to lukewarm. Stir the yeast into 1/4 cup warm water and let it stand for 5 minutes to dissolve. Add 3 cups of the flour and the dissolved yeast to the first mixture and beat vigorously for 2 minutes. Cover and let rise in a warm place until double in bulk. Stir the dough vigorously and add as much of the remaining flour as necessary in order to knead the dough. Turn out onto a lightly floured board, knead for a minute or two, and let rest for 10 minutes. Resume kneading until smooth. Shape dough as desired. Cover and let rise until double in bulk. Bake 425° for 12 to 15 minutes.

BEEHIVE OVEN - TAOS, NEW MEXICO

We all must be grateful for the scientific strides made in the last 100 years. The idea of running outside in freezing temperatures to stoke up this oven and bake is more than this person cares to fancy. Think of the reformation from the beehive oven to the microwave!

❖ ❖ ❖ ❖ ❖ ❖ ❖ ❖ ❖

Gere remembers -
DAD'S SUNDAY A.M. BREAKFASTS - *I remember DOLLAR PANCAKES. Dad would drop the tiniest bit of pancake dough on the skillet and make me pancakes the size of silver dollars. It was really fun to see how many you could stack up and how many you could eat. I always had DOLLAR PANCAKES with* real *maple syrup.*

BAKING POWDER BISCUITS, *so light and fluffy I thought they would float away, were another of Dad's Sunday a.m. specials. I especially liked to watch Dad knead the dough, roll it and cut those round biscuit shapes - cooked to a golden brown and eaten with lots of butter and honey and a huge glass of milk.*

BANANA BREAD _____ Momo
First started making this in 1976 and haven't quit yet - it's great

Mix well until blended:
1/2 cup margarine
1 cup sugar
2 eggs
Stir in:
3 Tblsp buttermilk and 1 cup mashed bananas
Sift together and stir in: •
2 cups flour
1 tsp soda
1/2 tsp salt
Then blend in **1 cup chopped walnuts**
Pour into well-greased loaf pan or bread pan. LET STAND FOR 20 • MINUTES BEFORE BAKING. Let bake one hour at 350° or until a • toothpick pushed in center comes out clean. You can double this recipe • and bake in small foil pans (4) and they make great gifts.•

❖ ❖ ❖ ❖ ❖ ❖ ❖ ❖ ❖

SIPPETS _____ Beanie Flynn
Wonderful served with casseroles, soups or salads

Pepperidge Farm THIN sliced white bread

Remove slices from loaf and cut diagonally and place close together on cookie sheet. Toast slices for 20 minutes at 250°, turn over and toast for an additional 25 minutes. Remove from oven. While still warm, spread each section with soft butter and sprinkle with SCHILLING SALAD SUPREME which can be purchased in any Spice section of local grocery. Place cookie sheet in refrigerator til butter is hard and then reheat bread at 300° oven til hot, or until ready to serve. Crusts may be trimmed, if preferred.

❖ ❖ ❖ ❖ ❖ ❖ ❖ ❖ ❖

Anyone can count the apples on a tree, but it
takes someone with vision to count the trees in an apple.
• • • • • •
One good thing can be said about kleptomania. If
you've got it, you can always take something for it.

RICH PLAIN ROLL DOUGH   Gere Simmons

1 cup milk, scalded
1/4 cup shortening (Crisco)
1/4 cup sugar
1 tsp salt
1 cake fresh or 1 pkg granular yeast
1/4 cup lukewarm water
1 well-beaten egg
3 1/2 cups flour

Combine milk, shortening, sugar, and salt; cool to lukewarm. Add yeast softened in lukewarm water; add egg. Gradually stir in flour to form soft dough. Beat vigorously; cover and let rise in warm place (82 degrees) until doubles in bulk, about 2 hours. Makes 2 dozen rolls.

CINNAMON BOW KNOTS   Helga Petersen

Divide RICH PLAIN ROLL DOUGH RECIPE in half (See recipe above) Roll dough on lightly floured surface into a rectangle 1/2 inch thick.
Cut 6 inch strips, 1/2 inch wide. Knot each gently. Flip flop each knot in melted butter. Then place knot in plastic bag filled with 1/2 sugar and 1/2 cinnamon and coat with sugar mixture. Place knots on greased baking sheet and let rise until doubled in bulk.
Bake at 375° for 10 to 15 minutes.
ESPECIALLY FOR MALCOLM
With Love,
Gere

❖ ❖ ❖ ❖ ❖ ❖ ❖ ❖ ❖

DUMPLINGS   Alta Korb
Makes 6 to 8 dumplings

3/4 cup of flour   1 egg
2 1/2 tsp baking powder   1 Tblsp soft butter
1/2 tsp salt   1/2 cup milk

Sift flour, baking powder, salt together.
Beat egg and add milk, butter, and then mix all ingredients together to a soft batter.
You can add parsley or poultry seasoning to these dumplings for added flavor. Cook about 12 to 15 minutes but <u>do not remove</u> the lid during the cooking.

ANGEL BISCUITS   Pat Lynn
This dough lasts in the fridge for two weeks!

Dissolve **1 envelope of fresh yeast in 1/2 cup warm water**
Sift together:
5 cups flour   **1 tsp baking soda**
1 tsp salt   **3 tsp baking powder**
1 Tblsp sugar

Cut in **3/4 cup Crisco shortening,** add yeast mixture and **2 cups of buttermilk.** Stir until well moistened with a good mixer. Grease a large bowl, put in dough and seal tightly. When biscuits are needed, remove a portion, pat out to 3/4" on a floured board and cut with a biscuit cutter. Brush tops with melted butter, and allow to rise 1-1/2 to 2 hours. Bake for 12 minutes at 400°.

❖ ❖ ❖ ❖ ❖ ❖ ❖ ❖ ❖

MELBA TOAST BASKETS
So delicious to serve creamed meats, fish, fowl or vegetables in these crisp little cups.

Preheat oven to 275°
Lightly butter white WonderBread on both sides from which the crusts have been removed.
Press into muffin tins letting the corners protrude.
Toast until golden and crisp and are best when used fresh.

NEW ENGLAND BLUEBERRY MUFFINS
Great-Grandmother Ida Dunnell

1/2 cup sugar	1/4 cup melted butter
1 cup milk	1 1/2 cups flour
3 tsp baking powder	1/2 tsp salt
1 egg	1/2 cup flour

1 cup blueberries drained and floured

Sprinkle **1/2 cup additional flour** over 2 cups blueberries and toss. Cream butter, sugar and egg. Mix well. Sift flour with baking powder and salt. Add to first mixture, alternately with milk, beating well. Turn blueberries that have been floured into batter and stir VERY carefully. Butter muffin tins and fill half-full with batter. Bake 375° for 20 minutes or til done. Makes about 22.

Great-grandmother Ida Ogden Dunnell always had a canary in a cage in her dining room called Jolly. Fun at her house was watching the goldfish in her garden pond, watering the lovely flower garden, watching Jolly ride around the house perched on top of her lovely white hair, and could she make beautiful clothes for our dollies! Having dinner at our Grandparents' house usually included Blueberry muffins. I loved to stay overnight with them in Minneapolis, and in my memory I can still hear the radiators sing in the morning, the low sounds of the busses going by the house at night, and her sweet voice singing hymns as we made the bed together after awakening. And she used in her bathroom green glycerin soap that you could see through! Two of her favorites were Sugared Grapefruit Peel and Coffee Ice Cream which to this day I demur. Grandfather, whom we all held in awe and a little terror, one Armistice Day descended the grand staircase into the living room playing a drum hooked onto his belt!

MARY AND IRENE
WITH MAMMY

Each new day comes with its prizes unassembled.
Be handy with your tools.

• • • • • •

We fail, not because our qualities are ordinary, but
because we let them remain so.

• • • • • •

What are you going to be doing in the next five seconds
that keeps you from smiling right now?

BISCUITS _____ Irene Savidge
Grandmother Irene Savidge, who was Aunt Jane Peters' mother, was well-loved by all the Peters. The flowers from her garden looked like pictures in a seed catalogue, and she was forever bringing arrangements a florist would have been proud to claim. On top of being pretty and most lovable, she was a world-class cook and dinner at her house was a work of art.

Sift together:
    2 cups flour   **4 tsp baking powder**
    1 tsp salt   **3 Tblsp sugar**
Cut into dry mixture:
    1/2 cup shortening
Drop into the flour and shortening mix
    Either **2 egg yolks or 1 whole egg**
    1/2 cup milk
Add a little milk and blend well. Add rest of milk and stir until well •
mixed. •
Put on floured board, pat out to 3/4" thick, and cut with large biscuit •
cutter. •
Bake at 400° for 12 minutes.•
GET OUT THE HONEY!!•
This recipe also makes the best **shortcake** for strawberries you ever•
ate!•

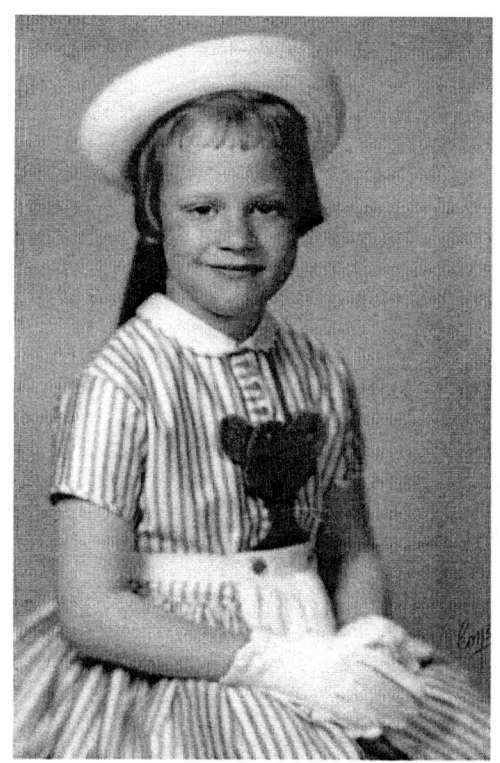

GERE

AMANDA BURKEY - Burkey was our babysitter and housekeeper on Alta Drive. She could bake white bread better and quicker than anybody I ever knew. It always fascinated me the way bread rose and puffed up. She also made the best Chocolate Chip cookies I ever tasted which Mother always tried to hide from my brothers and me (we always found them). Burkey had a love for the game of Yahtzee. I remember she would hold the Yahtzee cup and, stabilizing her elbow on the table, would shake the dice so hard SHE WOULD GET A BLISTER ON HER ELBOW. I give Burkey credit for my love for making bread.
- - - - - - Gere

WHOLE WHEAT BREAD - ORGANIC _____ Gere Simmons
This bread is truly addictive and a family favorite all through the year

2 pkg (cake) or 2 Tblsp dry yeast
1/2 cup lukewarm water
3 cups milk (scalded and cooled)
1 stick butter
1 cup molasses (or 1/2 honey - 1/2 molasses)
1 Tblsp salt
6 cups whole wheat flour
6 cups white flour

Start the milk on the stove on med/high heat. After scalding the milk, add the butter, salt and molasses. Stir until butter is dissolved. Let cool. In HUGE bowl add the lukewarm water and then the yeast. Stir with a fork until dissolved and leave alone until nice and bubbly. Then add cooled milk mixture and stir gently. Now add 6 cups whole wheat flour and stirring it up, slowly add approximately 4-5 cups white flour. For those of you who are non-bread makers it is best if the dough in the bowl is really soft and not too stiff. Now dump and spread out about 2 cups of flour on your working table and glomp the bread dough from the bowl onto this. If the dough is soft enough it will kind of ooze to the edge of the white flour and stick to your table. Quickly reach under the dough and turn it into the middle. If you've done it right, the flour from beneath the dough will allow you to do this without sticky business. Continue this KNEADING procedure until the dough becomes a smooth almost rubbery consistency; add white flour to the table as needed to prevent sticking. You are now working out all of your tensions and the smell of the bread will just send you. After dough is smooth and rubbery, place into a greased bowl and rub butter on top of dough so it doesn't dry out; cover with wax paper, put in warm place, let rise until doubled, about 2 hrs. Push down dough and separate into 4 portions. Place in greased loaf pan. Let rise until double in bulk. Put in 400° oven for 30-40 minutes (I double this recipe when I make it and get 8 loaves). IT'S SO GOOD, IT'S WORTH IT . . . !

❖ ❖ ❖ ❖ ❖ ❖ ❖ ❖ ❖

EVEN IF YOU'RE ON THE RIGHT TRACK•
YOU'LL GET RUN OVER IF YOU JUST SIT THERE.•

STARTER FOR SOUR DOUGH BREAD _____ Doug Peters

1 pkg dry yeast dissolved in 1/2 cup warm water
Carefully mix together until dissolved the following:
2 cups of water   2 cups of flour
1 tsp salt   3 Tblsp sugar
Then add yeast solution and mix thoroughly with the flour/water mixture and put in a covered plastic quart container, and seal with a cover. The starter will double in size overnight.
CAUTION: Starter may bubble over, so you should set the container in a bowl to catch the overload. When it goes over, just add a little more flour and stir. This will settle the starter. Store in the refrigerator for up to 3 months without spoiling.
Refresh your sour dough starter by adding additional water and flour to make up the volume you use in your bread. Let it set out in the kitchen for 2 or 3 days and it will work and get sour again. Then put it back in the refrigerator.

FAMOUS SOUR DOUGH BREAD_____ Doug Peters

2 pkg dry yeast dissolved in 1/3 cup warm water
1/2 tsp sugar
Warm 2 cups milk in a saucepan and pour into a large bowl that has added to it
1 Tblsp sugar
1 tsp salt
Stir this mixture until dissolved.
Add **1 1/2 Tblsp Mazola oil**
Then add yeast, warm water and sugar mixture. Stir well. When mixture cools, add **1 cup sour dough starter and mix well.**
Turn all of the above into the bowl of your Kitchen Aid mixer and put on the dough hook attachment.
Add **5 to 6 cups of unbleached flour**
This will make a fairly stiff dough. Dough will pull away from the sides of the bowl when enough flour has been added.
If you do not have a dough hook, remove dough from bowl and knead for 5 minutes until shiny.
Butter a large clean bowl, place dough in bowl, cover with plastic wrap and let rise for 1 1/2 to 2 hours in a warm place until double in bulk.
Punch dough down in bowl, remove and shape dough into 2 long French loaves and put on a cookie sheet that has been buttered and sprinkled with corn meal, lightly. *(continued on next page)*

Sprinkle a little corn meal on top of loaves, cover and let rise for 1 hour while preheating oven to 400°. After rising, make 3 diagonal slashes with a sharp razor blade in loaves. Bake for 30 to 35 minutes. Get out the butter and a knife!

❖ ❖ ❖ ❖ ❖ ❖ ❖ ❖ ❖

Louise and her husband Norman Filbert are referred to as Mr. and Mrs. Show Business in a 2-state area. Norman's talent as director-actor extraordinare has been heralded by every periodical and newspaper in the Middlewest while Louise' talents as hostess - gourmet cook have been preceded only by her very special talents as actress-singer. She is cleverness itself in the kitchen and the only person I ever knew that made her own croissants and they melted in your mouth. I have never decided whether I liked the Filberts' food better or their delightful conversation. Because of our friendship with these wonderfully talented people, Doug and I were able to exercise whatever limited talent we possessed (enforced by outrageous bravado) and dabbled our toes on the amateur stage. The excitement of those days is easily recalled. Chanticleer Theatre in Council Bluffs is a testimony to the hard work of a bright and talented couple and to Council Bluffs patrons who made a dream come true and brought Amateur Theatre to their city.

CHEEZY TOMATO GARLIC LOAF _____ Malcolm Peters •

1 stick butter   1/4 cup chopped parsley
6 med. tomatoes, (6 cups) skinned and chopped
3 small chopped onions (1 1/2 cups)   1 1/2 tsp oregano
4 cloves garlic finely chopped   1 tsp salt
1/4 tsp pepper

Cook ingredients over high heat for 45 minutes until sauce thickens. Slice one large loaf of Italian bread lengthwise and spread with tomato mixture. Top this with
1 10 oz. pkg of mozzarella cheese
1/2 cup Parmesan cheese

Bake for 45 minutes in a 400° oven until cheese is brown and bubbly. A real crowd pleaser if you have the time to do it!

CROISSANTS _____

3/4 cup butter   1 pkg active dry yeast
3 cups lightly spooned flour   3 Tblsp sugar
3/4 cup milk   1 tsp salt
1/4 cup warm water(105°-115°)   2 eggs
1 Tblsp cream

Work butter into 1/4 cup of the flour until mixture is a smooth paste. Place between 2 sheets of waxed paper and roll out to small rectangle. Chill for 1 hour.

When butter mixture is chilled, scald milk and cool to luke-warm. Measure warm water into a large, warmed mixing bowl, sprinkle with yeast, and stir until dissolved. Add sugar, salt, 1 beaten egg, milk, and 1 cup flour, and beat until smooth with an electric mixer or wooden spoon. Stir in remaining flour and mix until completely blended.

Turn out dough onto a well-floured board and roll out to a 12-inch square. Carefully peel waxed paper from chilled butter mixture and place it over the center third of rolled dough. Fold both ends of dough over butter mixture into thirds (like a business letter). Give dough a quarter turn (folds will be on right and left), roll out again to a 12-inch square, and fold in thirds as before. Turn, roll, and fold dough 3 more times. (Re-chill the dough if it softens while your are working with it. After 20 to 30 minutes in the refrigerator, it will be ready for you to continue with the recipe). Wrap in waxed paper and refrigerate for 3 hours (*Recipe can be prepared ahead to this point and held in refrigerator over-night or up to 12 hours*)   (continued on next page)

To shape croissants, divide chilled dough into thirds. Take each third in turn, refrigerating remainder, and roll out to a 12-inch circle. Cut into 8 pie-shaped wedges. Brush point of each wedge with a mixture of 1 egg beaten with cream. Beginning at the wide end, roll up each wedge tightly and pinch point to seal. Place on a greased baking sheet with the point underneath and curve to form a crescent. Cover with plastic wrap or towel and let rise in a warm place free from drafts until almost doubled, about 30 to 50 minutes. Brush each croissant with egg-cream mixture and bake in a preheated 375° oven for about 12 to 15 minutes or until lightly browned. Makes 24 croissants. *Baked croissants may be frozen for up to one month. Bring to room temperature; warm if desired.*

❖ ❖ ❖ ❖ ❖ ❖ ❖ ❖ ❖

As young marrieds in Council Bluffs, Iowa, eight couples agreed to form a monthly dinner club with the brilliant appellation of Supper Club, Incorporated. That club is the personification of loyalty and faithfulness.
Trips to Lake Okoboji for golfing, card playing and eating, plus long weekends at the Elms Hotel and Spa at Excelsior Springs in Missouri are part of the glue that cements our love for one another. And the yearly Christmas party with gift exchange that includes all the children and grandchildren is joyous. You can imagine the furor of party planning when one of the many children of that group declared nuptial intentions! That's where we shone! What a pleasure it has been to entertain those dear young people.
Well, here's a picture of that group looking younger and younger after 36 years of leaning over hot stoves to please the palates of SUP INC.

BISCUIT MIX

Doug and I used to buy this BISCUIT MIX from the ladies of the Council Bluffs Congregational Church and Lucy Beall Graeme was kind enough to give us the recipe.

4 cups flour	**1 tsp sugar**
2 Tblsp baking powder	**4 Tblsp dry milk**
1 1/2 tsp salt	**Generous 1/2 cup of Crisco**

Work with a pastry blender til all ingredients are like fine corn meal. Add 1 1/2 cups water to make 30 - 2 inch biscuits. Bake 10 to 12 minutes in a 450° oven.

❖ ❖ ❖ ❖ ❖ ❖ ❖ ❖ ❖

One of the stories that we love to recall about cooking as young brides concerns Martha Walsh who tried to feed us an appetizer of peeled uncooked shrimp.
"You mean, you have to COOK them?!!"
That dear girl is hard to match in the kitchen now and besides, she started baking Sour Cream Coffee Cakes for Christmas presents, and we all forgave her.

SOUR CREAM COFFEE CAKE   Martha Walsh

1 stick butter	**1 tsp vanilla**
1 cup sugar	**2 cups flour**
3 eggs	**1 tsp baking powder**
1 cup sour cream	**1 tsp soda**
1/2 tsp salt	

Filling: 3/4 cup brown sugar packed firm
                  2 Tblsp butter
                  1/2 tsp cinnamon
                  1/2 cup nutmeats, chopped

Cream sugar and butter and add eggs one at a time. Add vanilla. Add sour cream and dry ingredients alternating. Grease a bundt pan <u>well</u> and fill pan halfway with batter. Then top batter with half of filling. Add rest of batter and rest of Filling. Bake at 350° for 1 hour.

3 - 2 - 1 BREAD   Commodore Beaver

3 cups self-rising flour
2 Tblsp sugar
1 can regular beer

Mix ingredients thoroughly and pour into a greased bread loaf pan. Bake at 375° for 55 minutes or until done. Com says this is FAST - EASY - GOOD!

> As the man and wife left the restaurant, the wife flared furiously. "Why on earth did you give that cloakroom girl such an enormous tip?" she demanded.
> "Look at the hat and coat she gave me!"

ORANGE SWEETIE ROLLS   Gere Simmons•

1 1/4 cups milk, scalded	**1/2 cup shortening**
1/3 cup sugar	**1 tsp salt**
1 cake fresh or 1 pkg granular yeast	**2 well-beaten eggs**
1/4 cup orange juice	**2 Tblsp grated orange peel**
5 cups flour	

Combine milk, shortening, sugar, and salt; cool to lukewarm. Soften yeast in this mixture. Add eggs, orange juice and peel; beat thoroughly. Add flour; mix to soft dough. Cover and let stand 10 minutes. Knead on lightly floured surface. Place in greased bowl; let rise in warm place (82°) until double in bulk, about 2 hours. Punch down. Roll dough in an oblong shape 1/4" thick. Brush with melted butter; sprinkle with sugar. Roll and cut in 1-inch slices. Place, cut side down in greased baking pan or greased muffin pans; cover and let rise until double in bulk. Bake in moderately hot oven (375°) for 25 minutes. Remove from pans;cool and frost lightly with Orange Frosting. Makes 2 dozen.

Orange Frosting
NOTE: I added egg yolks and orange juice right off the bat, and had to add alot more confectioner's sugar than recipe called for. Experiment with this one . . .
1/4 cup butter
2 cups confectioner's sugar
2 egg yolks (may be omitted)
1 Tblsp orange peel
2 Tblsp orange juice

ZUCCHINI BREAD _____

2 cups zucchini grated	2 cups sugar
3 cups flour	1 cup Wesson oil
1 tsp salt	3 eggs beaten
3 tsp cinnamon	1 tsp vanilla
1/4 tsp baking powder	1 tsp baking soda

Blend sugar and oil and add eggs. Then stir in vanilla and zucchini. Mix dry ingredients and add to liquids. Bake at 325° for 60 to 70 minutes. This makes 2 loaves of bread.

GERE SIMMONS

Here comes Joy on Wheels - Gere Peters Simmons - the greatest story teller ever and her enthusiasm for life is incredibly contagious. The world is a festival for her and as Googah the Great, professional clown, has entertained young and old to resounding applause. She tries everything: a ham radio operator, she rides horses, snow skis, jet skis, can fish and hunt and makes sweetie rolls and breads nonpareil. And lock the doors to the Craft shops, she can CREATE anything. Lately, one of the Simmons' finest acts was to give us all little Katie - hard to follow that one!

HUSHPUPPIES   Johnny Peters•

1 1/4 cup corn meal   1/3 tsp garlic salt
3/4 cup flour   1/2 tsp pepper
3/4 tsp salt   2 cup minced onion
6 tsp baking powder   2 eggs
1 1/4 tsp sugar   1 cup milk

Mix dry ingredients and stir in onion. Separate eggs and beat the yolks into the milk. Stir liquid into dry ingredients. Beat egg whites to soft peaks. Add a light additional sprinkling of baking powder to egg whites just before you finish beating them. Fold carefully into batter stirring as little as possible. Drop by spoonsful into deep fat at 350° and cook about 5 minutes until brown.

❖ ❖ ❖ ❖ ❖ ❖ ❖ ❖ ❖

CAN CAN BREAD   Gere Simmons
Save your pound coffee cans!

1 envelope yeast   3 Tblsp sugar
1/2 cup warm water   1/8 tsp ginger
1 12 oz. can evaporated milk 4 cups flour
3 Tblsp Wesson Oil   1 tsp salt

Place warm water in bowl, add yeast and stir til dissolved. Let yeast foam up. Add milk, oil, sugar, ginger, salt. Stir until well mixed. Add flour gradually. Grease 2 one pound coffee cans and lids. Divide dough into each coffee can. Place lid on top and let rise, about 45 min. to an hour. When dough has risen to top, take off lid, place in 350° oven right side up for 40 minutes. Sometimes dough will cook up and over can and look like a mushroom cap. Take bread out of can while still hot-ish. This is a really heavy sweet bread with a ginger zing. WONDERFUL!

Wisdom isn't the acquisition of knowledge. It's knowing•
which knowledge is worth acquiring •
• • • • ••
Chinese Proverb: Worry is an old man with bended head,•
carrying a load of feathers which he thinks is lead •
• • • • ••
Monday is an awful way to spend one-seventh of your life •

Hazel Smith was Principal and teacher of Glendale Country school and the Smith family were homesteaders on a Council Bluffs farm ever since the 1840's. She had a wonderful asparagus bed that she shared with us, plus all kinds of fresh produce. After retiring from school, she ran a bakery out of her home and this was one of our favorite breads. Picnics at her home were a great treat.

SWEET RYE BREAD _____Hazel Smith

Mix together and let cool
1 cup scalded milk   **1/2 cup brown sugar**
1 tsp caraway seed   **1 Tblsp salt**
1/2 cup dark molasses
Then add
2 pkg active dry yeast in 1 cup warm water
2 Tblsp melted butter   **3 cups sifted all purpose white flour**
3 cups sifted rye flour

Mix three cups of white flour and then add enough rye flour to make a stiff dough. Turn the dough out on a floured board, cover and let rest for about 10 minutes. Knead lightly for 10 minutes. Place in greased bowl, cover and let rise until double in size, about 1-1/2 hours. Divide dough in half, shape into round loaves. Place on a greased baking sheet lightly sprinkled with corn meal. With a sharp blade, slash the top from center out to the edges. Brush top of loaves with egg white slightly beaten and diluted with a Tblsp of water. Bake at 375° for 40 to 50 minutes. Delicious toasted!

PUMPKIN BREAD _____Joyce Pogge •
Freezes well for gifts

3 1/3 cup flour   1 cup oil
2 tsp soda   4 eggs
1 1/2 tsp salt   2/3 cup water
1 tsp cinnamon   2 cups canned pumpkin
1 tsp nutmeg   1 cup chopped walnuts
3 cups sugar

Sift together flour, soda, salt, sugar, cinnamon and nutmeg into bowl. Make a well in center and add oil, eggs, water, pumpkin and nuts. Mix til smooth. Divide batter into 3 regular size loaf pans which have been greased and floured. Bake at 350° about 1 hour and 20 minutes. Cool slightly in pans, and turn out onto racks. Wrap in Saran Wrap and foil and freeze or refrigerate. If you use foil pans, they need not be greased or floured.

BUTTERMILK SCONES
Make the scones for tea time like a proper Scotch lassie

4 cups sifted flour	**2 tsp baking powder**
1 tsp baking soda	**1 1/2 tsp salt**
1/8 tsp mace	

Sift dry ingredients and cut in •
4 Tblsp shortening until mixture resembles coarse meal.•

1/3 cup sugar	**3/4 cup raisins**
1 1/2 cup buttermilk	

Stir into the coarse meal, sugar and raisins.•
Gradually add buttermilk mixing lightly with fork til dough sticks•
together. •
Turn out on lightly floured board. Divide dough into 4 parts and knead •
each part a minute. Then pat into 3/4" rounds. Arrange well apart on •
greased baking sheet and using floured knife, mark each round into •
quarters. Bake 400° about 30 minutes.•

GREELEY HERB BREAD
Momo's favorite

In **1/2 cup warm water put**
　1 Tblsp active dry yeast
　pinch of sugar
　1/8 tsp ginger
Transfer mixture to large bowl and stir in

2 cups warm milk	**1/4 cup melted butter cooled**
2 lg. eggs slightly beaten	**1 tsp nutmeg**
2 tsp crumbled dry sage	**4 tsp caraway seeds**
1 tsp salt	**6 1/2 to 7 1/2 cups all purpose flour**
1/2 cup sugar	

Knead dough on floured surface incorporating more of the flour as•
necessary to keep the dough from sticking for about 10 minutes. Put •
ball of dough in oiled bowl and let rise, covered with plastic wrap for 1 •
hour til double in bulk.•
Punch down dough, halve it, and form into 2 loaves. Put in oiled pans•
9 x 5 and let rise in warm place about 30 min. til double in bulk. Bake •
350° for 35 to 40 min. Let loaves cool in pans 10 min. and turn out on •
rack. This is wonderful toasted!•

17 MILE HOUSE CORNBREAD

On Vancouver Island there is a road tucked in that beautiful primeval forest that goes to Sooke & Metchosin from Victoria that has Inns along the way. They are called 2 Mile House, 11 Mile House, etc., and at 17 miles there is the 17 Mile House – a Country Pub, an historic Roadhouse established in 1894, and the charm of the exterior invites you in for darts or pool and delicious homemade meals. Here is their recipe for Corn Bread that they have given out a million times.

2 cups flour
1/2 cup sugar
8 tsp baking powder
2 cups buttermilk

1 1/2 tsp salt
2 cups cornmeal
4 eggs
1/2 cup melted butter

Mix all dry ingredients. Add remaining liquid ingredients. Do not overstir. Pour into greased 9 x 11 pan and bake 425° for 20 to 25 minutes.

AUNT DAPHNE'S SOFT CORNBREAD

3 eggs, beaten light
1 cup cornmeal
3 cups milk
1 tsp salt

1 scant tsp sugar
1 rounded tsp baking powder
1 Tblsp butter

Warm 2 cups of the milk, and stir into it gradually the cornmeal. Cook until it just begins to thicken, take off the stove and add the salt, sugar, and butter, and the remaining cup of milk. When cool, add the well beaten eggs, then the baking powder. Pour into a buttered baking dish, and bake in a hot oven 1/2 hour or more. Serve hot.

MARILYN AND DOUG

Tracy and Marilyn Diers were such magic people - everybody loved them. It seemed they were always right there to help friends through problems and were full of enthusiasm and imagination for community or social functions that demanded their time and talent. I loved Marilyn's positive action attitude - the impossible could always be accomplished. We had alot of fun together: skiing, sailing, flying on holidays, planting watercress, finding mushrooms, being partners in M & M Creations. The most heartbreaking funeral I ever attended was theirs - killed in a flaming plane crash.

SWEET BRAN MUFFINS   Marilyn Diers

2 cups of Nabisco bran
2 cups of boiling water
Soak these two ingredients together. •
Beat together •
1 heaping cup of Crisco
3 cups of sugar
Add **4 eggs**and then fold the bran mixture together with eggs, sugar and •
Crisco. Then add•
4 cups of flour
5 tsp baking soda
1/2 tsp salt
1 quart of buttermilk
4 cups ALL BRAN
2 cups of currants that have been soaked in hot water for 10 minutes and then patted dry.

The currants are delicious in these sweet muffins and I always bake them in LITTLE muffin tins at 400° for about 15 minutes. Nice for luncheon accompaniment with a salad.

❖ ❖ ❖ ❖ ❖ ❖ ❖ ❖ ❖

YORKSHIRE PUDDING   Maureen May

2 cups presifted flour
4 eggs
2 cups whole milk
1 tsp salt

Mix in Waring blender well. Put top on blender and refrigerate for at •
least 2 hours.•
Place 1 tsp of roast drippings in a 12 cup muffin tin. Get drippings red •
hot in 425° oven. Fill cups 1/2 full with batter and bake 20 to 30 •
minutes til brown and crispy to accompany meat.•

PENNY ROLLS _____ Kitty Lemen •

Boil **3 small potatoes,** mash when soft and turn into a 2 cup measuring•
cup. Fill to the 2 cup level with potato water. •
Dissolve **1 pkg of dry yeast with 1/4 cup water**
Beat **2 eggs** with mixer and add •
1/2 cup sugar
1 Tblsp salt
6 Tblsp melted butter
dissolved yeast
potato mixture
5 cups flour

Using an electric mixer, thoroughly mix after adding each cup of flour. Leave dough in bowl and grease top of dough. Let rise for 2 to 3 hours. Punch down, cover with a towel and put in the refrigerator overnight. WARNING: This dough is very sticky.

Butterscotch Topping

Melt **3 sticks butter**
Not quite a full box of brown sugar, about 15 ounces
4 Tblsp cream
Cook on stove until sugar melts. Place 1 Tblsp butterscotch topping in •
each cup of a large size muffin tin that has been buttered. Let topping•
cool.•
Divide dough into 2 even sections and roll each into a rectangular•
shape 18" long. Spread each section with melted butter, sprinkle with•
brown sugar and cinnamon, and roll up like a jelly roll.•
Slice 1" wide. •
Place on top of brown sugar mix in muffin tins and let rise for 1 to 2 •
hours. Bake 12 to 20 minutes at 400°. Remove from muffin tins after 5 •
minutes cooling period. This recipe makes 36 rolls•

Don't start making these! There will never be an end to it unless you're going for heavy credits!

CAKES

FROSTINGS

CAKES & FROSTINGS

Alvina's Date Cake	73
Angel Food Ambrosia	75
Apple Cake	62
Best Ever Rum Cake	74
Better than Sex Cake	63
Buttermilk Cake	63
Carrot Cake	71
Cheese Cake	71
Chocolate Chiffon Roll	73
Chocolate Frosting	76
Chocolate Fudge Frosting	60
Chocolate Pecan Icing	60
Chocolate Roll	77
Chocolate Sheet Cake for 24	60
Coffee Cream Cake	77
Decorator Icing	75
Great Grandmother Ada White Stickney's Marble Cake	69
Homemade Orange Cake	78
Ice Box Gingerbread	69
Jiffy Cake with Black Walnuts	68
Lemon Cake	70
Lovely Special Cake Decoration	64
Oatmeal Cake	62
Orange Cake	64
Penuche Frosting	61
Poppy Seed Cake	76
Sauce for Angel Food Cake	65
Spice Cake I	65
Spice Cake II	70
Sponge Cake with Filling	66
The Best & Easiest Frosting in the World	65
Ugly Duckling Pudding Cake	61
Waldorf Astoira Red Cake	72
Wellesley Fudge Frosting	68
Wellesley Tea Room Fudge Cake	68
You've Got to be Kidding! German Chocolate Cake	59

Matt, Billy, Kathleen & Brian's mother, Mary W. Peters, is the all-around champ cake baker and decorator in the birthday department. She could make any child's heart's desire from a Teddy Bear to a Dinosaur. At most of the family gatherings, she is asked to bring the dessert and everyone starts salivating the week before. It is always something incredibly rich and absolutely beautiful to look at. Her fingers are magic and her creative talents, limitless. Plants always respond to her sweet touch and she always has time for a hug and a talk. Referred to in the family as Mary the Good, we are not kidding - she is universally loved.

❖ ❖ ❖ ❖ ❖ ❖ ❖ ❖ ❖

YOU'VE GOT TO BE KIDDING! German Chocolate Cake _____

Prepare **one German Chocolate Cake mix** according to directions and bake in a 9 x 13 cake pan. When baked, remove from oven and pierce entire top of cake with a utility fork. Pour over the hot cake, **one can of condensed sweet milk** and set aside to cool completely.
When cool, pour over **one jar of Mrs. Richardson's (1 pint) Caramel Fudge Sauce.** Refrigerate.
When ready to serve, whip **one cup of whipping cream with 3 tsp sugar and 1 tsp vanilla.** Spread over cake.
Crush **4 Heath Old English toffee bars** into tiny pieces and sprinkle over top of whipped cream.
Cut and serve and listen to the groans.

CHOCOLATE SHEET CAKE FOR 24 — Nadine Morrow

2 cups sifted flour
2 cups sugar
1/4 cup plus 1 1/2 tsp cocoa
1/2 cup buttermilk
1 tsp vanilla

2 eggs
1 tsp baking soda
1 cup water
1 cup butter
1/2 tsp salt

Sift together flour, sugar, cocoa and salt in a large bowl and set aside. Combine water and butter in a heavy saucepan and bring to a boil. Remove from heat and pour into dry ingredients. Beating constantly, add eggs, one at a time. Beat after each egg. Dissolve soda in buttermilk and add vanilla to chocolate mixture. Beat well. Pour into a greased 15 x 10 jelly roll pan. Bake at 325° for 30 minutes. Spread hot icing over warm cake. Cool and cut. (See below).

WITH
CHOCOLATE PECAN ICING

1/2 cup butter
1/4 cup cocoa
1 1/2 cup chopped pecans

1/4 cup milk plus 2 Tblsp
1 tsp vanilla
1 16 oz. pkg powdered sugar, sifted

Combine butter, milk, and cocoa in heavy saucepan. Bring to boil. Remove from heat. Stir in powdered sugar, vanilla and pecans. Spread hot icing on warm cake.

Nadine says that she makes half again the proportions of the icing to cover the cake. What a confection! Here are total measurements if you want alot of frosting . . .

3/4 cup of butter
1/3 cup cocoa
2 cups chopped pecans

1/3 cup plus 2 Tblsp milk
1 1/2 tsp vanilla
1 1/2 lbs or powdered sugar, sifted

CHOCOLATE FUDGE FROSTING

6 Tblsp soft butter or oleo
1/2 cup cocoa
2 2/3 cup confectioner's sugar
1/3 cup milk
1 tsp vanilla and a pinch of salt

Mix til soft and fluffy - you may need a dash more milk. This makes 2 cups of frosting.

When Doug and I were newly married and lived on Perrin Avenue in Council Bluffs, we were neighbors to John and Freida Anderson who were retired farmers. In the evening, Freida would ask baby Duff and me to come over and watch her television set and just as soon as she'd get settled in her rocker, off she'd go to Dreamland. I understand that now. She just loved that undertone of a baby playing and someone in the house - She was a wonderful cook and came frequently to our door with delicious goodies. And flowers just loved to grow for her! What a treat to have someone like that living next door to the young bride.

UGLY DUCKLING PUDDING CAKE — Ann Powell
Gentle, sweet and beautiful, Ann Powell makes Thursday a halcyon day for me as she creates another miracle with my hair.

1 pkg. yellow cake mix
1 pkg. Lemon Instant Pudding & Pie Filling Mix
1 can 16 oz. Fruit Cocktail plus syrup
1 cup flake coconut   **4 eggs**
1/4 cup oil   **1/2 cup chopped nuts**
1/2 cup brown sugar

Blend all except the brown sugar and nuts. Beat 4 minutes at medium speed. Put in greased and floured pan 9 x 13 and sprinkle with brown sugar and nuts. Bake at 325° for 45 minutes, remove from oven and cool in pan for 15 minutes.
Spoon the following hot butter glaze over the warm cake and serve with Dream Whip or Whipped cream.

GLAZE:
Combine: **1/2 cup butter**
1/2 cup sugar
1/2 cup evaporated milk
Boil sauce in pan for 2 minutes and stir in
1 1/3 cup flake coconut

PENUCHE FROSTING

Melt **1/2 cup butter** and add **1 cup brown sugar.**
Bring to boiling; cook and stir 1 minute or til slightly thick. Cool 15 minutes.
Add **1/4 cup hot milk** and beat smooth. Beat in **1 3/4 cup sifted powdered sugar** til spreading consistency. Will frost a 2-layer cake.

OATMEAL CAKE — Marilyn Braasch

Mix and let stand for 20 minutes:
1 1/4 cup boiling water   1/2 cup melted margarine
1 cup oatmeal
Then add to oatmeal mixture
 1 cup brown sugar   1 cup white sugar
2 beaten eggs and beat well
Then add
1 1/4 to 1 1/2 cups flour   1/4 tsp salt
1 tsp baking soda   1 tsp cinnamon
1/4 tsp nutmeg
Mix well and bake for 35 to 40 minutes at 350°.

FROSTING:
6 Tblsp soft margarine   1/4 cup evaporated milk
1/2 cup brown sugar   1 cup coconut
1/2 cup chopped nuts
Mix and spread on hot baked cake and slip under the broiler until brown.

APPLE CAKE — Freida Anderson

Cream together
1 cup sugar   1/2 cup butter
Add one egg
Sift together **1 cup flour**
1 tsp soda   1 tsp cinnamon
1 tsp nutmeg   1 tsp salt
Add to butter and egg mixture and then stir in
3 cups peeled, chopped apples (not too fine)
1 cup broken nut meats
Bake one hour at 350°
Spread this sauce over the top after it has been baked.

SAUCE
1/2 cup butter   1/2 cup white sugar
1/2 cup brown sugar   1/2 cup cream
1 tsp vanilla
Top with whipped cream!

BETTER THAN SEX CAKE (Can you believe it?!)

1 pkg. yellow cake mix 20 oz. can crushed pineapple
1 cup sugar 6 oz. pkg. vanilla instant pudding mix
8 oz. container frozen whipped topping, thawed OR
1 cup real cream whipped with 1/4 cup confectioner's sugar and
1 tsp vanilla
1 cup chopped pecans 1 cup flaked coconut
Maraschino cherries

Prepare cake mix and bake in a 9 x 13 cake pan. Combine pineapple (undrained) with sugar and bring to boil and cook for 5 minutes. When cake is done, remove from oven and pour syrup over hot cake. Allow to cool completely.
A variation at this point is to slice three bananas over the top of the cake if you wish. Prepare pudding mix and stir in coconut. Spread over cooled cake. Be sure pudding is cool before you spread with whipped cream. Then sprinkle the nut meats on the whipped cream and decorate with maraschino cherries.

BUTTERMILK CAKE (a big cake!)

3 cups sugar 1/2 cup butter or margarine, softened
1/2 cup shortening 6 egg whites
4 cups CAKE flour 1 tsp salt
1 tsp baking soda 1/2 tsp baking powder
2 cups buttermilk 1 Tblsp vanilla
1 tsp almond extract

Grease and flour three 9" cake pans. Set oven to 350°. Cream butter, shortening and sugar til fluffy. Beat in egg whites one at a time, beating well after each addition. Sift flour with salt, baking soda and baking powder. Add alternately with buttermilk which has been mixed with vanilla and almond extract. Bake 15 minutes at 350°, then reduce oven to 325° and bake 15 minutes more. Test with toothpick to see if done. Cool completely on wire racks.

FROSTING

1/2 cup butter, softened 8 oz. cream cheese, softened
1 16 oz. pkg. confectioners' sugar 1 tsp vanilla extract
1 cup flaked coconut 1/2 cup chopped pecans

Mix all together, whipping with an electric beater til frosting is fluffy. Frost layers and outside of cake.

LOVELY SPECIAL CAKE DECORATION

Melt white chocolate in double boiler and tint with green food coloring, a lovely light green. Spread the tinted white chocolate on the BACK of 12 or more rose leaves. Chill. When ready to decorate, peel off and discard the rose leaves. Place 3 in a fan shape centered with 2 raspberries for a lovely effect.

❖ ❖ ❖ ❖ ❖ ❖ ❖ ❖ ❖

ANOTHER TRIUMPH WE HAVE KNOWN AND LOVED

CHOCOLATE DECADENCE

Mary Peter's favorite ORANGE CAKE

Make **one orange cake mix (box)** and split the two layers when cool.
ORANGE FILLING:
Mix **1 cup sugar**   **3 Tblsp cornstarch**
1/2 tsp salt
Stir in **3/4 cup orange juice**
1/4 cup lemon juice   **1/2 cup water**
Cook over heat until it boils.
Add carefully: **3 egg yolks   1 Tblsp grated orange peel**
Beat constantly and BOIL again for 1 minute. Cool mixture and divide and spread between 3 layers. *(see frosting on the next page)*

Then frost cake with:
THE BEST AND EASIEST FROSTING IN THE WORLD

1/2 cup egg whites at room temperature
1 1/2 cups sugar   **1/2 tsp cream of tartar**
1/2 cup of water   **1/2 tsp vanilla**

Beat egg whites to SOFT PEAKS. Cook sugar, water and cream of tartar to just 240° on your candy thermometer. Start beater fast on egg whites and SLOWLY pour in hot sugar/water syrup and beat these together to form stiff peaks. Add vanilla. Frost cake immediately and you may sprinkle cake with shredded coconut if you wish. Fabulous on chocolate cake!

SPICE CAKE   Belle Hess

1 1/2 cups sugar   **1/2 cup butter**
Add to the above mixture after it has been thoroughly creamed
3 eggs
Then sift together
1 tsp soda   **1 tsp cloves**
1 tsp nutmeg   **1 tsp allspice**
1 tsp cinnamon   **1 pinch salt**
2 cups sifted flour   **1 tsp baking powder**
Alternately add
1 cup milk

Bake in two 9" greased and floured cake pans at 350° for 30 to 35 minutes. Fill and frost with Penuche frosting - found in this chapter.

SAUCE FOR ANGEL FOOD CAKE

3/4 cup sugar   juice of 1 orange
1 Tblsp cornstarch   juice of 1 lemon
2 Tblsp flour in a little water   **2 eggs, beaten**
1 cup whipped cream

Cook all ingredients except cream in double boiler. Cool mixture and fold in whipped cream. Spoon over angel food cake for a lovely light dessert.

SPONGE CAKE with filling!!

Mrs. George Lemen, Sr., was Mary Wilcox Peters' grandmother. She was a marvelous cook and here is another of her very elegant desserts. Serves 12.

11 egg whites	1 cup cake flour
6 egg yolks, beaten	(sifted 6 times!)
1 tsp cream of tartar	1 tsp lemon juice
1 1/2 cups sugar, sifted 5 times	1 tsp vanilla

Beat egg whites until they form soft peaks. Sift dry ingredients together and fold in egg whites carefully. Fold in lemon juice and vanilla. Beat egg yolks til creamy and add. Bake in angel food cake pan for 40 minutes at 325° and 20 minutes at 350°. Let the cake cool.

FILLING:

5 egg yolks, beaten	2 tsp Knox gelatin
1 cup sugar	1/2 cup water
1 Tblsp flour	1/2 pint whipping cream
pinch of salt	1 tsp vanilla
1 1/2 cups milk	1 tsp lemon juice

Soak gelatin in 1/2 cup water. Combine 5 yolks, sugar, flour, salt and milk in top of double boiler and cook til thick. Mix in dissolved gelatin and cool the custard in the refrigerator. Do not let it get stiff. Add the whipped cream which has been flavored with the vanilla and lemon juice, folding carefully into the custard. Split cake horizontally through the middle and spread with cooled filling. Fill hole with filling. If there is any filling left, spread on top and sides.

You may frost this cake with either whipped cream or Seven Minute Frosting (See FROSTING listed with ORANGE CAKE).

❖ ❖ ❖ ❖ ❖ ❖ ❖ ❖ ❖

HOW TO BE A MILLIONAIRE

do I have to go to school tomorrow?

(Put a nickle in a jar every time you hear this phrase)

WELLESLEY TEA ROOM FUDGE CAKE___ The Original Recipe

2/3 cup butter	2 2/3 cups brown sugar, well packed
1 whole egg and 3 egg yolks, well beaten	
4 squares unsweetened chocolate	
2/3 cup boiling water	
1 1/2 tsp baking powder	2 2/3 cups sifted pastry flour
2/3 cup thick sour milk	1 1/4 tsp soda dissolved in milk
1 tsp vanilla	dash of salt

Cream butter and sugar; add eggs. Dissolve chocolate in boiling water; stir to consistency of thick paste and add to butter mixture. Add baking powder to flour; add alternately with milk (and soda). Add vanilla and salt. Bake in two 9" square pans in moderate oven. Fill and frost with your favorite chocolate frosting and chopped nuts. Serves 24.

WITH

WELLESLEY FUDGE FROSTING

4 squares Baker's chocolate	4 tsp light corn syrup
1 1/2 cups milk	1/4 cup butter
4 cups sugar	2 tsp vanilla
pinch of salt	

Place chocolate and milk in saucepan. Cook over low heat stirring constantly til blended. Add sugar, salt, corn syrup. Stir til sugar is dissolved. Boil over low heat stirring occasionally til small amount dropped into cold water forms a soft ball. Or 240° on your candy thermometer. Remove from heat & add butter and vanilla. Cool to lukewarm and beat til creamy. Spread between layers of cake, over top and sides.

JIFFY CAKE with black walnuts_____ Frieda Anderson

2 cups sugar creamed with **2 sticks of oleo margarine**

2 cups flour (sifted and measured)	1/4 tsp salt
1 cup black walnuts	1 tsp lemon extract
1 tsp vanilla	5 large or 6 small eggs

Beat at high speed for 5 minutes. Pour into greased 10" tube pan and bake at 350° for 1 hour and 15 minutes.

ICE BOX GINGERBREAD   Gladys Peters

Cream together
1/2 cup lard   **1/2 cup butter**
1 cup sugar
Add **2 beaten eggs**
Sift together and add to above ingredients
3 cups flour (scant)   **2 tsp cinnamon**
a pinch of salt   **1 Tblsp ginger**
1 tsp baking soda
Then add and mix well
1 cup boiling water   **1 cup dark molasses**

Grease and flour muffin tins and bake gingerbread muffins for 20 minutes in a 350° oven. You can keep this dough covered in the fridge for fresh muffins through the week.

❖ ❖ ❖ ❖ ❖ ❖ ❖ ❖ ❖

GREAT GRANDMOTHER ADAH WHITE STICKNEY'S MARBLE CAKE

This is the way the recipe came down to me from my mother and is the only touch I have with the dear great-grandmother other than her picture in the Stickney scrap book.

2 cups sugar   **1/2 cup butter**
1 cup cold water   **5 egg whites**
3 cups flour   **2 tsp baking powder**
3 tsp baking powder

Add **one square of Bakers chocolate** to half of the batter.

Well, this surely leaves the cook lots of room for improvising and I always wondered what Adah did with the 5 egg yolks that were left over. Maybe she made Hollandaise in her Cuisinart - tee hee.

LEMON CAKE   Lou Dixon and Marie Knudsen

1 pkg. Lemon Cake Mix   1 Pkg. Jello Lemon Instant Pudding
4 eggs   3/4 cup cooking oil
3/4 cup water

Mix well and pour into an ungreased loaf cake pan. Bake at 350° until top is done to touch. As soon as cake is out of the oven, punch holes with a fork into cake and pour on the following mixture:
1/3 cup orange juice and 2 cups powdered sugar that has been stirred til well dissolved.

SPICE CAKE

Cream together:
1 cup white sugar   **1/2 cup brown sugar**
1/2 cup butter
Add **2 eggs and 1 Tblsp vanilla**
Mix together in a bowl:
3 Tblsp commercial sour cream   **1 cup buttermilk**
1 tsp baking soda
Take **1 cup raisins,** wash them and cook them in a small amount of water until thick. Cool the mixture. Leave juice on raisins and dredge with **1/4 cup flour**
Sift dry ingredients:
2 1/4 cups flour   **2 tsp cinnamon**
1 tsp nutmeg   **1/8 tsp salt**
Alternate dry ingredients with buttermilk mixture.
Finally add **1/2 cup chopped nuts** and **cooked raisins**. Bake in 9" layer pan for 25 minutes at 350°.

QUICK CARAMEL FROSTING
1/4 lb. butter   **1/2 cup brown sugar**
1/4 cup milk   **2 cups confectioners' sugar**

Melt butter and brown sugar in pan, stirring til sugar is dissolved. Add milk and blend. Cool and then beat in confectioners' sugar til thick enough to spread.

CHEESE CAKE   Houghton Furr

This is the first cheese cake we ever ate and we still think it is one of the very best.

1/3 pkg. or 18 slices of plain zweibach, crushed
2 Tblsp sugar   1 tsp cinnamon
1/4 cup melted butter

Mix together and press into the bottom and sides of a well-buttered 9" spring form pan.

Cream together:

1 1/2 lbs of cream cheese   4 beaten egg yolks
1/2 cup sugar

Add **the juice of 1 large lemon plus the zest of one large lemon**
A dash of nutmeg   **1 tsp vanilla**

Beat the egg whites til almost stiff with **2 Tblsp of sugar** and continue beating til stiff and glossy. Fold meringue into the cheese mixture lightly and pour in prepared pan. Bake at 350° for 35 minutes.

TOPPING:
1 cup sour cream   3/4 tsp of vanilla
2 Tblsp sugar

Mix together and spread on top of hot cake. Slip back into oven and bake for 15 minutes more.

❖ ❖ ❖ ❖ ❖ ❖ ❖ ❖ ❖

CARROT CAKE   Mary Teigeler

1 1/2 cup Mazola oil   4 eggs
2 cups sugar   3 cups grated carrots, packed
2 tsp baking soda   2 cups flour
1 tsp salt   1 cup chopped nuts
2 tsp cinnamon   1 tsp vanilla

Beat eggs til fluffy. Add sugar gradually and mix well. Add oil and carrots. Blend dry ingredients together and slowly add to the mixture. Add nuts and vanilla; bake in 2 layers at 350° for 45 minutes.

FROSTING
1 8 oz. pkg cream cheese   1 lb. powdered sugar
1 stick margarine   2 tsp vanilla

You may add WELL drained crushed pineapple to the frosting if you desire.

A 2 1/2 day stop in New York before we went to St. Thomas Island for a winter vacation seemed justified, as our 3 high school children were just ripe for the magic of the largest city in the United States. Doug had made reservations at the Waldorf-Astoria. We arrived about 5:00 in the afternoon to be told that our 2 rooms were not available! But, with our permission, they would be putting us in a SUITE in the TOWERS!

I became positively giddy as we crossed the lobby to the private elevators that whisked us high above the city of New York to the door of the finest suite I have ever seen. A huge living room with library, grand piano, and fireplace, dining room that could seat 16, kitchen & servant quarters, separate bedrooms and baths for each member of the family! It was enormous and lush. We ran from room to room just to see it all.

Doug ordered Dom Perignon, Gere played the piano, we danced, sang, had dinner brought to the rooms, and to this day have not forgotten one moment of that glorious surprise.

THANKYOU, WALDORF-ASTORIA
Love, The Peters

WALDORF ASTORIA RED CAKE

1/2 cup shortening   **1 cup buttermilk**
1 1/2 cup sugar   **1 tsp soda**
2 eggs   **1 Tblsp vinegar**
2 1/4 cup cake flour
Make a paste of:
2 oz. Red food coloring   **2 Tblsp cocoa**
1 tsp vanilla   **1 tsp salt**

Cream shortening and sugar and add eggs. Add the paste of cocoa and food coloring. Alternately add buttermilk, flour and salt that have been sifted together. Fold in the soda that has been mixed with the vinegar. Put dough in three 8" cake tins and bake at 350° for 25 to 30 minutes.

FROSTING:
3 Tblsp flour   **1 cup milk**
1 Tblsp butter   **1 cup sugar**
1 Tblsp vanilla

Cook flour and milk until thick. Set aside and cool. Cream sugar and butter, adding sugar gradually. Add cooked ingredients and vanilla. Beat until frosting looks like whipped cream.

ALVINA'S DATE CAKE   Franny Farkle (Fran Day)

1 cup hot water   1 cup chopped dates
3/4 cup shortening   1 cup sugar
2 eggs   1 tsp baking soda
1 3/4 cup flour

Pour water over dates and shortening and set aside. Beat sugar and eggs. Blend in flour and soda. Blend in date mixture. Pour in greased 13 x 9 x 2 pan.

TOPPING:

1 cup chopped chocolate chips   1 cup chopped nuts
1/2 cup brown sugar

Sprinkle topping on cake and bake at 350° for 35 to 40 minutes. Cool. Serve like brownies with a blob of whipped cream. Serves 10 to 12.

CHOCOLATE CHIFFON ROLL

4 oz. semi-sweet cooking chocolate   3/4 cup water
1 2/3 cups sifted cake flour   1 1/4 cup sugar
2 tsp baking powder   3/4 tsp salt
7 egg yolks   1/2 cup salad oil
7 egg whites   1/2 tsp cream of tartar
1/4 cup granulated sugar, additional

Melt chocolate with water over low heat and then cool. Sift flour with 1 1/4 cups sugar, baking powder and salt in a large bowl. Make a well in the center of flour mixture. Add egg yolks, oil and chocolate. Beat on low speed of mixer for 2 minutes.

Combine egg whites and cream of tartar at high speed until foamy. Add remaining 1/4 cup sugar, two Tblsp at a time, beating thoroughly, until mixture forms stiff peaks. Fold chocolate mixture into egg whites. Divide batter between two 15 x 10 jelly roll pans greased and lined on the bottom with greased wax paper. Bake 18 to 20 minutes at 350°. Cool in pan 3 minutes before removing.

Sprinkle confectioners sugar on 15 x 10 towels. Loosen cakes from pans and immediately invert. Remove paper quickly and trip crisp edges. Roll each cake, starting on small side and rolling towel with cake. Cool on rack for 45 minutes. Unroll and fill with brandied apricot cream. Chill for 2 hours and slice to serve.

BRANDIED APRICOT CREAM
Whip **3 cups whipping cream with 4 tsp sugar**
Add 2 tsp of good Cognac and beat til soft peaks form.
Fold in **at least 1 cup of apricot preserves** and fill and frost the roll.

BEST EVER RUM CAKE

1 tsp sugar
1 cup dried, mixed fuit
1 tsp soda
2 eggs, large
1 oz. lemon juice

1 bottle **Rum**
2 cups brown sugar
1 cup butter
1/2 cup baking powder
1/2 lb. mixed nuts

Before starting, sample Rum to check quality. It should be smooth and not at all harsh to the palate. Select a large mixing bowl, measuring cup, etc. Check Rum again. It must be just right. To be sure Rum is of proper quality, pour level cup of Rum into a glass and drink it as fast as you can. Repeat.
With electric mixer, beat 1 cup butter in a large fluffy bowl. Add 1 seaspoon of thugar and beat again.
Meanwhile, make sure Rum is still OK right. Try another cup. Open second bottle i-fxx, ifff, if necessary. Add eggs, 2 cubs fried druit and beat til high. If druit gets stuck in beeters, pry loose with drewscriber. Sample Rum again, checking for tonscisticity. Next, sift 3 cups pepper or salt, really doesn't matter. Sample Rum.
Sift 1/2 pint lemon juice. Fold in chopped butter and strained nuts. Add 1 bablespoon of brown thugar or whatever color you can find. Wix mel. Greese oven. Turn cake pan to 350 degrees. Check Rum again and bo to ged.

Another Triumph
Mary W. Peters

DECORATOR ICING

Here's a recipe for icing for successful cake decorating when using a decorating tube. It can be stored in the refrigerator for a week if necessary. Makes 3 cups.

1/2 cup vegetable shortening (solid)
1 tsp vanilla
2 Tblsp milk
1/2 cup butter or margarine
4 cups sifted confectioners' sugar (1 lb)

Cream butter and shortening. Gradually add sugar, 1 cup at a time. When well beaten, add milk and beat on high speed til light and fluffy. Tint any color you wish with drops of food coloring. For chocolate icing, add **6 Tblsp unsweetened cocoa.**

ANGEL FOOD AMBROSIA

What to do with the leftover Christmas peanut brittle

1 10" Angelfood cake
1/4 cup cold water
8 egg yolks
2 cups whipping cream
1/2 lb peanut brittle candy, finely crushed
1 envelope gelatin
2 Tblsp Bourbon
1 cup powdered sugar

Slice angelfood cake in 3 sections crosswise. Soften gelatin in cold water and dissolve over low heat. Add the Bourbon whiskey. Beat the egg yolks until they are THICK. Gradually beat in the sugar. Stir in the gelatin and finally fold in the whipped cream that has been beaten stiff. Chill all until slightly thickened. Spread frosting on each layer and sprinkle with crushed peanut brittle. Stack layers and frost rest of cake with frosting and sprinkling on rest of peanut brittle. Chill for 2 or 3 hours.

❖ ❖ ❖ ❖ ❖ ❖ ❖ ❖ ❖

I just saw lovely Julia Childs interviewed on telly in 1990, looking as bright and spry as always. She declared, in this age of abstemious dining, that if you don't get the proper amount of butter, whipped cream and gravy in your body, your vitamins will simply not assimilate properly. Isn't that good news?

CHOCOLATE FROSTING
To drizzle over dessert cream puffs

3 ox. Semi-sweet chocolate
2 Tblsp butter
Melt together and spoon over filled eclairs or cream puffs and let drip down the sides!

❖ ❖ ❖ ❖ ❖ ❖ ❖ ❖ ❖

THE TROUBLE WITH OLD AGE IS -
EVERYBODY IS A CHIEF AND THERE ARE NO INDIANS

To divide a portion of food in two parts and keep peace in the family, let one person cut and let the other person have first choice
... Warren Connell

❖ ❖ ❖ ❖ ❖ ❖ ❖ ❖ ❖

POPPY SEED CAKE — Phyllis Weinberg

3/4 cup poppy seeds soaked in 3/4 cup milk overnight
1 1/2 cups sugar   **3/4 cup butter**
Cream butter & sugar and add the poppy seeds & milk, alternately with
2 cups Cake flour   **2 tsp baking powder**
1/4 tsp salt
After cake has been beaten together, fold in **4 beaten egg whites** to dough. Bake in THREE 8-inch cake pans at 350° for 25 minutes.

FILLING
Cook together until spreading consistency
1/2 cup sugar   **1 1/2 cups milk**
1 Tblsp corn starch   **4 egg yolks**
Then add
1 tsp vanilla and 1/4 cup chopped nuts
Put the layers together with the filling and frost the whole cake with whipped cream. This is a bridge club favorite.

CHOCOLATE ROLL   Betty Cutler

Betty Cutler, full of sunshine and solicitude, puts on a dinner party smoother than anyone I know. Her wonderful giggle is mainline infectious and best of times are mini-vacations with she and Bill at their cottage at Okoboji.
Betty says that this recipe came from her Mother, Muriel Ross and has always been a family favorite. The Supper Club is crazy about it also.

5 eggs, separated
Sift together
1 cup powdered sugar   1 tsp vanilla
3 level Tblsp cocoa   1 heaping Tblsp flour
Stir dry ingredients into beaten egg yolks. Add vanilla. Fold into well-beaten egg whites. Pour into 10 x 15 greased cake pan and bake 30 minutes at 300°. May take slightly longer cooking time. Allow to cool. Whip **1 cup whipping cream** and sweeten slightly. Spread on cake and roll toward you and place on cake plate. Frost with your favorite chocolate frosting. Refrigerate.

COFFEE CREAM CAKE   Maxine Watson

8 oz. marshmallows
1/4 cup instant coffee combined with 1 cup water
1 Tblsp cocoa combined with 1 Tblsp hot water
2 cups heavy cream, whipped
1 tsp vanilla

In a sauce pan place marshmallows, coffee and cocoa mixture. Heat over a low flame til marshmallows melt completely. Transfer to mixing bowl and cool Beat for 2 to 3 minutes til mixture is light in color and smooth. Whip cream and vanilla and combine with the coffee mixture.
Line and 8" or 9" spring form pan with **Sponge cake or lady fingers.**

Pour coffee mixture into spring form lined with cake and sprinkle top with **1 bar of shaved sweet chocolate (dark)**

For a birthday party:
Pipe rosettes of **1 cup heavy whip cream** whipped with **1 Tblsp of sugar** onto a greased cookie sheet, one for each year and one for good luck. With a birthday cake candle, make an indentation in the center of each rosette. Set cookie sheet in freezer. When ready to serve, place frozen rosettes on to cake and set a candle in each one.

Norrie and Tidy Swan included Doug & me, the Connells, Kissingers & Pauleys on a White Water Raft trip on the Colorado River in Utah, tenting at night on the banks of the Canyon. That boffo trip gave us all a reason to have a higher regard for one's tenacity of spirit.
The trip outward bound was made in the Pauley's customized bus for which I would have traded our own home! First stop was at the Kissinger's mountain cabin in Poudre River Canyon, in the Rockies. There was a trout stream in their back yard and tackle was flashing through the air as a gentle snow shower gave us all some indication of the lack of control we had over the weather the first week of September in the mountains. Arriving in Utah, gear was loaded into rafts, good-byes were said to civilization, and nature's bounteous beauty reinforced by whitewater thrills was the bit between our teeth.
It is lovely to know people who can survive wet sleeping bags through a night of Stygian blackness while icy rain weakens the stakes of tiny pup tents. I feel that the bottom line of this trip was to see if AARPIES could take it and keep their mouths shut. Frankly, we've never stopped talking about it and we'd do it all over again with the darling people.

HOMEMADE ORANGE CAKE

2/3 cup butter   **Grated zest of 1 large orange**
2 cups sugar   **1 cup milk**
4 whole eggs   **2 1/2 cups pastry flour**
2 rounded tsps of baking powder

Cream butter and sugar well, then add the beaten yolks. Add alternately the flour, which has been well sifted with the baking powder, and the milk. Lastly, fold in the four egg whites, which have been whipped stiff with a pinch of salt. Bake in three layers, at 350° for 25 minutes.

Candy

CANDY

Almond Butter Crunch	82
Best Ever Peanut Brittle	81
Candy Apples	85
Fudge for Christmas	85
Glazed Walnuts	82
Great Toffee Candy	82
Kiwi Dreams	86
Mocha Truffles	85
Old Fashioned fudge	81
Peppermint Fudge	84
Soft Pralines	81

SOFT PRALINES   Ninette Beaver

3 cups sugar	3/4 cup milk
1/2 tsp baking soda	2 tsp butter
2 cups pecan halves	1 1/2 tsp vanilla

Cook sugar, milk, baking soda over low heat, stirring occasionally until mixture reaches soft ball stage – 240°. Remove from heat, add butter, vanilla and pecans. Beat until candy loses its "glossy" look. Working fast, drip by spoonfuls onto waxed paper and let cool.

❖ ❖ ❖ ❖ ❖ ❖ ❖ ❖ ❖

BEST EVER PEANUT BRITTLE   Jere Mitten

Jere and Ham Mitten asked our children to their house one Christmas vacation to learn how to make peanut brittle and we're all still talking about how lovely they were to do that. One of our nicest Christmas memories.

1 cup white sugar	1/2 cup Karo white syrup
1/2 cup water	1 tsp salt

Boil ingredients to soft ball (240°) stage. Add **1 cup RAW peanuts, shelled and skinned.** Turn heat down to medium and cook to 320°. Remove from stove and add **1 tsp butter, 1 tsp vanilla and 1 tsp baking soda.** Stir REAL FAST and pour out on foil or a marble slab and pull out the edges til very THIN. That's what made her peanut brittle so good.

❖ ❖ ❖ ❖ ❖ ❖ ❖ ❖ ❖

OLD FASHIONED FUDGE

3 cups sugar	1/2 cup white Karo syrup
3/4 cup rich milk or cream	2 squares chocolate

Combine in pan and cook til mixture forms a soft ball by dripping 1/2 tsp of chocolate syrup in a cup of cold water. When soft ball forms, add **butter the size of a walnut, and 1 tsp vanilla.** Let cool and beat until thick. Turn into a buttered pan. You may add ½ cup of nuts if you wish.

ALMOND BUTTER CRUNCH

1 1/2 cups butter
1 cup sliced raw almonds
1/2 cup finely ground pecans or walnuts
2 cups sugar
1 1/2 cups semi-sweet chocolate chips

Melt butter over low heat in a heavy saucepan; do not boil. Add sugar and boil over medium heat stirring, until candy thermometer says 260°. Add almonds and continue stirring (mixture will be very thick). When thermometer reaches 295° pour candy on lightly greased 11x17 pan spreading candy thin with back of spoon. Work QUICKLY. Melt chocolate chips over low heat; when candy has cooled slightly, spread chocolate on top. Sprinkle with ground nuts while chocolate is still melted! Allow to harden for several hours and then break into pieces. Store in fridge. Makes about 2 pounds. What a Christmas present!

❖ ❖ ❖ ❖ ❖ ❖ ❖ ❖ ❖

GLAZED WALNUTS   Ninette Beaver

1 1/2 cups sugar
1 1/2 tsp vanilla
1/2 cup sour cream
3 cups walnut or pecan meat halves

Cook sugar and sour cream to soft ball stage – 240°. Remove from heat and stir in vanilla and then the nuts. Spread walnuts on waxed paper to cool.

❖ ❖ ❖ ❖ ❖ ❖ ❖ ❖ ❖

GREAT TOFFEE CANDY   Wilcox Family

2 cups chopped pecans
1 1/2 cups brown sugar
1 cup butter
1 6 oz. pkg. of chocolate chips

Spread nuts on bottom of 9x13 pan. Boil sugar and butter for 10 minutes, stirring constantly. Pour over nuts and let stand for a few minutes. Sprinkle chocolate chips over hot toffee. When chocolate has melted, spread evenly over toffee. Crack into pieces when cold.

❖ ❖ ❖ ❖ ❖ ❖ ❖ ❖ ❖

The Douglas Peters family lived for 16 years in an old English Tudor home in Fremont, Nebraska that was referred to as The Olde Haslam House; credits to the former owners that built the house in 1929. The attic was floored with boards from a platform built in Fremont City Park to showcase the famous evangelist Billy Sunday when he came to town to preach.

The house had mullioned windows whose metal created a fortress-like atmosphere and precipitated the departure of the previous owners, who had washed enough window panes to last them a lifetime. It was surrounded by huge pines and deciduous trees that were home to large families of squirrels. Our hunting dogs spent a lot of time twitching in their sleep. The garbage cans usually held one a week – a present to the family from a happy dog.

I learned to hate squirrels. The chimney served as an Interstate for them and a sooty, crazy squirrel is hard to deal with in a family of hunters. Mac blasted one on the attic steps that lay dying of heat prostration. Vish, the dog, cornered one on the sun porch in an overstuffed chair and was so confounded that it did not move, that they just sat and stared at each other. Doug shot one in the library that was sitting on top of an oil painting, missed, but brought him down with another blast as he perched on the hand-blocked linen drapes. I left the pepper holes in the walls for some years; it was great cocktail conversation.

There was also a wall in Duff's room that hummed every spring. A huge nest of honey bees called it home.

In the dark of night, a terrible storm came up that sent us flying to close the windows. I had just taken my hands off Mac's metal bedroom windows when lightening struck the roof, traveled across the peak, down past Mac's window, and jumped over to the huge tree just outside. The deafening sound plus the brilliance of the flash sent Mac and I into each other's arms, from which we did not soon release. It makes me shake again in the retelling.

GRANDMOTHERS

Don't forget to have a taffy pull when the kids come over to spend the night.

Or make caramel apples – Remember what fun that was?

Have you toasted marshmallows in the fireplace? - You can buy inexpensive wiener forks at any outlet store you have on hand.

Don't spend a lot of time on meals, because they won't like it – it's not like their Mother fixes it!

Don't even bother to ask them what they want – if it's got sugar or carbonation in it, they'll love it.

If the weather is nice, a walk to the park is good for both of you, taking a back-pack-snack!

And the best of all – an afternoon at the ZOO.

And try to take them just one at a time – competing for your attention wears them out and they have SO MUCH to talk about.

Try not to say the word NO.

Let them sleep with you if they are little.

PEPPERMINT FUDGE (Glady's mellow mints)

1 cup milk
1/3 cup white corn syrup
2 1/2 lb. Hershey Milk Chocolate, grated (40 oz.)
1/2 tsp peppermint oil (from drug store)
Bring milk and syrup to boil and turn fire low. Add grated chocolate slowly stirring well. Then add peppermint, turn into buttered tins and refrigerate. Add nuts if desired and cut in squares.

MOCHA TRUFFLES

In a 2 quart pan melt over low heat
1 8-oz. Package chocolate semi-sweet squares
Remove from heat and stir in
1/3 cup condensed sweet milk
1 Tblsp Kahlua or coffee liquer
1/4 tps almond extract
Refrigerate for about 40 minutes or until mixture is easy to shape into balls. Dust hands with cocoa. Shape 1 teaspoonful of chocolate mixture into a rounded ball and roll in more cocoa. Makes about 30 truffles. Store in a covered container.

CANDY APPLES

Scant 2 cups white Karo syrup **1 pound of sugar**
1/3 stick butter or margarine **dash of salt**
1 can condensed milk **20 apples medium size**

Wash and remove stems from apples. Insert stick in stem part of apples. Sticks can be purchased at meat markets. Combine in a pan: white syrup, sugar, butter and ½ of the can of milk. Cook over medium heat stirring constantly. When mixture begins to thicken, add <u>remainder</u> of the can of milk and continue cooking to soft ball stage (235°). Test by spooning caramel over the apple. Once the caramel will hold on the apples, spoon on QUICK before it sets. Place on buttered cookie sheets or in buttered cupcake papers.

FUDGE FOR CHRISTMAS   Mom Schenck

12 oz. Semi-sweet chocolate pieces
12 oz. German Sweet chocolate pieces
1 pint marshmallow cream   **2 cups nut meats**
4 1/2 cups sugar   **1 large can evaporated milk**
1 pinch salt   **2 Tblsp butter**

Put chocolate pieces, marshmallow cream and nut meats in a large bowl. Boil sugar, salt, butter and evaporated milk 6 minutes. Pour boiling syrup over ingredients in bowl. Beat until chocolate is all melted and pour in pan. Let stand a few hours before cutting. Store in a metal box to keep moist.

When Ford Motor Company hired Jonette Beaver as the first female executive in their corporate structure, her mother Ninette and I had to go back to Detroit and get this dear girl settled into her new life experience.

On the way, we stopped in Chicago at NBC headquarters, as Ninette had just finished a novel on Caril Fugate, partner-in-crime to the Starkweather murders in Lincoln, Nebraska. She was the primary television news interviewer for that story, and being with her at NBC news headquarters was like walking into a movie script. I was spellbound.

In Detroit, Jonette, Ninette and I took an Olympic gold in laughing while we were settling the young exec's apartment, and chicken was the word (we ate a lot of it) that turned the key in the ignition. We had a REALLY good time.

❖ ❖ ❖ ❖ ❖ ❖ ❖ ❖ ❖

KIWI DREAMS

4 medium Kiwi fruit pared and sliced in ¼ inch slices
1/4 lb. White chocolate – good quality

Drain kiwi on paper towels. Melt chocolate over boiling water until smooth and let stand about 5 minutes. Pat kiwi dry with paper towels and dip each slice in chocolate, covering halfway. Put on wax paper and refrigerate one hour. Place in gold fluted petit fours cups.

Casseroles, Quiches & Crêpes

CASSEROLES, QUICHES & CREPES

Aunt Grace's Egg Casserole 101
Baked Breakfast Soufflé 98
Baked Chicken Salad 90
Chafing Dish Scrambled Eggs 89
Cheese Soufflé 94
Cheese Strata with Ham 98
Cottage Cheese Eggs 100
Crab Meat Casserole 94
Don Juan Pie 102
Eggplant Casserole Peters 91
Escalloped Pineapple 100
Great Lasagne 97
Hot Fruit 93
Impossible Quiche 101
More Please 103
Moussaka 104
My Kids' Favorite Casserole 97
Party Chicken Lasagne 90
Peters Pork and Putt Bean Casserole 92
Quiche Lorraine 99
Reuben Casserole 92
Scrambled Egg Casserole for 20 93
Spinach Quiche without Crust 103
Turkey Tetrazzini 105
Wile Rice Casserole 89

WILD RICE CASSEROLE   Alice Mendenhall

Take **1 3/4 cups of wild rice** and cook it until it is light and fluffy. Then add the following ingredients to the rice, mix and place in a casserole and put in a 350° oven for 1 hour.

1 large chopped onion	**1 chopped green pepper**
1 tsp sage	**3/4 cup chopped celery**
1 tsp salt	**2 Tblsp melted butter**
1/2 cup sherry	**1 beaten egg**
1 can mushroom soup	**1 small pkg. slivered almonds**

For those hard-to-open jars, put on a pair of rubber gloves or wrap a couple of rubber bands around the lid.

To separate stamps that are stuck together, put in the freezer.

CHAFING DISK SCRAMBLED EGGS

9 eggs   **1 large can evaporated milk**
1/2 tsp salt   **1/4 tsp pepper**
1 Tblsp chopped chives   **1 Tblsp butter**
1 3-oz. pkg. of cream cheese

Beat together eggs, evaporated milk, salt, pepper and chives. Melt 1 Tblsp butter over hot water in a chafing dish. Add eggs and cook 15 minutes. Do not stir. Open chafing dish and stir once, cover and cook again for 15 minutes more. Cut cream cheese into chunks and fold into eggs. Cover and cook til cheese begins to melt – just a minute or so. Makes 6 to 8 servings.

One of the most difficult instruments to play well is second fiddle.

* * * * * * *

Among the many things money won't buy is what it used to.

* * * * * * *

Wisdom has been defined as knowing the difference between pulling your weight and throwing it around.

BAKED CHICKEN SALAD — Joyce Pogge

This recipe is simply wonderful for a large luncheon where you want to be a part of the action. Can be prepared the day before with the potato chips garnished before baking on the day of the party.

2 cups of chopped chicken	**2 cups chopped celery**
salt and pepper to taste	**1 pkg. slivered almonds**
2 cans Cream of Chicken soup	**2 Tblsp lemon juice**
3/4 cup mayonnaise	**4 tsp scraped onion**
3 hard boiled eggs, sliced	

Make a layer of 1 cup chicken, 1 cup celery, and 1/2 pkg. of almonds in a large baking dish. Combine salt, pepper, soup, lemon juice, mayonnaise and onion. Place half the egg slices and half the soup mixture over chick in dish. Repeat process. Top with **2 cups potato chip crumbs.** Bake at 375° for 20 minutes and plan on 12 servings.

❖ ❖ ❖ ❖ ❖ ❖ ❖ ❖ ❖

PARTY CHICKEN LASAGNE — Jane S. Peters

12 oz. Lasagne noodles	**1 can Cream of Mushroom soup**
1/2 tsp salt	**2/3 cup milk**
1/2 tsp poultry seasoning	**1 16-oz. Cream style cottage cheese**
1 1/3 cup chopped onion	**1/4 cup minced parsley**
6 oz. Cream cheese, softened	**1/3 cup sliced green olives**
1/3 cup chopped green pepper	**4 cups cooked diced chicken**
Pimento for garnish	

Cook noodles in boiling salted water til tender. Drain, rinse in cold water. Mix soup, milk, salt and seasonings in saucepan and heat. Beat cheeses together. Stir in olives, onion, parsley, and green pepper. Place half of noodles in baking dish, spread half of cheese mixture, half of chicken, half of soup mixture. Repeat layers and top with a mixture of **5 oz. of grated Parmesan cheese and 1/4 cup fine bread crumbs browned in 2 Tblsp melted butter.** Bake in 9x12 dish, at 375° for 30 minutes.

Delores Borman is the ultimate trip partner. If they call up and say Delores is going, be sure and sign up – it's going to be FUN! Especially remembered are trips for the girls to the Ozarks for power shopping and general craziness. Delores is also a very bright bridge player; but (I hate to get into this) she purloins recipes and passes them off as her own. She got caught in a nasty little caper that involved the NonPareil Newspaper and an Eggplant Casserole. And here it is:

EGGPLANT CASSEROLE PETERS

Peel and slice rounds of a **large eggplant** into ½ inch slices. Dip into batter of **2 egggs beaten with 4 tsp milk** and then dip into **crushed soda cracker crumbs,** coating well. Fry until brown on both sides in **1/2 bacon grease and 1/2 butter.** Remove slices from frying pan to casserole and overlap. Prepare cheese sauce:

2 Tblsp butter	**1 tsp Worcestershire sauce**
2 Tblsp flour	**dash of Tabasco**
1/2 tsp salt	**1 cup grated sharp Cheddar cheese**
1 1/2 cups milk	

Pour sauce over casserole. Bake at 350° until bubbly hot, about 30 minutes. Sprinkle with paprika.

REUBEN CASSEROLE _____ Ruth Smith

2 lbs corned beef, cooked and cut into bite size pieces (can use two 13 oz. cans corned beef)
4 cups sauerkraut, drained and chopped (2 7-oz. cans)
1 pint sour cream
1 chopped onion
6 cups or 1 1/2 lbs grated Swiss cheese
1 1/2 sticks butter
9 slices of dark rye bread, cubed (enough bread to cover)

Grease 9x12 casserole. Mix sauerkraut, sour cream, and onions. Spread over bottom of casserole. Then add corned beef and then cheese. Top with a covering of rye bread. Pour melted butter over all and cover with foil. Bake at 350° for 45 to 60 minutes until hot. Freezes well and feeds 10 to 12.

❖ ❖ ❖ ❖ ❖ ❖ ❖ ❖ ❖

My dear girlfriends will remember as young brides in the 1950's at our house, that I tapped on a glass while at the luncheon table so that I could be sure that I had everyone's attention.

"Girls, sin has crept into Council Bluffs! Doug told me yesterday that the dear little old ladies at Axelsen's Bakery were running a gambling den and that they were stuffing lottery sheets in the hot chocolate eclairs."

The laughing just died down in 1989, but I can still remember the chagrin I felt that day for having been so betrayed by my husband. That disastrous day was compounded with the realization that Creamed Sweetbreads in patty shells are not everyone's luncheon favorite and Meringues cannot be made in humid weather.

You see, we've all had our moment on the block.

PETERS PORK AND PUTT BEAN CASSEROLE _____

1 16-oz. can cut green beans	1 16-oz. can cut wax beans
1 16-oz. can lima beans	1 31-oz. can pork and beans
1 24-oz. can chili beans	1 6-oz. can tomato sauce
1 6-oz. can tomato paste	1 cup brown sugar
1 small onion, chopped	1 green pepper, chopped

16 oz. mild Italian sausage skinned, chopped, browned

Mix all together and bake at 250° for 4 hours.

SCRAMBLED EGG CASSEROLE for 20 _____

Heat together until melted:
4 cups milk   salt and pepper as you wish
1 8-oz. cream cheese **1/2 cup butter**
Beat in 30 eggs
Bake at 350° for 20 minutes and then stir eggs. Then bake for 10 minutes more.

In the last 3 or 4 minutes of baking, you may mix into the eggs cooked bacon, ham or sausage for an extra hearty breakfast casserole.

❖ ❖ ❖ ❖ ❖ ❖ ❖ ❖ ❖

HOT FRUIT_____ Alice Mendenhall

1 can pears, drained
1 can pineapple chunks, drained
1 can sliced peaches
1 small bottle of maraschino cherries, drained
Arrange all fruit in a baking dish and spread with the following:
1/2 cup butter mixed with 1/2 cup brown sugar to which has been added
1 tsp curry powder.
Sprinkle over fruit and bake for 1 hours at 300°.

CHEESE SOUFFLÉ

This is a strata, is easy and simply delicious

4 slices of day old bread from a large loaf rather thick slices (That's what my recipe says!)
1/2 lb. Sharp Cheddar cheese, shredded
3 eggs, beaten
2 cups of whole milk
1 tsp dry mustard
1/2 tsp salt and some fresh ground pepper

Cut off crusts and butter bread. Cut in cubes. Butter casserole baking dish, put half of bread on bottom, then half of the cheese and repeat bread and cheese in another layer. Beat eggs, add mustard, salt, pepper and milk. Pour over bread and cheese and let stand at least 2 hours and better if overnight. Set in pan of hot water and bake for 2 hours at 300°.

❖ ❖ ❖ ❖ ❖ ❖ ❖ ❖ ❖

CRAB MEAT CASSSEROLE — Momo
Serves 8

5 Tblsp butter
3 Tblsp flour
2 cups milk
Make a white sauce of the above and then add:
1/2 tsp celery salt
1 Tblsp minced parsley
2 Tblsp minced onion
1 Tblsp grated orange rind (optional)
1 Tblsp minced green pepper
Remove from heat and add:
2 Tblsp sherry
1 whole pimento minced
1 dash hot sauce
1 tsp salt and a dash of pepper
Carefully turn in **1 beaten egg** and stir together and add **1 lb. of crab meat.** Put in a 2 quart casserole and sprinkle with bread crumbs that have been sautéed in **1 Tblsp butter.** Bake at 350° for 15 to 20 minutes to heat through.

BELOVED CABIN ON THE PLATTE RIVER

The Fourth of July has held a special fascination for the Peters men. The principal reason for Douglas Peters to own a cabin on the Platte River was to have a place for family and friends to gather for picnics in the summer, but especially a safe haven for a bang-up Fourth of July. And I mean, the male members would start ordering from Fireworks catalogues in April and May, readjusting selections, getting permits, chortling over large delivered boxes filled with fireworks that would be laid out, checked and rechecked.

Hardly a child through the years could bear to miss the Fourth of July. Always cole slaw, ribs, chicken, beans, and brownies and ice cream. And bring your friends! The booming and banging would go on into the late hours.

At the end of the evening, a huge bonfire in the pit and singing the old songs. Lots of people stayed overnight in tents or sleeping bags. It was always great fun. Now they are all old enough to bring their own children.

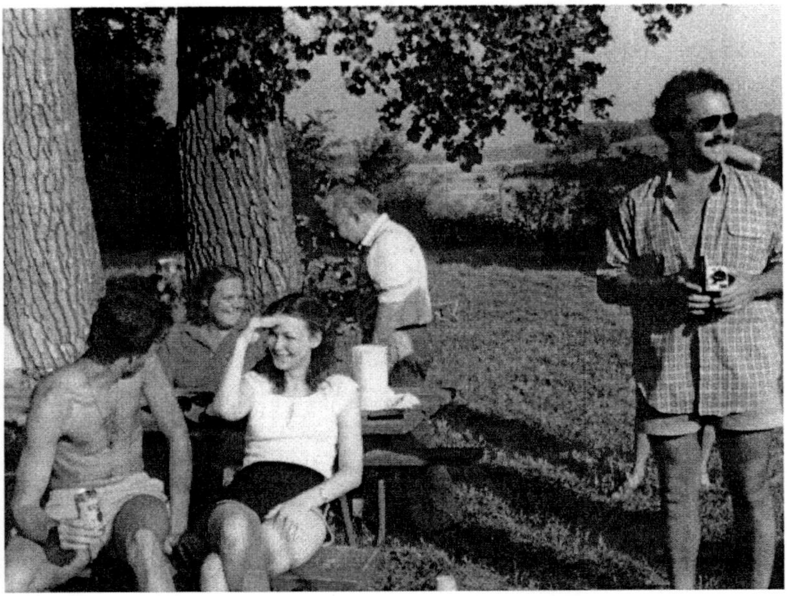

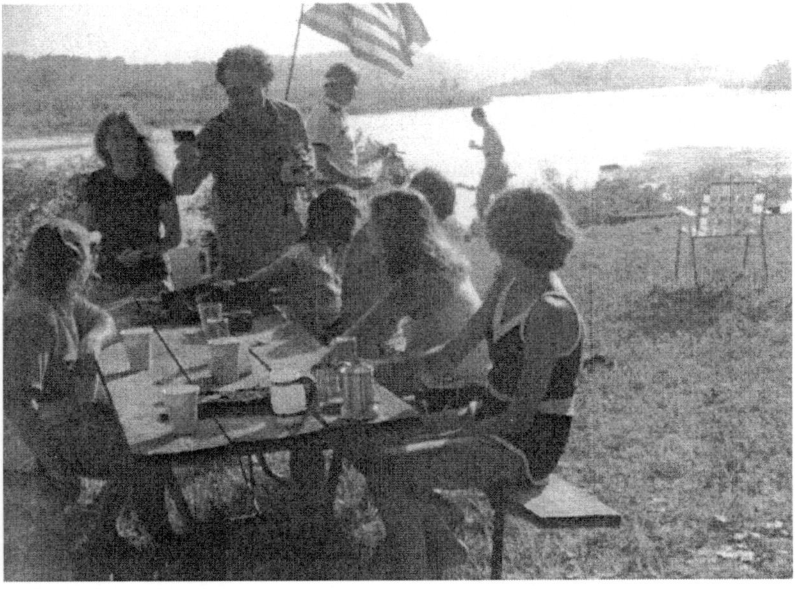

GREAT LASAGNE

In 2 Tblsp of oil brown:
2 lbs coarse ground beef
1 cup chopped onion
1 Tblsp salt
1/2 Tblsp pepper

Cook for 30 minutes:
1 15-oz. can tomato sauce
1 12-oz. can tomato puree
2 15-oz. cans tomatoes
salt to taste
2 Tblsp chopped parsley
1 Tblsp oregano
1 Tblsp basil
1 cup water

Mix together:
1 large cottage cheese large curd, drained well
1 small cottage cheese large curd, drained well
3 small eggs beaten
3/4 cup grated Parmesan cheese
salt to taste

3 packages sliced Mozzarella cheese, cut in 1/3 strips to place across casserole
2 packages lasagne noodles – cook in kettle of boiling water to which has been added **1 Tblsp salt and 2 Tblsp oil.**
When tender, drain, put in cold water and then dry.
Layer the above ingredients starting with tomato sauce in the bottom of a greased casserole. This recipe will make 2 casseroles and freezes very well. Be sure and top the prepared casseroles with more Parmesan cheese when all the layers have been added.

MY KIDS' FAVORITE CASSEROLE   Irene Peters

Brown **1 lb. hamburger with 1 medium chopped onion**
Pour into skillet with hamburger and onion:
1 can tomato soup
1 can water
Sprinkle in **1 cup your choice noodles** and cover pan. Cook on low until noodles are tender. Pour in
1 can corn, drained
Put all ingredients in a casserole. Add
1/2 lb. chopped cheese of any type, or mixed!
1 small chopped green pepper
1 or 2 tomatoes, chopped
A couple shots of Worcestershire sauce
Bake at 325° for 1 hour.

BAKED BREAKFAST SOUFFLÉ

1 1/2 pounds bulk sausage
9 eggs, slightly beaten
1 1/2 tsp dry mustard
4 slices white bread cut into cubes and crusts trimmed from bread
1 1/2 cups grated Cheddar cheese
3 cups whole milk
1 tsp salt

Brown crumbled sausage and drain well. Mix eggs, milk, and seasonings. Stir in bread, sausage, and cheese. Pour into a well-greased 9x13 pan, cover the casserole and refrigerate overnight. Bake uncovered at 350° for about 50 minutes. Shake pan to see if soufflé is set. Let rest a few minutes and cut to serve 12.

❖ ❖ ❖ ❖ ❖ ❖ ❖ ❖ ❖

CHEESE STRATA WITH HAM   Martha Walsh
Serves 10 to 12 people

6 plus slices of bread, crusts removed and cut in triangles. (Enough to cover the bottom of a 9x12 baking dish and also another layer)
3 1/2 cups of cut-up ham   10 oz. sharp Cheddar cheese, shredded
1/2 tsp onion, grated   10 oz. Swiss cheese, shredded
3 cups milk   6 eggs
1/2 tsp dry mustard   3 cups corn flakes, crushed
1/2 cup melted butter

Start layering bread, ham, cheese and repeat to make two layers in casserole pan. Mix mustard, milk, beaten eggs, onion and pour over layers. Chill overnight. Remove from fridge and melt butter to which crushed corn flakes are added. Spread over casserole. Cover lightly with foil and put in a 375° oven and bake for 50 to 60 minutes. Let rest for 10 minutes before serving.

QUICHE LORRAINE

This recipe comes from Carol Harvey's sister who lives in New York and Italy; it is just right.

1/4 lb. bacon, cut in 14 inch strips and fried crisp and drained
Sauté **1 Tblsp chopped shallots with 1/2 medium onion**
Grate **1 1/2 cups Gruyere cheese (none other will do).** Layer this in a 9" deep-dish pie shell that has been baked for about 4 minutes (to seal the crust so it will stay flaky). Beat together:
4 eggs
salt and pepper to taste
1 cup whipping cream
2 Tblsp dry vermouth
3-4 grinds of fresh nutmeg
Bake at 375° for 24 to 30 minutes. Test for firmness. Let pie set up for 5 to 10 minutes before cutting. Serves 6 to 8 people.

The John Pogge family of seven were about the best fun ever. What wonderful summer memories of that House of Happiness on the Fremont Lakes, with kids in the sand and water and the eternal spaghetti and brownies.
Joyce is the best cook ever and the first person I knew who took the quantum leap into the 21st century and mastered the Microwave!

RECIPE FOR LIFE

4 cups of love
3 cups of forgiveness
5 spoons of hope
4 QUARTS of faith

2 cups of loyalty
1 cup of friendship
2 spoons of tenderness
1 BARREL of laughter

Take love and loyalty, mix it thoroughly with faith; Bend the above with tenderness, kindness and understanding; Add friendship and hope, sprinkle abundantly with laughter . . .
Serve daily with generous helpings!

COTTAGE CHEESE EGGS   Dr. A.T. Harvey

Sauté   **1/4 lb. dried bbef cut in thin strips**
         4 Tblsp finely minced green onions in
2 Tblsp butter in the top pan of a chafing dish over low heat until the onions are lightly browned. Remove the pan from heat and place it over the hot water pan of the chafing dish. Blend:
1/2 cup cottage cheese with 6 well beaten eggs and beat til very smooth. Pour this mixture over the beef and onions and cook until the eggs are thick and soft. Serve on toasted English muffins that have been sprinkled with paprika.

❖ ❖ ❖ ❖ ❖ ❖ ❖ ❖ ❖

ESCALLOPED PINEAPPLE

4 cups bread cubes
2 cups sugar
1 #2 1/2 can crushed pineapple, undrained

a little milk
3/4 cup butter
3 eggs

Moisten bread cubes with just enough milk to moisten them. Set aside. In another bowl, cream sugar and butter. Add eggs, beating after each one. Fold in bread cubes and pineapple. Bake in a 7x12 casserole at 350° for 1 hour until golden brown. Serve warm.

❖ ❖ ❖ ❖ ❖ ❖ ❖ ❖ ❖

IMPOSSIBLE QUICHE

12 slices bacon, fired crisp and crumbled
1 cup Swiss cheese shredded (4 oz.)
1/3 cup chopped onion
2 cups milk
1/2 cup buttermilk baking mix for biscuits
4 eggs
1/4 tsp salt
1/8 tsp pepper

Heat oven to 350°. Lightly grease large pie plate. Sprinkle bacon, cheese and onion over bottom of pan. Place remaining ingredients in blender and blend on high speed one minute. Pour into pie plate and bake 50 to 55 minutes until set in center. Let stand 5 minutes before cutting.

AUNT GRACE'S EGG CASSEROLE   Martha Walsh

Who can remember Aunt Grace Hughes Caughlan besides Martha, who said that she had beautiful hands! And she surely did leave a recipe for the best brunch dish that was ever put together. We ALL have this recipe and have used it lots. Aunt Grace suggested that women will eat three halves, but you can count on the men eating four halves!

Hard boil enough eggs to feed your company and devil the centers with mustard, mayonnaise and Worcestershire sauce. Place halves in a large casserole and make a medium thick white sauce, enough to bathe the eggs well. To this white sauce, add diced smoked ham and fresh sautéed mushrooms. Add lots of Parmesan cheese to this sauce. Pour over the eggs in the casserole and cover the top with bread crumbs that have been browned in butter. Bake in a 350° oven until bubbly – 1/2 hour.

DON JUAN PIE   Ruth Smith
Ruthie says this is really MAGNEEEFICO!

Sauté 2 medium onions
Add 2 small cans green chilies, diced
4 cups Enchilada sauce (green chili salsa)
4 cups Snappy Tom tomato juice – simmer 20 minutes
4 cups grated Velveeta cheese
4 cups heavy cream
Mix above ingredients in a double boiler til cheese melts. Bake a **4 to 5 lb. chicken** in the oven wrapped in foil. When the chicken is tender (about 2 hours) remove all meat from bird. Or simmer 4 chicken breasts and cut up. Sauté **2 dozen frozen corn tortillas (Ricardo's)** in bacon fat just a few minutes on each side to soften. Spoon in sauce on bottom of casserole, layer tortillas, chicken, sauce and repeat this process til ingredients are used up. Bake at 350° til bubbly. *Serves 12.*

When it comes to a really fun couple, pull out the big purple ribbon for Ruth and Joe Smith. Everybody had more crazy times and laughs with these two good friends – always full of imagination, energy and enthusiasm. Their kitchen on Prairie Hills Lane was generally full of people discussing the party last night, state of your health, and the plans for tomorrow. They spent a lot of time in Acapulco getting tans and improving their Spanish, and entertaining Joe's wonderful relatives from Tennessee (dig in your cleats)!

MORE PLEASE _____Sarah Ginn
Here is a noodle and hamburger and cheese casserole that surpasses the average expectation. But one just simply must use Tillamook cheese from Oregon.

1 large pkg. of noodles	3 cloves garlic, chopped
3 1/2 lbs of good hamburger	1 Tblsp chili powder
2 large green peppers, diced	1 tsp pepper
2 tsp oregano	1 Tblsp parsley
2 tsp salt	3 small cans tomato paste
2 large chopped onions	3 small cans water
2 cans mushrooms	2 cans tomato sauce
2 Tblsp sugar	2 large cans whole tomatoes
1 lb. of Tillamook cheddar cheese	2 med. jars green stuffed olives

Brown onion, peppers and garlic in olive oil. Brown hamburger and drain. Add all ingredients together except noodles and cheese. Simmer the above ingredients together for four hours. Then combines sauce with cheese and noodles. Put in casserole and refrigerate overnight. Reheat in medium oven for 1 hours – 350°.

❖ ❖ ❖ ❖ ❖ ❖ ❖ ❖ ❖

SPINACH QUICHE without crust _____ Glenna Spetman

1 Tblsp butter, in which you sauté
1 large onion, chopped
1 pkg. frozen chopped spinach (thaw and squeeze dry in paper towel)
3/4 lb. Swiss or Muenster cheese, shredded
5 eggs beaten
salt and pepper

Bake at 350° for 40-45 minutes in buttered 9-inch pie pan. You may sprinkle crumbled cooked bacon or sautéed mushrooms on top if you wish.

❖ ❖ ❖ ❖ ❖ ❖ ❖ ❖ ❖

MOUSSAKA
Lamb and eggplant married in a lovely tomato sauce

Buy **2 egg plants** and peel them. Cut 12 slices 1/2 inch thick, salt them and brush both sides with **1/2 cup melted butter.** Place on baking sheet and broil on both sides til nicely golden.

In **2 Tblsp of butter**, sauté
1 chopped clove of garlic (or more if you love it)
1 1/2 lbs of lean lamb cut in chunks
1 cup of chopped onion
Cook until brown. And then add
1/2 tsp oregano   **1 tsp basil**
1/2 tsp cinnamon   **1 tsp salt**
dash of pepper   **2 cans of 8 oz. tomato sauce**
Simmer for 1/2 hour, and then stir into the sauce
2 Tblsp pulverized bread crumbs
Make a cream sauce in another pan of
2 Tblsp flour
1/2 tsp salt
2 cups of milk. Then stir in carefully
2 beaten egg yolks
In order to put this casserole together, have a 2 quart dish or even better, a 12x7½x2. Grease casserole and put 6 slices of eggplant in dish and sprinkle with a 1/4 cup of the following cheese mixture:
1/2 cup Parmesan cheese grated, mixed with 1/2 cup grated Cheddar cheese.
Put meat sauce over eggplant and cheeses, sprinkle with 1/4 cup mixed cheeses. Put remaining 6 slices of eggplant over meat sauce and sprinkle with 1/4 cup mixed cheese. Cover all with cream sauce and sprinkle with 1/4 cup mixed cheese. Bake at 350° for 35 to 40 minutes til hot and this will serve 12 as it is rich.

TURKEY TETRAZZINI   Momo

Cook together for 2 minutes but do not brown:
2/3 cup butter
1/2 cup flour
Add:
1 cup hot milk
1 cup hot chicken bouillon
1/2 tsp salt
1/8 tsp nutmeg
1/2 tsp white peper
1/4 cup dry sherry
Then add carefully:
3/4 cup heavy cream
Sauté in butter:
1/2 lb. sliced mushrooms
1 green pepper, diced
1 medium onion, diced
Dice:
3 1/2 cups of cooked turkey (can substitute chicken)
Cook until soft:
1 pound of spaghetti and drain

Grease casserole and cover bottom with thin layer of sauce. Then add layer of spaghetti, turkey and vegetables, cover with sauce and sprinkle liberally with **grated Parmesan cheese.** Repeat process until ingredients are all used and top with more **grated Parmesan**. You can refrigerate or freeze at this point. This serves 6 to 8 people. To reheat: place in 350° oven for 1/2 hour. When reheating, check to see if casserole is moist – if not, add a little more cream and move ingredients slightly with fork. This dish should be moist but not runny.

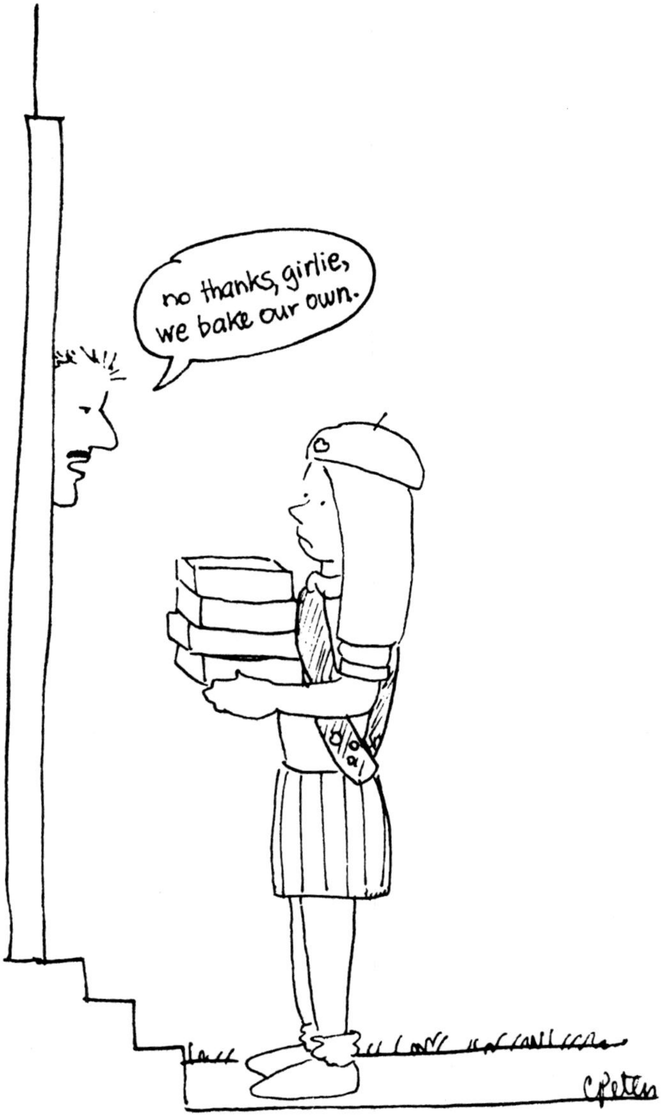

COOKIES

COOKIES

Aunt Lillie's Date & Orange Slice Bar 119
Brown Sugar or Vitamin Good For You Cookies 111
Brownies 122
Butter Pecan Turtle Cookies 108
Cake Brownies 121
Chocolate Brownies 122
Chocolate Drop Cookies 114
Chocolate Krinkles 117
Coconut Cookies 126
Cookies for Sobbing Boys 112
Date Pinwheels 123
Easy Chocolate Frosting (for cookies) 114
Fast Chocolate Crackles 124
Fast Cookies 108
Gingerbread Cookies 115
Gooey Marshmallow Puffs 114
Gumdrop Mince Meat Cookies 113
Humdingers 113
Icebox Cookies 121
Impossible Brownie Pie 124
Malcolm Sugar Cookies 123
Oatmeal / Chocolate Chip / Nut Cookies 121
Oatmeal Carmelitas 119
Oatmeal Lace Cookies 120
Pecan Slices Superb 127
Peters Christmas Ammonium Carbonate Cookies 118
Peters Christmas Butter Cookies 117
Potato Chip Cookies 119
Pumpkin Bars 115
Soft Chewy Chocolate Chip Cookies 112
Soft Ginger Cookies 118
Sour Cream Cookies 113
Toll House Golden Brownies 112
White Sugar Cookies 126
Yum Yum Eze Cookies 108

BUTTER PECAN TURTLE COOKIES

CRUST:
**2 cups all purpose flour   1 cup firmly packed brown sugar
1/2 cup butter, softened**
Combine crust ingredients until particles are fine. Pat firmly into an ungreased 13 x 9 x 2 pan and sprinkle
1 cup whole pecan halves over the unbaked crust.

CARAMEL LAYER:
**2/3 cup butter   1/2 cup firmly packed brown sugar
1 cup chocolate chips**
Combine butter and brown sugar in a saucepan and cook until the mixture boils. Boil for 1/2 to 1 minute, stirring constantly. Pour evenly over the crust and pecans. Bake at 350° for 18 to 22 minutes til caramel is bubbly and crust golden brown. Remove from oven and immediately sprinkle entire surface with chocolate chips. Allow to melt slightly and gently swirl as they melt. Cool and cut into 3 dozen bars.

YUM YUM EZE COOKIES   Phyllis Weinberg

My Fremont bridge partner, Phyl always brought a plate of these cookies to the Peters for Christmas. It was hard for me to share them with the children - I told myself she was MY friend and she actually meant them for me and I ate them guilt-free. Really she OWED them to me - for all that we went through at the gaming tables.

3/4 cup brown sugar   2 sticks butter
Cook for 13 to 14 minutes. Add
2 small packages sliced almonds and mix together.
Spread a 10" by 15" sheet pan, with an edge, with **Cinnamon Crisp graham crackers.** Spread over crackers butter/sugar mix. Bake for 13 minutes at 350°. Cut into 1 by 2 inch bars.

FAST COOKIES

Add **2 eggs and 1/2 cup cooking oil** to **any flavor cake mix** and you have a quick batch of cookies. Raisins, nuts or coconut can be added, if desired. Drop by teaspoonfuls onto slightly greased cookie sheets and bake at 350° for 8 to 10 minutes. How's that Grandma?

GRANDMA DUNNELL - *Overnighters at Grandma Dunnell's were just grand. I always could have more than one of the best Rootbeer floats I ever tasted and a VITAMIN cookie. Grandma taught me how to make stringers of paper doll cutouts from fan-folded magazine pages. We would take the most wonderful nature hikes & she taught me about butterflies, leaves, flowers, and a love for nature. At night, Grandma and I would snuggle in her bed together and watch the Johnny Carson show. She would let me smell her bottle of camphor (that was used for everything) and she always had a stash of mentholyptus throat lozenges which I never wanted to try. In the morning, she would make blueberry pancakes and blueberry syrup from REAL blueberry juice which always impressed me. After breakfast, Grandma would take me to her big bureau and open the top drawer and, wrapped in a scarf, was her special stash of firecrackers. She would give me one ladyfinger (which seemed to me like a stick of dynamite) to throw into the flames of the trash burning drum on the lot of her duplex. Mr. Yates, her crabby neighbor, always yelled about that!   - - - - - Gere*

BROWN SUGAR or VITAMIN GOOD FOR YOU COOKIES ____
Grandma Dunnell's recipe

5 small eggs or 4 large eggs
2 cups brown sugar
1 tsp baking soda

1 cup butter
1 tsp vanilla (or 2 tsp)
1/2 tsp salt

Beat together and add at least **4 cups flour.** Pat out with hands on floured board and cut with a big cookie cutter. Put **walnut half or large raisin** in the center. These are for the children to pick out and discard. Bake at 350° for 10 minutes or so.

None of the rest of us really knew Grandfather Douglas Peters except his family as he died when he was only 44. This handsome man was much beloved by his peers and spoken of with great affection by them. John and Tuds recall that his humor departed twice -- and then the hair brush was applied with vigor.
Once, the boys found their father's 22 pistol, had a little target practice and managed to kill 4 or 5 of his English Calling ducks which were very fine live decoys.
Another time concerned a Cowboy and Indian foray on the front porch which also involved the same 22 pistol which they had been forbidden to touch. As John leaped for an attack from behind the corner of the porch brandishing the gun, their father drove his car into the driveway.

COOKIES FOR SOBBING BOYS (Butterscotch)

1 cup butter & lard
2 cups brown sugar
2 eggs
1 tsp soda
3 1/2 to 4 cups of flour

1 tsp cream of tartar
1 tsp vanilla
1/2 tsp salt
1 cup fine nut meats

Cream shortening and sugar. Add beaten eggs and mix together well. Add vanilla, nut meats and dry ingredients sifted together. Add last of flour and mix with hands. Divide dough in four parts. Roll in a long roll and wrap in wax paper. Chill. Slice and bake at 375° for about 12 minutes until brown.

❖ ❖ ❖ ❖ ❖ ❖ ❖ ❖ ❖

TOLL HOUSE GOLDEN BROWNIES

2 cups unsifted flour
2 tsp baking powder
3/4 cup brown sugar, firmly packed
1 12-oz. pkg. chocolate chips
1 tsp vanilla

3 eggs
3/4 cup sugar
1 tsp salt
3/4 cup softened butter

Beat til creamy white and brown sugar and butter and vanilla. Add eggs one at a time and beat well after each addition. Add flour, baking powder and salt. Spread evenly in 15 x 10 pan and bake at 350° for 30 to 35 minutes.

❖ ❖ ❖ ❖ ❖ ❖ ❖ ❖ ❖

SOFT CHEWY CHOCOLATE CHIP COOKIES

3/4 cup Butterflavored Crisco
1 1/4 cups brown sugar, firmly packed
2 Tblsp milk
1 Tblsp vanilla
1 egg
1 3/4 cups flour

1 tsp salt
3/4 tsp baking soda
1 cup pecan pieces
1 cup semi-sweet chocolate chips

Cream Crisco, sugar, milk and vanilla til creamy. Blend in egg; finally flour, salt and baking soda. Add chocolate and nuts and drop by rounded tablespoons 3 inches apart. Bake 375° for 8 to 10 minutes, 11 to 13 minutes for CRISP. Cool on baking sheet for 2 minutes before removing.

HUMDINGERS   Jane Peters Bourland

From our cousin from Peoria, Illinois. She's the one that makes pancakes in tiny iron skillets in butter, removes them from the pan, dredges them with powdered sugar and squeezes lemon juice over them for breakfast. ---- ooooohhh!

1/2 lb. of butter creamed with
5 Tblsp sugar
Sift in **2 cups of cake flour** and mix well. Then add **2 tsp vanilla** and **1 1/2 cups well chopped pecans**
Roll into small balls and bake in 350° oven for 25 to 30 minutes. Remove from oven and roll in powdered sugar while still hot. When cold, roll in powdered sugar again. Store in a tin if you have any cookies left.

GUMDROP MINCE MEAT COOKIES   Viola Beats

1 cup shortening   1 cup granulated sugar
1 cup brown sugar   2 eggs
2 1/2 cups sifted flour   1 tsp salt
1/2 tsp soda   1 tsp cinnamon
1 cup mincemeat   1 cup finely chopped walnuts
2/3 cup finely cut green and red gumdrops
NOTE: When cutting gumdrops, use a little flour to prevent sticking to knife.

Thoroughly cream shortening, sugars, and eggs together. Sift dry ingredients together. Dredge mincemeat, nuts and gumdrops in 1/2 cup flour mixture; stir remaining dry ingredients into creamed mixture. Stir in floured gumdrop mixture. Shape into rolls, 2" in diameter or wrap in waxed paper and chill overnight. Cut in thin slices and place on ungreased cookie sheet. Bake in preheated 375° oven 6 to 8 minutes. Makes 7-8 dozen.

SOUR CREAM COOKIES   Jerry Dodson

1 cup sugar   1/2 cup butter
1/2 cup sour cream   1 tsp soda
1 tsp vanilla
Add enough flour (1 1/2 cups) to make a soft dough

Roll thin, put on cookie sheet and sprinkle with sugar and nutmeg. Bake in a moderate oven.

GOOEY MARSHMALLOW PUFFS   Cory Peters
These are fun to make with little kids 'cuz they are sweet, fast, and EEEEEzy.

Marshmallows	Butter
Sugar	Refrigerator Biscuits
Cinnamon	

Roll out the refrigerator biscuits, separately, until they are a little larger than a silver dollar and place them on a cookie sheet. Mix together the cinnamon and sugar in a bowl. Take a marshmallow and dip in the butter, which has been melted, and then roll in the sugar/cinnamon to coat thoroughly. Put each marshmallow on a biscuit and wrap the dough around it. Bake at 325° until golden brown or until the marshmallow is yummy gooey. Great to eat hot, or let cool and eat later. Ummmm.

CHOCOLATE DROP COOKIES   Mrs. Jessup

1 cup sugar	1/2 cup butter
2 squares Bakers chocolate	2 eggs
1/8 tsp salt	1 tsp vanilla
1 1/2 tsp baking powder	1 scant tsp cinnamon
3/8 cup of milk (less than 1/3 cup)	1 3/4 cup flour
1 cup walnuts, coarse chopped	

Beat eggs, salt and sugar together. Add milk and mix. Melt chocolate and butter in double boiler. Add to egg mixture. Then add flour and baking powder, vanilla and nuts. Drop spoonfuls on cookie sheet the size of a walnut. Bake between 350° and 375° for about 10 minutes. Frost with chocolate frosting: see below.

EASY CHOCOLATE FROSTING

6 Tblsp soft butter or oleomargarine	1/2 cup cocoa
2 2/3 cup confectioners sugar	1/3 cup milk
pinch of salt	1 tsp vanilla

You may need an extra tablespoon of milk for good spreadability. This makes 2 cups of frosting.

GINGERBREAD COOKIES _____ Irene (Bangaw) Savidge

1 cup molasses
1 cup packed brown sugar
1 cup lard
Put in saucepan, place on stove and bring to a boil. Add:
2 cups flour and cool mixture. Add
1 beaten egg and 1 Tblsp vinegar

Sift together:
2 1/2 cups flour	**1 tsp cinnamon**
2 tsp baking soda	**2 tsp ginger**
1 tsp salt	**1/2 tsp allspice**
1/2 tsp nutmeg	**1/2 tsp cloves**

Add more flour if needed for stiffness. Roll VERY thin, cut with round cookie cutter and bake in 350° oven til done - around 5 minutes.

PUMPKIN BARS _____

2 cups flour	**2 tsp baking powder**
1/2 tsp salt	**1 tsp soda**
2 tsp cinnamon	

Mix all ingredients together and add
4 eggs, beaten	**1 cup nut meats if you wish**
1 cup Mazola oil	**2 cups sugar**
2 cups of canned pumpkin	

Mix together well and bake in a 11 x 17 pan for 30 minutes at 350°.

PUMPKIN BAR FROSTING:
When bars are cool, spread with the following frosting:
1 small pkg. Cream Cheese	**1 stick margarine**
1 Tblsp cream	**1 tsp vanilla**
1 1/2 to 2 cups powdered sugar	

An Episcopal diocesan Bishop went to an unfamiliar church to celebrate the Eucharist. There was a microphone on the altar, and, uncertain whether it was switched on, he tapped it gently with no result. Leaning close to it, he said in a loud whisper which echoed around the church, "There is something wrong with this microphone."

The well-trained Episcopal congregation replied, "And also with you."

Douglas Peters, called Poppo by his grandchildren, is in charge of Christmas cookies. He makes the dough and operates the cookie press and oversees the decoration. His expertise is impeccable and we bow to him and his artistry.

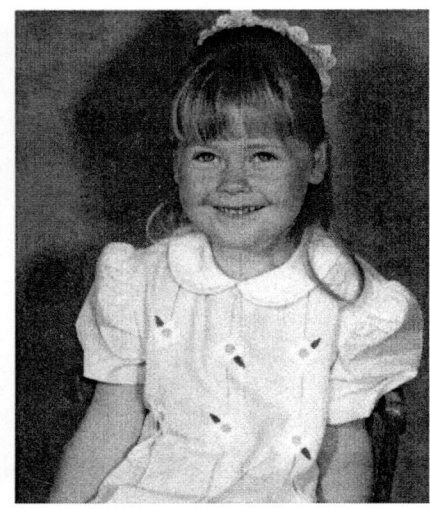

POPPO'S COOKIE HELPER
KATHLEEN

CHOCOLATE KRINKLES   Mary W. Peters

Thoroughly cream:
1/2 cup shortening   **1 2/3 cups granulated sugar**
2 tsp vanilla
Beat in **2 eggs**
2 squares baking chocolate, melted
Sift together **2 cups sifted flour**
2 tsp baking powder   **1/2 tsp salt**
Add alternately with **1/3 cup milk**
1/2 cup chopped pecans
Chill for 3 hours, form in 1-inch balls and roll in confectioners sugar. Place on greased cookie sheet and bake in 350° oven for 15 minutes. Cool a little before removing from cookie sheet. Makes 48.

PETERS CHRISTMAS BUTTER COOKIES

Daphy and Gladys started these cookies and the whole family began to make and decorate them. You really need a cookie press and several people to decorate and box them - all the while saying "Ooooh, this is the best batch we've ever done!"

Cream **3/4 lb. of butter**   **1 cup sugar**
When smooth add **2 beaten eggs**
Finally add **4 cups of flour**   **2 tsp vanilla**
Force the dough through a cookie press onto cookie sheets, decorate with many kinds of colored Christmas sugars and store bought decorations, letting artistic license carry you to extremes. Kids go crazy! Bake in 275° oven til just barely tan on edges.

CLAIRE PETERS AND KATHLEEN PETERS
COUSINS

PETERS CHRISTMAS AMMONIUM CARBONATE COOKIES

Though these cookies smell like baby's diapers when cooking, they are the most satisfactory cookie around. Ask your druggist to grind you a few ounces of Ammonium Carbonate in a jar and don't forget to let all the little kids have a big whiff before using! Never fails to convulse a grown-up. Also, the kids remember it all their lives. The old recipe states that this cookie should be ROLLED 1/8 inch thick, brushed with the white of an egg and sprinkled with :

1 Tblsp cinnamon **1 Tblsp sugar**
2 Tblsp finely chopped nuts

However, we all just simply decorated them just like the butter cookie, using the cookie press. Cream:

3/4 lb. of butter **1 cup sugar**

When smooth, add **2 eggs, beaten**
Finally, add **4 cups of flour** **2 tsp ammonium carbonate**
Bake in a 350° oven between 12 and 15 minutes. These do not brown.

❖ ❖ ❖ ❖ ❖ ❖ ❖ ❖ ❖

SOFT GINGER COOKIES   Daphy Peters

1/2 cup shortening   **1 cup dark molasses**
1/2 cup butter   **2 large eggs**
2 cups sugar   **1/2 tsp salt**
2 Tblsp ginger   **3/4 cup boiling water**
2 Tblsp baking soda
And, get this, enough flour for a soft dough!!

When I made these cookies, around 6 cups of flour created a dough barely firm enough to get out of the bowl, but soft enough to have fun juggling the cut cookies to the baking tins. Don't make these if you are a newly-wed. Wait til you're a grandma - they're real show business with lots of flour and dough and odd shapes etc., etc.

Cream sugar and shortening. Add eggs, molasses, salt and ginger. Dissolve the soda in the hot water. Add to the mixture with enough flour for a soft dough. Roll out 3/8 inch thick and cut with a 2 1/2 inch cookie cutter. They spread. Preheat oven to 400 degrees and bake them at 350°. They usually take 15 to 17 minutes. Store in covered tin to keep soft.

AUNT LILLIE'S DATE & ORANGE SLICE BAR *My favorite Aunt*

Filling:
1/2 lb. dates (1 cup)	2 Tblsp flour
1/2 cup sugar	1 cup water

Cook ingredients until thick. Let cool.
Batter: Cream
3/4 cup shortening	1 cup brown sugar
2 eggs	

Add:
1 tsp soda in 2 Tblsp hot water	1 tsp vanilla
1 3/4 cup flour	pinch salt

Put 1/2 the batter in greased 9 x 13 pan. Cover with **15 oz. pkg. of orange slices** cut in half lengthwise. Spread on 1/2 cup nuts and then date filling. Top with remaining batter. Bake at 350° for 40 minutes. Cool and cut into bars.

OATMEAL CARMELITAS

Combine in a large bowl
2 cups flour	**2 cups quick-cooking rolled oats**
1 1/2 cups firmly packed brown sugar	**1 tsp soda**
1/2 tsp salt	**1 1/2 cups butter, melted**

Take one-half of crumbs and press into an 11 x 11 pan and bake at 350° for 10 minutes. Sprinkle over baked crust:
1 cup chocolate chips   1/2 cup chopped nuts
Mix together:
3/4 cup of caramel ice cream topping with 3 Tblsp flour
Drizzle this over the chocolate & nuts. Sprinkle remaining crumbs over caramel topping. Bake at 350° for 15 to 20 minutes til golden brown.

POTATO CHIP COOKIES   Pat Linn

1 lb. Imperial margarine	**1 cup sugar**
1 1/2 Tblsp vanilla	
Add **3 cups flour**	**2 cups chopped pecans**

2 cups crushed (not too small) potato chips
Drop by spoonfuls on cookie sheet and flatten with a fork or by hand. Bake at 350° for 10 to 15 minutes til just tan around the edges. Wait a minute to remove them from the cookie sheet or they will break. Sprinkle with powdered sugar from a dredger.

Daphne and Gladys Peters, maiden Aunties, were extra Mothers to us all. Held in special reverence for their enthusiasm and unconditional love, they were most dearly loved by us. Their personal elegance was a standard to be mirrored and they left a pattern we hold in high regard.

GLADYS PETERS
with Douglas III

DAPHNE PETERS

OATMEAL LACE COOKIES _____ Daphne Peters

Sift together
1/2 cup flour   **1/2 cup sugar**
1/4 tsp baking powder
Stir into the above mixture
1/2 cup quick oats   **1/3 cup honey**
2 Tblsp heavy cream   **1 tsp vanilla**
2 Tblsp corn syrup

Mix together until blended well. Drop on ungreased cookie sheet by 1/2 teaspoonfuls, 3" apart. Bake at 375° for 6 to 8 minutes until light brown. Let stand for a few seconds before removing from pan. Makes 6 dozen cookies. Lovely with iced tea and little girls in pink dresses.

CAKE BROWNIES

4 squares of baking chocolate
1 cup milk
1/2 cup margarine
2 cups sugar
3 eggs

1 1/3 cup flour
1 tsp baking powder
1/8 tsp salt
2 tsp vanilla
3/4 cup chopped walnuts

Melt chocolate in milk over low heat and cool. Cream margarine and sugar; add eggs and chocolate mixture. Add remaining ingredients. Bake in a greased and floured 9 x 12 pan for 40 minutes at 350°.

ICEBOX COOKIES   Fan Belden

1 cup butter
1 cup lard
1 cup sugar
1 cup New Orleans molasses
1/4 tsp cinnamon

4 cups bread flour
1 tsp soda
1/4 tsp ginger
1/4 tsp salt
1 cup broken nut meats

Sift all dry ingredients together. Blend butter, lard and sugar. Add molasses, then flour and then nuts. Make two rolls in waxed paper and put into icebox for 24 hours. Slice thin cookies, bake medium oven (350°) and watch carefully. They brown easily.

OATMEAL/CHOCOLATE CHIP/NUT COOKIES___Malcolm Peters

1 cup margarine   1 cup white sugar
1 cup brown sugar
Cream the above together and then add and beat together
2 eggs   1 tsp vanilla
Sift
1 1/2 cups flour   1 tsp baking soda
1 tsp salt
Add to cookie mixture and beat. Then stir in
3 cups oatmeal   1/2 cup nutmeats (your choice)
1 cup chocolate chips
Bake at 375° for 10 to 12 minutes. Mac says these are great for the duck blind.

BROWNIES Paula Schenck Reynolds

1/2 cup butter or margarine
1 tsp vanilla
2 squares melted chocolate
1/2 cup nuts

1 cup sugar
2 eggs
1/2 cup flour

Blend ingredients well. Bake at 325° for 30 to 35 minutes in an 11 x 7 greased pan. It can be doubled and put in a 9 x 13 pan.

I do truly believe that next to religion, which varies for each one of us in its meaning and scope, a love of birds and flowers is the nearest thing to an eternal joy and comfort that we mortals can obtain on earth.

Youth flies, age comes, health departs, children grow up and vanish, old friends pass away, the eyes grow weak and reading becomes a chore instead of a pleasure; but unless we grow both blind and deaf, birds and flowers remain to enchant us. Religion is an inward consolation, but God sends us visible signs of His compassion from without when we rejoice in nature.

(ISD)

❖ ❖ ❖ ❖ ❖ ❖ ❖ ❖ ❖

CHOCOLATE BROWNIES Mary W. Peters

4 eggs
2 cups sugar
2 tsp vanilla
1 1/2 cups flour

4 squares chocolate
1 cup oleo margarine
1 cup chopped walnuts
1 tsp salt

Cream together the eggs and sugar, add the flour and salt. Melt chocolate and margarine in double boiler. Cool and add to above mixture along with nuts and vanilla. Grease and flour an 11 x 15 pan and bake for 25 minutes ONLY at 325°.

FROSTING:
Combine **1/4 cup margarine**   **1 cup sugar**
1/4 cup cocoa   **1/4 cup milk**
1 Tblsp light corn syrup
Bring to a rolling boil and cook one minute. Add vanilla and beat. Spread on cool brownies.

MALCOLM SUGAR COOKIES — Maggie Peters

3 1/4 cups flour	2 eggs
1 1/2 cup sugar	1/2 tsp salt
2/3 cup shortening	1 tsp vanilla
2 1/2 tsp baking powder	2 Tblsp milk

Cream sugar and shortening and add eggs. Mix rest of ingredients well and shape into ball. Wrap in saran wrap and chill in refrigerator, at least 3 hours. Heat oven to 400°. Grease cookie sheets. Divide dough in half and roll on flour dusted surface to 1/4 inch thickness for soft cookies and wafer thin will produce crisp cookie. Cut with floured cookie cutter, place on sheet and sprinkle with sugar. Cook 8 to 10 minutes.

Malcolm says this is a favorite in the duck blind to keep warmth in the bones and is just outstanding in every way.

DATE PINWHEELS

2 1/2 cups sifted flour	2 eggs
1/2 tsp salt	2 Tblsp cream
1/2 cup shortening	1 tsp vanilla
1 cup sugar	1/4 tsp soda

Sift flour, soda and salt. Cream shortening and sugar until light and fluffy. Add eggs, cream and vanilla, then add dry ingredients and mix well. Chill dough. Roll dough very thin and cover with date filling. Roll up like a jellyroll and slice. Bake at 400° for 8 to 10 minutes.

DATE FILLING

1 1/2 cups dates, finely chopped	**1/2 cup sugar**
1/2 cup water	**2 Tblsp lemon juice**

Cook slowly and stir constantly till mixture is thick. Cool and then spread on cookie dough.

> What will sustain me in my last moments
> is an infinite curiosity as to what is to follow!
> (ISD)

FAST CHOCOLATE CRACKLES
Fun for kids to make

1 regular package Devil's Food cake mix
2 eggs, slightly beaten   1 Tblsp water
1/2 cup solid vegetable shortening   Confectioner's sugar

Combine cake mix, eggs, water and shortening and mix with a spoon til well blended. Shape dough into balls the size of a small walnut and roll in powdered sugar. Put on greased cookie sheets and bake 8 to 10 minutes in 375° oven. Makes about 4 dozen.

❖ ❖ ❖ ❖ ❖ ❖ ❖ ❖ ❖

IMPOSSIBLE BROWNIE PIE   Mary Kay Semrad
There are people who spread the joy and Mary Kay Semrad wins a Blue for Zest for Life. It is such a pleasure to be with someone who finds outrageous humor in almost every situation -- Why do I have the feeling that this Brownie Pie will explode in the oven?

4 eggs
4 oz. of semi-sweet baking chocolate, melted and cooled over double boiler
1/2 cup Bisquick
1/2 cup brown sugar, packed
1/2 cup granulated sugar
1/4 cup soft butter or margarine
1 tsp vanilla or rum
3/4 cup chopped nuts (Walnut or Pecan)

Beat together all ingredients except chopped nuts. Grease a 9 inch pie plate and fill with batter. Sprinkle on chopped nuts and bake at 350° for 30 to 35 minutes until knife inserted in middle comes out clean. *Wedges served with ice cream and hot fudge sauce makes the Birthday Bridge Club girls inhale deeply and attack.*

In 1965, a horseback riding trip out of Yellowstone Park into the wilderness of Wyoming for 10 days, was one of our family's most unforgettable vacations. Our children, Duff, Gere and Mac were old enough to manage a horse, sleep in a tent, go toity outdoors, and hold a fishing pole. On that unforgettable trip, we all learned to eat cumin. Cookie, the cook, was from the Middle East and put cumin in everything. It's not bad. I still use a little in meat loaf now and then and I recommend it.

Food never tasted better than on that trip. Really being starving hungry and eating food prepared and served out of doors is an experience unparalleled and always remembered. Every day was full of physical activity and we all came to the campfire with no complaints about the plate of food given us. And O, the fresh trout! And after a week of the perfect tranquility of the deep woods, the agony of returning to the assault of the sounds of civilization almost made us frantic to find that silence again.

Kids: Your horses were --

Jumper - Mac *Sandy - Mom*
Queenie - Gere *Clipper - Dad*
Tiger – Duff

COOKIE

WHITE SUGAR COOKIES _____

Cream together
1/2 cup butter   **1 cup sugar**
Add **1 egg** and mix well.
Stir in **2 cups sifted cake flour**   **1 tsp baking powder**
1/4 tsp salt
Mix well and refrigerate dough. When cold, roll pieces of dough in balls and squeeze flat. Sprinkle each cookie with a mixture of the following topping:
1/4 cup sugar mixed with 1 tsp cinnamon
Bake at 350° for 10 to 12 minutes.

And this is Tweetie Bird, Steve and Gere's daughter. Can you imagine trying to concentrate on anything else when an angel like this one descends?

COCONUT COOKIES _____ Mom Schenck

1/2 cup butter   **1/2 cup brown sugar**
1 cup and 1 Tblsp sifted flour
Cream and spread mixture on a greased cookie sheet. Spread thin. Bake 10 minutes at 375°.
Beat **2 eggs** well and add
1 cup brown sugar   **1/2 tsp baking powder**
2 Tblsp flour   **1 1/2 cup coconut**
1/4 tsp salt   **1 tsp vanilla**
1/2 cup walnuts
Spread this mixture on the cookie sheet dough that has been baked. Bake these cookies at 375° until brown and cut into squares.

MIME - Spending the night with Grandmother Jerry Peters Dodson was such a treat for me. I remember the bed I slept in was always so fresh and crisp feeling. I always had a baby pillow to cuddle as I slept, that smelled like violets. In the morning I would hear Mime shuffling her slippers on the floor and she would be making that funny noise like she was trying to whistle a tune, but didn't want to wake you up; so it sounded like the wind blowing through the trees. Breakfast started with half a grapefruit which I loved to attack with the sterling silver pointed-tip spoon. Then a scrambled egg with a piece of Stouffer's coffee cake, 2 - 4 slices of bacon covered with a candy coating of brown sugar from being slow-broiled, and cocoa made really rich with vanilla and whipped cream. And all the while that I'm eating this glorious breakfast, Mime is telling me the grandest made-up stories about the figurines she has placed especially on the center of the table for me to view. Then we would spend the day shopping or playing lots of Gin Rummy and I would win all of her pennies from her. - - -- Gere

PECAN SLICES SUPERB _____ Jerry Dodson

1 cup flour, sifted twice   **1/2 cup butter**
1 Tblsp brown sugar
Cut butter into flour as pastry and pat into 10 x 10 cake pan and bake 5 minutes at 350°. Cool.
FILLING:
1 1/4 cup brown sugar, scant   **1 cup broken pecans**
1/2 cup shredded coconut   **2 round Tblsp flour**
1 tsp baking powder   **1 1/2 tsp vanilla**
Add 2 beaten eggs.
Mix together, pour over pastry and bake in 350° oven for 20-plus minutes.
Frost cooled slices with a powdered sugar frosting of
2 cups powdered sugar
3 to 4 Tblsp fresh lemon juice
2 Tblsp soft butter

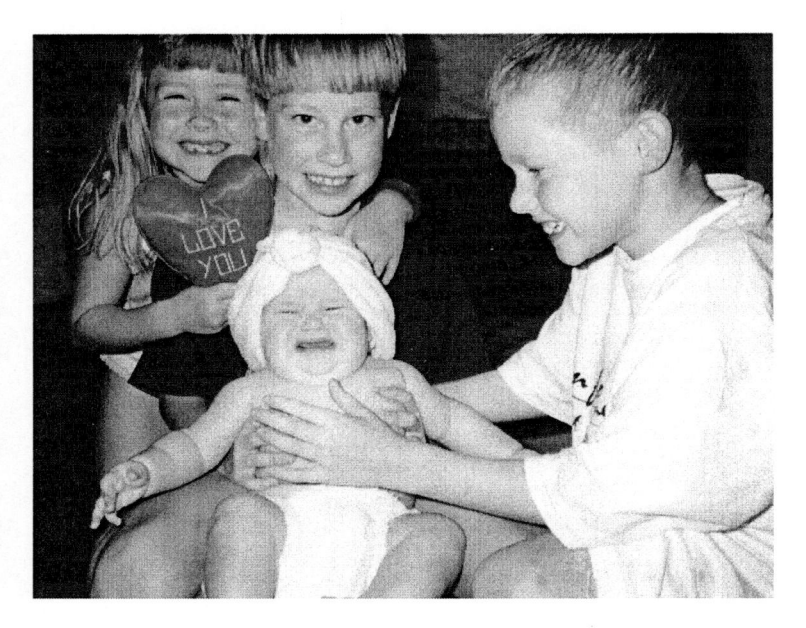

The GRAND VIZIER BRIAN
wants his Mama

Desserts

DESSERT

Apple Crisp	149
Bananas Flambé	140
Bavarian Cream	154
Blueberry Slump	144
Bread and Butter Pudding	135
Caramel Custard	135
Cherries Jubilee	153
Chocolate Bavarian Cream	132
Chocolate Hush Dessert	147
Chocolate Mousse	136
Christmas Steam Puddings	138
Cottage Pudding	151
Crème Patissiere	137
Crepe Suzette Sauce	143
Crepes	143
Date Raptures	142
Fat-Fatty Coconut Fruit Dessert	131
Fresh Strawberry Tart	137
Grand Marnier Soufflé	142
Lemon Angel Pie	144
Lemon Curd Tarts	152
Meringue Torte	138
Mincemeat Crepes	143
Miniature Tart Shells	152
Old Fashioned Vanilla Ice Cream	149
Orange Marshmallow Pudding	131
Pear Tart	133
Pineapple Ice Cream	148
Poached Peaches	134
Poached Peaches Princessa Margaretha	139
Pots De Crème Au Chocolat	136
Raisin Bread Pudding	151
Rhubarb Oatmeal Crunch	149
Rice Pudding	140
Rum Pudding with Cherry Sauce	146
Sneaky Dessert	147
Spanish Cream	153
Trifle for Myriads	150

FAT-FATTY COCONUT FRUIT DESSERT _____ Cory Peters
1 pkg. (8 oz.) cream cheese, softened
1/3 cup sugar
2 Tblsp Rum
3 1/2 cups whipped topping
1 can 8 oz. crushed pineapple in syrup
2 2/3 cups flake coconut

Beat cream cheese, sugar and Rum until smooth. Fold in 2 cups of whipped topping, pineapple with syrup and 2 cups of coconut. Spread in 8" layer pan lined with plastic wrap. Invert pan onto serving plate; remove pan and plastic wrap. Spread with remaining whipped topping and sprinkle with remaining coconut. Freeze until firm. Cut into wedges and garnish with pineapple or cherries. I also like to eat some of the pineapple and replace it with mandarin orange slices (before you initially fold it in with other ingredients, of course!).
NOTE: The actual act of cutting this dessert into wedges causes most of the calories to leak out, so eat as much as you want!

ORANGE MARSHMALLOW PUDDING _____
1 lb. marshmallows
Juice of 6 large oranges
Combine in double boiler til marshmallows are dissolved. Add **1 envelope of Knox gelatin** that has been dissolved in **1/4 cup of cold water.**
Combine this mixture and when it begins to congeal, whip with beater til frothy.
ADD: **grated rind of 1 orange and 1 pint of heavy cream, whipped**
Fold together carefully, put in melon mold and refrigerate.

SAUCE
1 cup sugar
1/3 cup butter
1/2 cup water
Cook and add **2 Tblsp cornstarch** that has been dissolved in a little cold water.
Cook for 5 minutes, then add the **juice of 2 oranges, juice of 1 lemon, and grated rind of 1 lemon and 1 orange**. Bring to boil again and serve hot.

CHOCOLATE BAVARIAN CREAM _____

Put **1 Tblsp of gelatin** in **1/4 cup cold water** and let dissolve. Make custard of the following ingredients over a double boiler:

2 egg yolks   **1/2 cup sugar**
1 cup milk   **1 square bitter chocolate**

Add the gelatin while it is still hot, let it dissolve and then strain and cool the custard. When the custard begins to set up in the refrigerator, whip **1 cup of whipping cream** and carefully fold into the gelatin mixture. Place in a mold rinsed in cold water and refrigerate, til set.

❖ ❖ ❖ ❖ ❖ ❖ ❖ ❖ ❖

Invite a friend to
HAVE A FEAST OF REASON AND A FLOW OF SOUL

❖ ❖ ❖ ❖ ❖ ❖ ❖ ❖ ❖

Grandmothers are Mothers who get a second chance

❖ ❖ ❖ ❖ ❖ ❖ ❖ ❖ ❖

SPONGE CAKE
Borrow the ingredients from a neighbor!

❖ ❖ ❖ ❖ ❖ ❖ ❖ ❖ ❖

BILL'S VERY OWN

PEAR TART
Douglas Peters, II
A real favorite

Pate sucree:
1 3/4 cups flour
1 1/4 sticks unsalted butter plus 2 tsp butter, well chilled & cut into 1/2" pieces
1/4 cup sugar
2 egg yolks
1/4 tsp water
4 drops vanilla

Combine flour, butter and sugar in processor, turning on/off til mixture's like corn meal. Add yolks, water and vanilla and mix til dough is crumbly. Gather dough into a ball and flatten into a disc, wrap in plastic and freeze 30 minutes or refrigerate overnight.

Filling:
1 cup plus 3 Tblsp sugar   **6 Tblsp flour**
3 eggs   **1 1/2 sticks butter**
2 perfect Bartlett pears, peeled, cored, and quartered lengthwise

Combine sugar, flour and eggs in large bowl and whisk til smooth. Melt butter in medium skillet over high heat til foamy and golden brown. Slowly whisk melted butter into sugar mixture. Set aside.

Divide dough in 4 pieces. Knead each piece between fingers until malleable but still cold; do not over-work. Roll all of dough out on lightly floured surface into circle 1/8 inch thick. Lift dough onto rolling pin and transfer to 11" tart pan. Carefully press dough into pan, removing excess around edges and refrigerate for 15 minutes.

Preheat oven to 375¡. Cut pears crosswise into slices 1/8" thick. Gently open slices into fan shape. Arrange pears in crust in flower petal pattern. Pour melted butter mixture over pears. Bake til crust and filling are brown, about 1 hour. Serve warm or room temperature. Sprinkle top with powdered sugar.

❖ ❖ ❖ ❖ ❖ ❖ ❖ ❖ ❖

Laura Byers said her Mother referred to her as
PERFECT – AND THE PATTERN LOST

POACHED PEACHES   Mary Peters
The almond extract is the secret to a beautifully light dinner finale that is also a most attractive presentation.

Pick out **8 choice ripe peaches,** scald the peaches and peel them. Divide in two and poach in a 5 quart dutch oven in the following bath:

6 cups water
1/4 cups sugar
1 Tblsp vanilla

Boil the water and sugar until dissolved and add the vanilla. Add the peaches and heat to boiling. Reduce the heat, cover and cook 5 to 10 minutes, basting now and then. Remove from heat, drain and cool.

ALMOND SAUCE
Mix 1 Tblsp cornstarch
3 Tblsp sugar
1/8 tsp salt, and add:
2 cups whole milk
Cook over a double boiler til sauce thickens just slightly. Then carefully add:
2 beaten egg yolks
1/2 tsp almond extract
Cook over double boiler til sauce thickens slightly again, but DO NOT BOIL.

STRAWBERRY PUREE
Wash and de-stem **1 pint of choice strawberries** and pat dry. With **2 Tblsp of sugar**, puree strawberries in a blender til smooth.

To serve:
Place several spoonfuls of sauce on a dessert plate til bottom is covered. Place peach half, cut side down on sauce and spoon a ribbon of strawberry sauce over each service. This recipe can also use Bartlett pears as a substitution when peaches are unavailable. But the quality of the fruit is important!

> Left over Coca-Cola will clean the corrosion off your battery terminals and make the toilet bowl sparkle. What's it do to your stomach?

CARAMEL CUSTARD

Custard is such a lovely texture to eat. Good for a sick person, old ones can gum it, little ones think it's ice cream, and it makes gourmands roll their eyes.

HOW TO CARAMELIZE A MOLD
Find a 6-8 cup mold.
1/2 cup sugar
2 1/2 Tblsp water
In a saucepan swirl water and sugar until liquid is clear. Then boil, swirling pan, til sugar has turned caramel-brown, 2 to 3 minutes. Immediately pour caramel into mold turning in all directions to film bottom and sides of mold. When it ceases to run, reverse mold onto a plate.
5 large eggs
4 egg yolks
3/4 cup sugar
3 3/4 cups hot milk
1 1/2 tsp vanilla

Beat eggs and slowly add sugar. When foamy, add hot milk very slowly. Add vanilla. Put in mold with caramel, set in pan of boiling water, bake in lower half of oven, about 40 minutes at 350°. Custard is done when knife comes out clean. Put in pan of cold water for 10 minutes and reverse on plate to unmold.

BREAD AND BUTTER PUDDING ___ The great Ritz Hotel, London
1 cup whole milk   **1 cup heavy cream**
One half a vanilla pod   **8 slices of bread, crusts removed**
5 eggs   **1 cup sugar**
1/4 cup raisins   **Fresh nutmeg and unsalted**
butter for buttering bread slices

Butter the bread, remove the crusts and cut in triangles. Butter an ovenware dish and in a saucepan bring to a boil the milk, cream, and vanilla pod. Set aside. Beat together the eggs, sugar and raisins well and as you layer the bread in the casserole, cover with the egg, sugar, raisin mixture. Let stand 7 or 8 minutes. Finally, top with milk/cream, place casserole in a hot water bath and bake in a 325° oven for 45 to 50 minutes, or until the custard is FIRM when you shake and touch the pudding. Please don't forget to dust the top of the pudding with nutmeg before baking.

POTS DE CREME AU CHOCOLAT   Jane S. Peters

6 oz. Bakers semi-sweet chocolate
2 egg yolks
2 eggs
1 tsp vanilla

2 Tblsp Kahlua liquer
3 Tblsp orange juice
1/4 cup sugar
1 cup heavy cream

Melt the chocolate in the Kahlua and orange juice and set aside to cool. Put the egg yolks and eggs in the top of a blender with the vanilla and sugar. Blend for 2 minutes at medium speed. Add the heavy cream and blend on medium high for another 30 seconds. Add the melted and cooled chocolate and blend til smooth. Pour into a bowl or 6 individual cups and refrigerate for several hours or overnight.

CHOCOLATE MOUSSE   Nancy Jenkins
I cannot count the times I have served this dessert at our dinner parties. I love show business and it is lovely to have the mousse and whipped cream delivered to the table in silver bowls so that I may serve everyone's dessert plate. Topping off each serving with a candied violet is the coup de grace.

Separate **4 eggs** and let egg whites come to room temperature. In double boiler melt **6 oz. semi-sweet chocolate** and **5 Tblsp butter** over hot, not boiling, water.
Using a wooden spoon, beat in the egg yolks separately after cooling the chocolate mixture. Beat well. Add **2 Tblsp extra-fine cognac**. Beat whites til they form peaks and fold into the chocolate mixture. Put in silver bowl and chill 24 hours. Serve with sweetened whip cream. *Double this recipe to serve 12.*

Peters house in the honey locust forest - Omaha

FRESH STRAWBERRY TART
A favorite dessert of Doug Peters

1 10" fully-baked pastry shell
2 Tblsp sugar
1 qt. large ripe handsome strawberries
2 Tblsp Kirsch or Cognac
1 1/2 to 2 cups chilled creme patissiere
1 cup red currant jelly

CRUST:
2 cups sifted all-purpose flour
1/4 lb. chilled butter, cut into 1/2" bits
1/2 tsp salt
3 Tblsp chilled vegetable shortening
2 pinches of sugar
5 Tblsp cold water

Rub flour and fat and all ingredients but water rapidly between fingers til fat is the size of oatmeal flakes. Add water and shape into a ball. Place dough on lightly floured board and with heel of hand smear bits of the pastry down board away from you in a final blending of fat and flour. Scrape up, knead briefly into a ball, sprinkle with flour and wrap in wax paper. Refrigerate for 2 hours or overnight. Roll out dough quickly so it will not become soft. Roll into a circle 1/8 inch thick and place in a 10" metal flan pan with a false bottom. Bake 7 to 10 minutes at 400° til tan.

CREME PATISSIERE:
1 cup sugar
2/3 cup sifted flour
5 egg yolks
2 cups boiling milk

Beat sugar into egg yolks for 3 minutes til it forms a ribbon. Beat in flour. Add milk VERY slowly, beating all the while. Into a 3 qt. saucepan, put patissiere and start to cook it stirring constantly with a wire whip. When boil is reached, cook 2 to 3 minutes more. Do not burn! Remove from heat and add:

1 Tblsp butter and 3 Tblsp of Kirsch or Cognac

Next, wash and hull the strawberries quickly and set on rack to dry. Boil currant jelly, sugar and liqueur to 228°. Paint interior of pie shell with jelly mixture to waterproof and let dry for 5 minutes. Spread a 1/2" layer of patissiere on the pastry shell. Arrange the berries in a design with the largest berries in the center. Warm the jelly glaze if it has hardened and spoon or paint a thin coat of glaze over the berries. Forks poised, everyone?

MERINGUE TORTE

This is a recipe from Kate Peters who was a sister-in-law of M.C. Peters and she lived in California. Found this in Daphne and Glady's Cook Book.

4 egg whites	1 cup sugar
1/2 tsp salt	1/4 tsp vanilla extract
1/4 tsp Cream of Tartar	1/4 tsp almond extract

Beat egg whites til frothy. Add salt and Cream of Tartar and continue beating til mixture stands in peaks. GRADUALLY add sugar a Tblsp at a time and then add flavoring. Turn into well-buttered 9 " pie pan and bake one hour at 275°. When cold, place in refrigerator for 24 hours - this is important as this treatment makes a tender fluffy meringue. Make a depression bringing up the sides of the meringue before baking so that the shell can be filled with berries and whipped cream, or sherbet, or fruit, especially peaches.

CHRISTMAS STEAM PUDDINGS

2 cups bread crumbs, ground fine	
1/2 cup butter	1 cup brown sugar
1 cup raisins	1 cup chopped dates
2 cups milk	1 cup chopped nuts
2 tsp cinnamon	1 tsp nutmeg
1 tsp dissolved baking soda	1 egg

And a small amount of mixed citron fruit, chopped.

After mixing dough, fill 1# coffee cans 3/4 full, and put in a covered kettle that has been filled half-way up the coffee cans with water. Set the coffee cans on jar tops in the water to lift up from kettle bottom. Let the water just boil and steam for 3 hours.

SAUCE

1 cup sugar	1 Tblsp flour
1/4 tsp salt	

Add **1 cup boiling water** and cook til thick and clear. Cool slightly and add: **1 Tblsp butter**
1 tsp Demarara rum

> In the game of life, as in other sports, you can pick out the winners - they are the ones who aren't complaining about the officiating.

POACHED PEACHES PRINCESSA MARGARETHA
John Peters
This is John's favorite dessert

1 fresh peach per person. Poach in slightly sugared boiling water, flavored with a vanilla bean for 2 minutes. Skin peaches and leave in liquid. In a chafing dish, put 1 Tblsp each per person:
Strawberry jam
Bar-Le-Duc jam (or Currant)
Greengage plum jam
Add peaches, drained. Pour on 2 Tblsp each per person:
Cognac and Kirsch, set alight.
Vanilla ice cream on each plate. Ladle peaches over it and sprinkle with toasted, slivered almonds.

JOHN

Rare it is, at the Clan gatherings, that John M. Peters does not lead us all in song. From college rondelets to the best of Barbershop, we all join in, improving year by year as the harmony swells.

Christmas would not be complete without The Chili Supper and Caroling Party started 40 years ago with everyone outfitted in Santa Claus hats and still going strong. Neither snow nor cold can stay us from our appointed rounds and we now number, friends included, about 50.

❖ ❖ ❖ ❖ ❖ ❖ ❖ ❖ ❖

Add a lump of butter or a few tsp of oil to water when you cook rice, noodles or spaghetti. Water will not boil over kettle nor will contents stick together.

Keep cookies fresh and soft by placing one or two slices of apple in the cookie jar.

BANANAS FLAMBE   Malcolm Peters
The first thing to do is assemble friends for a great big feast with lots of booze and wine and Peters story-telling and fabricating. Then go to the kitchen to prepare the finale.

In a large skillet melt **1 stick of no-salt butter** and **a big fist-full of brown sugar** with **a generous sprinkling of cinnamon**. Warm sauce, then add a **good shot of brandy** to loosen it a bit. Split **four bananas** lengthwise and then halve them. By now **your vanilla ice cream** should be scooped onto the dessert plates. Add bananas to sauce and cook 1 minute. Do not overcook or they'll get mushy!! Pour another shot of brandy over the bananas and move gently. Flambé at tableside for OOH'S and AAH'S. Spoon over ice cream and serve immediately with aperitifs.

RICE PUDDING
You will scream and cry for more!

1/2 cup sugar	2 slightly beaten egg yolks
1 Tblsp flour	2 1/2 cups scalded milk
1 Tblsp cornstarch	1 cup cooked rice
1/4 tsp salt	1/4 cup raisins
1/2 cup cold milk	1 tsp vanilla

MERINGUE:

2 egg whites	1/4 cup sugar
few grains salt	1/2 tsp vanilla

Mix sugar, flour, cornstarch and salt. Stir in cold milk and egg yolks. Add scalded milk and rice. Cook in double boiler JUST until it starts to thicken. Add raisins and vanilla. Pour in 2 quart baking pan and set in larger pan of boiling water. Bake at 325° for 20 minutes.
Meanwhile beat egg whites and salt til frothy. Gradually beat in sugar and vanilla until stiff peaks form. Pile onto hot pudding and bake 20 minutes more or til browned.

Honesty is not only the best policy;
It is basic in character building.

+ + + + + +

It is difficult, nay impossible, to cook without a good wire whisk. No cream sauce, gravy or patissiere should be made without one, unless you have a compulsion for repentance.

Grandfather Richard Dunnell was part of that elitist generation where the males grew up with no knowledge of the inside of a kitchen. Furthermore, they did not CARE to know. But there were 2 desserts that were favorites that he would put together when our Mother took to her bed.

CHOCOLATE PUDDING
Get one box of Jello Chocolate Pudding and follow the directions. Put in bowls for each person present.

CANTALOUPE A LA MODE
Get one cantaloupe, cut it in half, remove the seeds, and put a scoop of vanilla ice cream in the center, sit on the front steps and eat.

❖ ❖ ❖ ❖ ❖ ❖ ❖ ❖ ❖

Love is by far the most important thing of all. It is the Golden Gate of Paradise. Pray for the understanding of love, and meditate upon it daily. It casts out fear. It is the fulfilling of the Law. It covers a multitude of sins. Love is absolutely invincible. There is no difficulty that enough love will not conquer; no disease that enough love will not heal; no door that enough love will not open; no gulf that enough love will not bridge; no wall that enough love will not throw down; no sin that enough love will not redeem. It makes no difference how deeply seated may be the trouble, how hopeless the outlook, how muddled the tangle, how great the mistake; a sufficient realization of love will dissolve it all. If only you could love enough you would be the happiest and most powerful being in the world.

DATE RAPTURES_____Gertrude Schenck's

Sift together:
1 cup sifted flour   **1/2 tsp salt**
1/2 tsp baking powder   **1/2 tsp soda**
Then add: **1 egg**
1/2 cup oleo   **1/3 cup buttermilk**
1/2 cup sugar   **1 Tblsp orange rind (grated)**
Beat until smooth and blend **in 1 cup of dates, cut fine**. Pour into greased muffin cups 2/3 full. Bake 350° for 30 minutes. When done, pour over cakes:
3/4 cup orange juice in which you have dissolved
1/4 cup sugar
Let juice soak into cakes and serve hot, topped with whipped cream.
Serves 6

And what with the Peters family do without
GRAND MARNIER SOUFFLE_____ Serves 8

2 cups milk   **5 egg yolks**
3/4 cup sugar   **7 egg whites**
1/3 cup flour   **2 oz. Grand Marnier**
2 oz. butter

Beat egg whites until stiff. Heat milk, add sugar, stir and bring to a boil. Mix melted butter with the flour and stir into the boiling milk, constantly stirring until thick and creamy. Off the fire, add the Grand Marnier.
Beat the egg yolks til lemon in color and add to the mixture, stirring constantly. Gently fold in the beaten egg whites. Pour into a buttered and sugared soufflé mold. Preheat oven at 400° and bake for 25 minutes. Serve immediately, after breaking the center open with 2 serving spoons.

How about CREPES SUZETTE for dinner? Here's a recipe that's easy - ---- I mean EEEEEEEEZZEEEEE.

CREPES _____ Mary Peters

Get out your Waring blender and whir on high for 1 minute:

1 cup cold water   **2 cups sifted flour**
1 cup cold milk   **4 Tblsp melted butter**
4 large eggs   **1/2 tsp salt**

Refrigerate the blender-full of batter for at least 2 hours or longer. Heat a 6 - 7" non-stick skillet til it begins to smoke after you have painted the pan with cooking oil. Immediately put in about 1/4 cup of batter and tilt pan to cover bottom with batter. Cook about 1 minute til tan, turn and cook other side. It will be spotty. Slide crepe onto plate and separate with wax paper. Can be frozen if you make ahead. Grease pan after every crepe.

CREPE SUZETTE SAUCE _____ Mary Peters

In a large fry pan melt:

1/2 cup butter   **juice of 1 orange and its grated rind**
1/2 cup powdered sugar   **3 Tblsp cognac**
3 Tblsp Grand Marnier

After butter, sugar and orange juice have cooked up into sauce, add liquors & heat again til sauce gets hot. Put match to sauce and let flame, briefly. Put crepes in sauce individually and handkerchief fold each one, so that they are covered with sauce. Plan to serve two crepes per person. You can <u>double</u> or <u>triple</u> this recipe easily - the sauce is the BEST PART!

MINCEMEAT CREPES _____

Use the crepe recipe listed above

1 pkg. 9 oz. condensed mincemeat
3/4 cup water
1 cup fresh orange juice
3 Tblsp Grand Marnier

Crumble mincemeat in a frying pan, add water, break up lumps, bring to a boil and boil 1 minute. Add orange juice, Grand Marnier and stir. Put each crepe (two for each person) in the sauce and fold in quarters. Put on heated plates and spoon sauce over crepes.

Okay! You Peters Children, I'm Putting It IN! And I don't care what you say!

BLUEBERRY SLUMP (sometimes called Grunt or Flummery) _____
This dessert is older than New England. Irrespective of the fact that I have taken alot of abuse through the years for this recipe, as it was regarded as my greatest culinary failure, I will include it for all of you to try.

**4 cups blueberries
8 slices buttered bread
1 cup sugar**

Wash the berries, put in saucepan with sugar and cook over low heat to simmering point, about 10 minutes. Butter bread generously and trim crusts. Line baking dish with bread, cutting slices to fit. Pour portion of berries and juice over bread and continue with alternate layers of bread & berries ending with fruit and juice. Bake at 350° for 20 minutes. Chill in refrigerator. Serve with whipped cream flavored with nutmeg.

❖ ❖ ❖ ❖ ❖ ❖ ❖ ❖ ❖

LEMON ANGEL PIE _____ Daphne Peters

**4 eggs, separated   1/2 tsp cream of tartar
1 1/2 cups sugar   1 lemon, juice then grate the peel
1/4 cup water   1 cup whipping cream, whipped**

Beat egg whites til frothy; add cream of tartar; beat til stiff. Add 1 cup of sugar gradually, beating constantly. Beat until glossy. Line bottom & sides of a 9" pan with this meringue. Bake 1 hour in a 275° oven. Cool. Beat egg yolks til thick and light. Add remaining 1/2 cup sugar, lemon juice, lemon peel and water. Cook over hot water, stirring constantly, til thick. Cool. Spread half the whipped cream in meringue shell. Add lemon filling, spreading evenly. Top with remaining whipped cream. Chill 24 hours.

When Aunt Daphne and Gladys asked Doug and me to motor to Florida with them in February, 1957, we jumped at the chance. We were to meet Daphy's old Brownell Hall school chum and her husband who were moored up at Key Largo and then fly on to Cuba. The day before we arrived in Havana, Insurrectionist students had been machine-gunned in the streets by Cuban soldiers. The steps of the Palace were stained with their blood as they had tried to gain entry to kill Juan Batista, hoping their hero, Fidel Castro, would ascend to power. Soldiers with guns and bandilleros stood in the streets as our taxi passed. Our vacation there was uneventful and splendid. Havana, Cuba was very beautiful with parts of the city very old, especially the walled harbor and Morro Castle. It was one of the great cities of Latin America, considered the "Key of the New World" with its many harbors, absolutely perfect climate year-round and limitless produce and raw materials. It was a superb vacation area for tourists and the night club shows and music were unparalleled. We considered ourselves very fortunate to have seen that great city before it was closed to the world.

RUM PUDDING _____ Irene Savidge

This is one of the great recipes of all time. The Pete Peters children refuse to partake of Christmas dinner if it does not include Rum Pudding. It has now become an Institution and no matter what condition one's digestive system after partaking of Christmas dinner, there is ALWAYS room for a little Rum Pudding. Thankyou, Bangaw....

Cook in a double boiler until the mixture coats the spoon:
1 cup whole milk   **2 egg yolks**
1/2 cup sugar   **1/8 tsp salt**
Add:
1 Tblsp Knox gelatin that has been dissolved in 1/3 cup milk
Stir together until smooth. Cool. When mixture begins to thicken, Add:
4 Tblsp Myers Jamaica Rum   2 beaten egg whites
Let thicken again and fold in:
1 cup whipping cream that has been whipped stiff
(Fold in egg whites and whipped cream to keep pudding light.) Pour into ring mold that has been rinsed with cold water and shaken to remove excess water and place mold in refrigerator overnight.

CHERRY SAUCE

1 can sour red pie cherries, drain off juice into a double boiler and add to juice: **2 Tblsp cornstarch**
Cook up cherry juice and cornstarch until thick and clear.
Then add: **1/2 cup sugar**
Few drops of red food coloring
A bit of brandy or Cherry liquer
Add pie cherries. Keep this sauce warm in the double boiler for serving with the cold pudding.

Irene presented this on a silver platter surrounded with fresh holly and the hot cherry sauce in a footed bowl in the center of the ring mold ...WOW!

CHOCOLATE HUSH DESSERT   Joani Mitten
Joani says this is an olde recipe that was used for dessert bridge parties and was always a groaning success ....

1 Angel Food cake	12 oz. chocolate chips, semi-sweet
4 large eggs, separated	pinch of salt
2 Tblsp sugar	2 cups whipping cream
1 tsp vanilla	

Break angel food cake in half. Put one half of cake, broken into pieces, in the bottom of two greased 8 x 8 x 4 baking casseroles. In a double boiler, melt 2 cups of semisweet chocolate chips and remove from heat and cool a little. Stir into chocolate: 4 egg yolks that have been beaten. Beat 4 egg whites with 2 Tblsp of sugar and a dash of salt until stiff. Fold into chocolate mixture starting with 1/3 of the egg whites that have been stirred into the chocolate to loosen its consistency. Whip 2 cups of whipping cream and add vanilla. Fold carefully into the chocolate mixture. Put half of chocolate over the bottom layers of Angel food cake and repeat the process once again. Refrigerate overnight. To serve, top with sweetened whipping cream and we will all hope that you do not have to cook for the family that evening. Just give them the rest of the dessert and stand back. It makes loads.

❖ ❖ ❖ ❖ ❖ ❖ ❖ ❖ ❖

SNEAKY DESSERT   Malcolm Peters
This started back in the 60's

Quietly take a large bowl and fill it with any flavor of ice cream, being careful not to let anyone know you're in the fridge, cause you didn't finish your dinner or are already too fat. Quietly get out the Nestle's Quik cocoa mix and get a scoop or 23 and shovel it over your slowly-melting mountain of joy. Then sneak it into the bedroom where the TV is operating and slowly mix the dessert up, not letting anyone see the dust cloud of powdered chocolate rising from your mad-cap stirring. When your chocolate soup is of the desired consistency, drink it down and slide the bowl under the bed as if nothing has occurred. Then when someone calls out "Hey! Does anybody want any ice cream?" you can yell "You bet! And how about a little Quik on top for me, too."

TWINK, CHIP & BABY

DAD'S FAVORITE ICE CREAM -*Homemade ice cream was quite a special thing to make in the Peters' household. Dad's favorite was vanilla and we made it one hot summer day while sitting on the porch at Alta Drive. We all took turns turning the cranker and really got pooped. When the ice cream was ready we had to go inside to eat dinner first. Dad left the ice cream in its long, metal cylinder to "marry" on the front porch until dessert time. While eating dinner we heard the loudest clang-banging racket. We all went to look and there was our German Shorthair "ChocolateChip" (no pun intended) with his head STUCK inside the ice cream drum. I can't remember if there was any left for us ....   Gere*

PINEAPPLE ICE CREAM _____ Gere Simmons

2 cups sugar
1 tsp lemon juice
2 quarts of cream
6 eggs
2 Tblsp vanilla
1/2 tsp salt
15 oz. pineapple rings (mushed)
1 small can crushed pineapple

Mix all ingredients in a bowl. Place in ice cream mixer. Churn til set. YUMMY!

❖ ❖ ❖ ❖ ❖ ❖ ❖ ❖ ❖

OLD FASHIONED VANILLA ICE CREAM for a ONE GALLON FREEZER

4 eggs
2 cups of sugar
Beat eggs til foamy and gradually add sugar. Beat til thickened.
Then add: **2 cups of whipping cream**
3 Tblsp of vanilla
Mix above together well and pour into freezer container and fill with whole milk til 3/4 full, and stir well. Follow instructions on ice cream maker for freezing ice cream - this makes 4 quarts.

STRAWBERRY
Wash, hull, and crush **1 quart of strawberries, 1/2 cup sugar**. Chill, add to above.

PEACH
Pare, slice & **mash 3 lbs (12) peaches**. Stir in **1/4 cup sugar & a dash of salt**. Cover and let stand til sugar is dissolved & add to above recipe.

RHUBARB OATMEAL CRUNCH

2 heaping cups of cut up rhubarb; Place in 9 1/2 x 5 1/2 bread pan and sprinkle on:
1 1/2 Tblsp sugar
1 1/2 Tblsp flour
Melt 1 stick butter in pan on stove and add:
1/2 cup frm-packed brown sugar
1 cup oatmeal
Mix well and spread over rhubarb. Bake at 350° for 35 minutes til bubbly and serve warm with soft vanilla ice cream.

APPLE CRISP   Louise Filbert's Mom

With pastry cutter, cut until pea size:
1 cup flour   **1/2 cup brown sugar**
1 stick butter
In a 9 x 9 pan, slice **6 medium tart, crisp apples** until pan is half-filled. Squeeze over **1 Tblsp of lemon juice, 1 cup sugar**, and a **good sprinkling of cinnamon and nutmeg**. Cover with topping and bake for 50 minutes at 350° until it bubbles. This is even better the next day reheated and don't forget to serve warm with ice cream!

Turning 40 for me was just too terrible. So I took up skiing at Crescent Hills outside Council Bluffs as a psychological barricade to Father Time. What a panacea! Soon, the whole family learned on that little primitive hill with the rope tow and we all graduated to Aspen and Snowmass. Doug and the children soon surpassed me, but, through the years, that sport brought me more pleasure with the family or with a bunch of girlfriends than any activity I've ever embraced. To be mature and physically careless on the slopes was euphoric.
That reminds me, I must try again to find someone to drive me in a Racing car.

TRIFLE for Myriads _____
This recipe will fill up a large punch bowl and feed 15 or 20 guests

Make **2 pound cakes (box mixes will be fine)** and let them age about 3 days. Cut into 2-inch fingers and drizzle with **1/2 fifth of sherry.** Let steep for 1/2 a day. Meanwhile, make **up 4 small packages of Jello French Vanilla pudding (not the Instant variety).** Whip **1 qt. whipping cream** and flavor with at **least 1/2 cup of Grand Marnier liqueur.**
Frost the pound cake fingers with **1 12 oz. jar of good apricot preserves**
Open **2 31-oz. cans of Wilderness Cherry Fruit filling.**
Start with the vanilla pudding and simply make layers of the above ingredients so that all the flavors will be closely incorporated. Do not stir. This is a very pretty dessert and heroic to serve.

COTTAGE PUDDING   Irene Dunnell

Cream:
1/4 cup shortening
3/4 cup sugar
Add:
1 egg	**1/2 tsp salt**
1 3/4 cup flour	**3/4 cup milk**
3 tsp baking powder	**1 tsp vanilla**

Put batter in a greased 8" x 8" pan and sprinkle sugar over the batter. Bake in a 350° oven for 30 minutes. Serve hot with the following sauce.

LEMON SAUCE
1 big hunk of butter	**1 round Tblsp flour**
Juice of 1 lemon	**rind of 1 lemon, grated**
1 cup of water	**1/2 cup sugar**

Cook until thickened and add more lemon if desired. Spoon hot sauce over pudding.

RAISIN BREAD PUDDING   Irene S. Dunnell
A favorite of my Mother's

Remove crusts from **8 slices of bread** and butter them with **1/4 pound of butter**. Cut into pieces. Soak **1/2 cup raisins** in hot water for 10 minutes. Drain and pat dry. Butter a 9 x 9 baking dish or pan. Place bread in casserole and sprinkle with **1 tsp cinnamon.**

Heat **3 cups of milk with 2/3 cup granulated sugar** in a double boiler, so that sugar dissolves. Add **4 beaten eggs** carefully to the hot milk. Flavor with **1 tsp vanilla** and pour over bread in the casserole. Add 1/2 cup raisins. Place in a pan of hot water and bake in a 350° oven about 30 to 40 minutes until custard is set and lightly browned on top. You may serve warm with heavy cream or soft vanilla ice cream!

MINIATURE TART SHELLS _____
3 cups sifted flour
1 cup shortening
1 1/2 tsp salt
6 Tblsp cold water
Sift flour and salt. Cut in shortening until the size of large peas. Sprinkle water over mixture and mix thoroughly until a smooth dough is formed. Roll on floured surface to 1/8 inch thickness. Cut into 2 1/2 inch rounds and fit into 1 3/4 inch muffin pans. Prick well. Bake at 450° for 10 to 20 minutes til golden brown. Makes about 4 dozen.

❖ ❖ ❖ ❖ ❖ ❖ ❖ ❖ ❖

And now you can make

LEMON CURD TARTS _____ Kay Schenck
grated rind of 2 lemons   **1 cup butter**
1/2 cup lemon juice   **4 eggs, well beaten**
2 cups sugar
4 dozen miniature baked tart shells, cooled

Combine lemon rind, lemon juice and sugar in top of double boiler. Add butter. Heat over boiling water stirring til butter is melted. Stir in eggs. Continue cooking, stirring constantly til mixture is thick enough to pile slightly, about 15 minutes. Cool thoroughly. Spoon filling into tart shells.

CHERRIES JUBILEE

2 Tblsp butter
2 Tblsp sugar
1 tsp each grated orange rind and lemon rind
1/4 cup each orange juice and lemon juice
1/4 cup Kirsch (cherry brandy)
3 cups black Bing cherries, pitted and drained
1/4 cup warm Brandy
Vanilla ice cream

In a skillet or chafing dish, melt butter over high heat. Blend in sugar and heat til mixture boils. Stir in grated rinds and simmer til mixture is light brown. Stir in juices and cook til it bubbles. Add Kirsch and cherries and stir gently. Pour in warm Brandy and ignite and stir til flame dies and serve over vanilla ice cream.

SPANISH CREAM   Jerry Peters Dodson

Scald **3 cups of milk** and add:
1 cup sugar
2 Tblsp gelatin
Add: **3 egg yolks very carefully**
Cook all of this over a double boiler until the custard coats the spoon. Then remove from heat and add:
1 tsp vanilla
2 Tblsp sherry
1 cup crushed macaroons
Cool this quickly while stirring in a bowl of ice. Then fold in:
3 beaten egg whites
Pour into a mold and refrigerate until set.
Serve with sweetened whipped cream.

BAVARIAN CREAM   Jerry Peters

Soak **1 Tblsp unflavored gelatin in 1/4 cup cold water.** Dissolve by setting cup in a container of hot water.
Beat until light:
5 egg yolks
1/4 cup sugar
Add gelatin mixture and **1 1/2 tsp vanilla**
In separate bowl whip egg whites until stiff and **add 1/8 tsp salt**
Whip in slowly **1/4 cup sugar**
In separate bowl whip til stiff **2 cups heavy cream**
Combine all ingredients lightly and place pudding in a wet mold. Chill thoroughly. Unmold and serve with crushed fruit or foamy sauce.

THINGS I PRIZE
Henry Van Dyke

These are the things I prize and hold of dearest worth:
Light of the sapphire skies,
Peace of the silent hills,
Shelter of the forests, comfort of the grass,
Music of birds, murmur of little rills,
Shadows of cloud that swiftly pass,
And, after showers,
The smell of flowers
And the good brown earth –
And best of all, along the way,
    Friendship and mirth.

MEAT

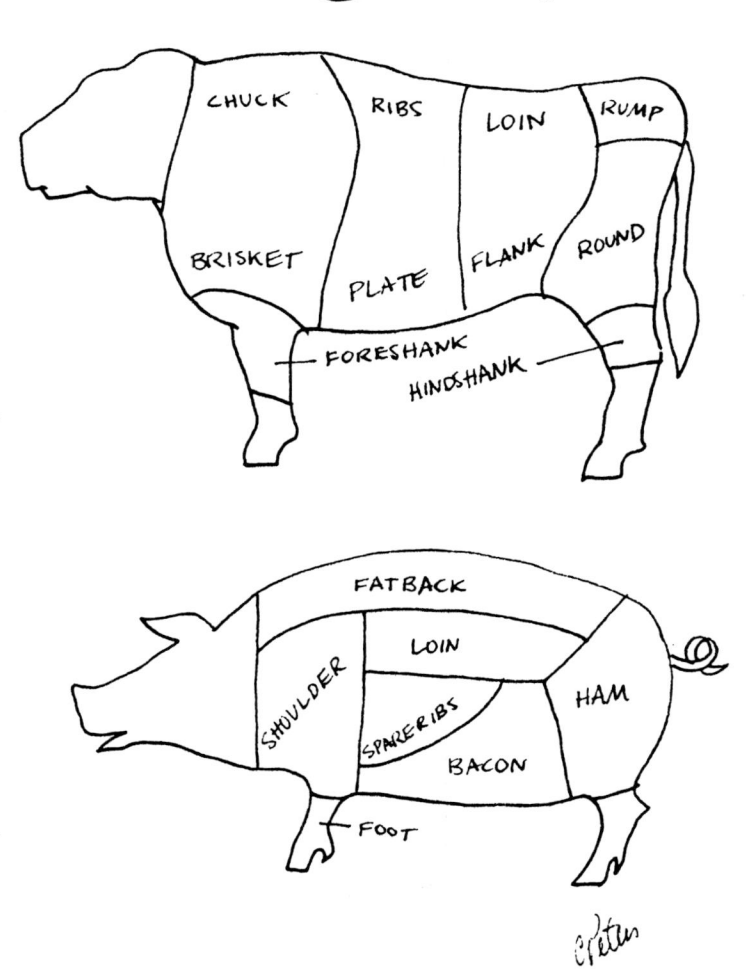

MEAT

Beef Stroganoff 166
Beef Stroganoff 169
Cheese Burgers 165
Chinese Pork with Sweet and Sour Sauce 164
Cooking and Uncooked Ham 163
Crock Pot Roast Beef 169
Easy Beef Brisket 165
Fleischlabalan 170
Good Old Pot Roast 161
Ham Balls 164
Ham Loaf 158
Ham Loaf for Easter 166
Ham Meat Loaf 170
New England Boiled Dinner 165
Olde Tyme Barbeque Beef Brisket 171
Pirogi 171
Roast Beef 168
Roast Leg of Lamb 159
Steak Diane 160
Steaks in Cognac 157
Tender Loving Care of Nebraska Beef 172

MALCOLM PETERS

STEAKS IN A BLIZZARD _____

Steaks in a blizzard are easier than most think. Just remember to stand away from flare-ups and to drop and roll if you feel rather hot all of a sudden. A cute hat from Peru will improve your odds of successful barbecuing as the gods will be watching you! The shovel is to keep a path clear to the bar inside. This truly is the most important tool in winter steak cooking. You see, it takes several Scotches to even consider venturing outside to cook the steaks, anyway.
Grill steaks on one side, turn and when they become shiny on reverse side, remove from fire and they will be medium rare. Who cares? You've been drinking Scotch anyway, haven't you?   ---- Mac

STEAKS IN COGNAC _____A.T. Harvey

Roll the steaks on both sides in freshly ground pepper. Pan grill them in very, very hot butter. Then add a glass of Cognac to the pan and set it afire. When the blaze has gone out, remove the steaks and add a glass of white wine or vermouth and another tablespoon of butter to the sauce. Beat it up with a fork and serve the steak and the sauce on buttered toast. A glass is about the size of a small liqueur glass, or an ounce.

HAM LOAF   Angela Bennett

1 cup bread crumbs	3 eggs, beaten
1 can tomato soup	1/2 tsp sage
1 small onion, grated	1/2 lb. of ground ham
3/4 lb. of ground fresh pork	

Mix together all ingredients and mold into one large or two small loaf pans. Place pan(s) in water bath and bake at 300° for 1 1/4 hours.

SAUCE:
2 Tblsp sugar   **1 egg, well beaten**
2 Tblsp vinegar
Cook these three ingredients for a minute or two until thick and then cool. Then add
1 cup whipping cream, whipped
1/2 cup horseradish
This sauce keeps a long time.

Beef Tenderloin with puffed pastry Courtesy Chef Peters

ROAST LEG OF LAMB

Cut peeled cloves of garlic into 4 or 5 slivers, cut pockets into the leg of lamb with a sharp knife and insert at least a dozen slivers into the lamb.

Rub ground pepper into the roast on both sides. Salt entire leg with Lawry's Season Salt and pat in.
Dredge entire leg with flour and place in large roasting pan.
Cover top of lamb with prepared mustard.
Sprinkle rosemary herbs over the mustard.
Peel small potatoes for each guest and a few for the pot and par boil for 10 minutes.
Peel onions and parboil. Cool, cut in half so that each guest has an onion half. Place these around the roast and salt and drizzle with a little oil so they will brown while roasting.

You may also use this procedure with carrots and place them in the roasting pan, if pan is large enough.

Our family loves lamb chops pink when prepared, but our family always served leg of lamb well done, so that the meat was tan all the way through. It does not toughen the meat to so cook. A leg of spring lamb at room temperature should take about 3 to 3 1/2 hours at 325° to cook thoroughly.

Strain off grease and make plenty of lamb gravy to serve with roast and don't forget the mint sauce; recipe for sauce in another section.

Another method of cooking roast leg of lamb:
Bring lamb to room temperature.
Preheat oven to 500°.
Bake lamb for 20 minutes, turn oven off and let stand in oven, door closed, for 3 1/2 hours. No peeking!!

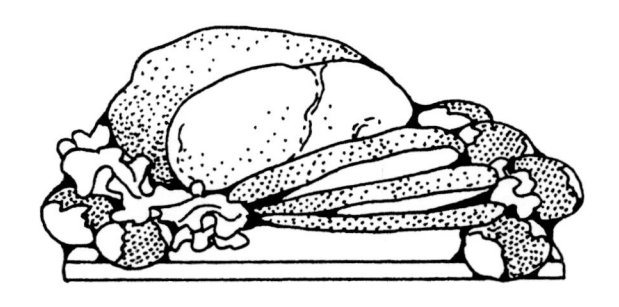

YOU SEE - - -
THIS IS THE SORT OF THING
WE'RE DEALING WITH HERE AT THIS HOUSE . . .

❖ ❖ ❖ ❖ ❖ ❖ ❖ ❖ ❖

At one time in the late 50's, we were dinner hosts at home to two German journalists, one of whom rather enjoyed his Brandy too much. As the dessert course arrived at the table, I watched with horrified glee as Otto, my dinner partner, ladled from the salt dish spoonful after spoonful of salt into his after-dinner coffee.
I do not consider myself a naughty person, (full of fun, yes) yet I do recollect the stoicism with which I watched the man and I was powerless to speak. His first sip was reward unimaginable.

STEAK DIANE_____

Trim steaks and salt and pepper.
Cook in **4 Tblsp butter** until medium rare.
Pour in **1 pony of Cognac** and flame.
Remove steak and add **1 Tblsp Worcestershire sauce**
1 Tblsp prepared mustard
1/2 can of Brown Sauce
Cook this down, add a little salt and serve.

GOOD OLD POT ROAST   Momo

Mom, start this in a roasting pan or Dutch oven early in the morning and by dinner time, you won't even whimper when the kids ask you if Teddy, Eddy and Freddy can stay over for dinner. There's plenty for everyone and is especially nice for getting a hot meal into a fast-paced family who are making deadlines. This food can be reheated and abused and simply gets better.

1   5 to 6 lb. pot roast of chuck (whatever looks good at the market)
3 Tblsp oil
Brown roast on both sides in Dutch oven really well in hot grease and add **2 Tblsp Kitchen Bouquet** meat enhancer to both sides of roast. Then chop
1 large onion
3 large cloves of garlic
Add to meat in pan and cook for 5 minutes.
Season meat with **1 tsp fresh ground pepper.**
Add 1 large can of stewed tomatoes
1 green pepper cut up
3 large onions quartered
6 large carrots scrubbed and halved
6 potatoes peeled and cut in halves
Sometimes I add **2/3 can of beer or 1/3 cup of Bourbon** to roast for a wonderful flavor. Don't worry - the alcohol cooks off!
Put the covered pan in a 300 to 325° oven and just let it cook slowly for 5 or 6 hours: - when meat is tender - stop cooking. Season the pot with Lawry's Season Salt toward the end of the cooking period.

To serve: Put roast and veggies on large platter and thicken pan juices with cornstarch diluted in water for a lovely gravy. Can be rewarmed in pot endlessly.

I became involved with the Dunnell geneology, which had never been traced beyond my Great-grandfather Mark Dunnell. After 12 years of researching, I completed the line and found our illustrious predecessor Henry, in York, Maine in the year 1636, having left Scotland with his young son Thomas, aboard the ship BONAVENTURE from the port of England.

He was an early settler in the Casco Bay area of Maine and to see that area and find the houses and walk the lands owned by his descendants was the dream that kept me struggling. 1983 was the year of fulfillment and the pleasure of those days in that lovely State with its rock bound coast and majestic sea is a memory worth the effort of those many years of work.

It was in Maine that New England boiled dinner Maine-style was brought to my everlasting attention and I was also able to surfeit an uncontrollable demand for the best of all foods - boiled lobster.

The picture below is the Dunnell manse in Minnesota that has been moved to the Steele County Fair Grounds in Owatonna as the dominant structure in their Village of Yesteryear. It was originally built in 1868-69 by Great-grandfather Mark Dunnell who served in Congress for 12 years.

Grandma D. says: Old age begins when your descendants outnumber your friends!

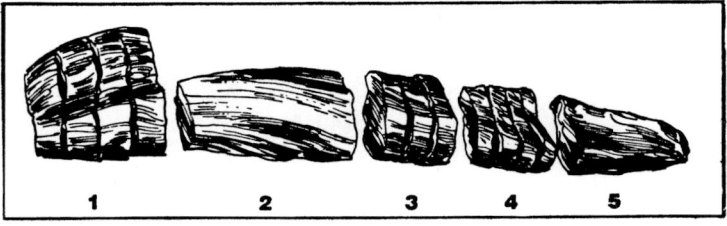

Beef tenderloin . . .Illustration at top is the whole tenderloin. The numbered illustration shows the tenderloin cut for use as multiple meals. The French terms for the numbered sections are: 1. biftek, 2. Chateaubriand, 3. filet steak 4. tournedos, 5. filet mignon. Any portion of a tenderloin would make a wonderful steak.

❖ ❖ ❖ ❖ ❖ ❖ ❖ ❖ ❖

COOKING AN UNCOOKED HAM

Find a nice 14 pound uncooked fresh or "green" ham. Trim the fat to 1/8" and score the fat in a pretty diagonal diamond pattern centering each with whole cloves.
Make a glaze of the following:
1 cup brown sugar
1/2 cup sherry
1/4 cup honey
1/4 cup Dijon mustard
Spoon the glaze over the ham and bake in a 350° oven for 20 minutes.
Reglaze the ham, turn oven to 325° and bake 20 minutes.
Reglaze the ham and turn oven to 300° and bake for 3 hours.
Reglaze ham and bake 15 minutes more. If you're not sure, put a thermometer in it but not near the bone as you will not get an accurate reading.

CHINESE PORK WITH SWEET & SOUR SAUCE_____ _Fran Day

Dredge **4 whole pork tenderloins in**
2 Tblsp flour
Brown in **5 Tblsp butter** in frying pan. then add
3 green peppers sliced in strips
1 medium onion diced
3/4 cup of crushed pineapple
1/2 tsp salt and dash of pepper
1/2 can Campbell's consumme
Cook mixture for 1/2 hour covered. Then stir in and cook for 15 minutes more the following ingredients that have been stirred together
3 Tblsp cornstarch
1/4 cup vinegar
1 tsp Soy sauce
1/2 cup brown sugar, packed

Serve with 3 cups of hot rice using recipe for Fried rice in this Cookbook.

HAM BALLS _____ Carol Harvey
This recipe makes 20 balls

1 1/2 lb. LEAN ground ham
1 lb. LEAN ground pork
1 1/2 cups crushed cracker crumbs
1 Tblsp dry mustard
1 cup milk
1 small onion chopped fine
2 eggs

SAUCE:
3/4 cup hard packed brown sugar
1/2 cup vinegar
1/2 cup water

Put sauce and balls in heavy skillet and cover with tight lid. Bake in 350° oven for abut 1 1/2 hours or you can cook over low heat on top of stove same length of time. If glaze becomes too thick, thin with a little water.

A NIZE, EASY BEEF BRISKET NEVER HOIT

One 3 to 3 1/2 lb. fresh beef brisket
1/2 cup brown sugar
1 envelope regular onion soup mix
1/2 tsp garlic powder
3/4 cup catsup

Seal beef brisket in heavy foil in a roasting pan with all ingredients spread over. Bake at 325° for 3 to 3 1/2 hours til brisket is tender. Skim fat from sauce, slice beef and serve with sauce. Potato latkes are marvelous with this.

NEW ENGLAND BOILED DINNER

1 1/2 lb. smoked pork shoulder butt (ask your butcher)
1 1/2 head of cabbage, cut in wedges
1 small onion, stuck with 2 cloves
4 ribs of celery
8 cups of water
1 bay leaf
2 sprigs of thyme or 1/2 tsp
3/4 lb. of turnips
2 leeks split
2 allspice
4 pepper corns
4 sprigs of parsley
4 carrots

Bring to a boil and simmer for 10 minutes. Add turnips and carrots and a potato for everyone and simmer for 30 minutes more. Vegetables should be tender. Unload on a big platter.

CHEESE BURGERS   Delores Borman

2 lbs ground chuck beef
8 oz. frozen onions, chopped (2/3 of a package)
1 1/2 lbs Velveeta cheese, cut in small cubes
2 small cans chopped olives

Brown onions in pan in small amount of oil. Add beef and brown. Then drain all fat from onions and beef. Add cheese until melted, add olives and heat for 10 minutes. Cool. Fill 2 dozen bakery hot dog buns with beef mixture, wrap in foil and freeze. To use: heat at 350° for 30 minutes.

BEEF STROGANOFF — Wanda Larsen, consummate ski partner

2 lbs. boneless beef cut in thin strips
Coat beef strips well with
1/2 cup flour   1 tsp salt
1/2 tsp Accent   1/8 tsp pepper
Brown in **1/2 cup butter** and add
1/2 cup shallots or onion
When very, very brown, sprinkle in rest of flour and brown. Add
3 cups bouillon or consumme and simmer 1 hour. If needed, add more liquid.
Brown **1/2 lb. fresh mushrooms in butter** and drain.
Blend **1 1/2 cups sour cream with 1/2 tsp Worcestershire sauce or 1/2 cup sherry** and add to meat mixture carefully. Add mushrooms and heat but do not boil.
Serve with rice sprinkled with chopped fresh parsley.

❖ ❖ ❖ ❖ ❖ ❖ ❖ ❖ ❖ ❖

HAM LOAF FOR EASTER — Joani Mitten
Get out your old fashioned tea towels girls!

1 1/2 lb ground pork
1 lb. ham, ground
1 green pepper chopped fine
1 cup bread crumbs
1 cup milk

Mix together well and mold into a loaf and place in an old sugar sack (made of tea towels) 3 to 3 1/2 inches in diameter. Place in kettle with water to cover to which **1 cup of vinegar** is added and boil gently for 3 hours. When cooked, remove from sack and serve with the following sauce.

Cook the following in a double boiler until thick:
1/2 cup tomato soup   **1/2 cup vinegar**
1/2 cup prepared mustard   **1/2 cup sugar**
1/2 cup butter   **3 beaten egg yolks**

Bill Schenck and Doug Peters invented grilling. In 1953 in Omaha at the old Peters house on Ridgewood Road, the boys converted a Maytag washing machine into a roaring inferno, slapped an old oven rack over the top, and grilled some lovely steaks from SAC Air Base commissary into indistinguishable black lumps. As newly marrieds, the Schencks and the Peters thought that charcoal broiled meat meant charcoal black. As our palates refined and the price of meat went up, a good deal more finesse was applied and both the men turned out to be Class A artists at the console of the Weber . . . . until Kay wrote in the early 80's that - BILL HAD LOST HIS WILL TO GRILL ------!
However, Bill remains in my heart, championship stuff, and he still makes the best mixed drink in the world. Looks cute on a camel, too.

Artist's Signature MRP

age 11

Matthew Robert Peters

ROAST BEEF _____ Jane Peters
You won't believe it!!

Bring ANY SIZE roast to room temperature. Preheat the oven to 375°.
Season roast.
Place roast in oven and bake for one hour. Turn oven off.
DO NOT OPEN THE OVEN DOOR FOR AT LEAST FOUR HOURS
or more.
When getting ready to serve guests - - -
Turn oven back on to 375° and cook for 1 more hour. Let roast rest for
1/2 hour and serve Medium Rare as if by magic.

BEEF STROGANOFF   Jane Peters

1 Tblsp flour
1/2 tsp salt
1 lb. of beef cut in 1/4 inch strips. The more expensive the beef, the more tender will be the dish.
Combine flour and salt and dredge the meat in this combination.
Then sauté the beef in **2 Tblsp butter** until brown.
In another pan sauté until tender
1 cup thinly sliced mushrooms
1/2 cup chopped onion
1 large clove garlic, minced
Remove vegetables from pan and combine
2 Tblsp butter with 3 Tblsp flour and cook roux until well mixed about 3 minutes.
Add
1 can beef broth
1 Tblsp tomato paste
Stir and cook until thick and then add vegetables and meat that have been pre-cooked. Stir together and add
1 cup sour cream
2 Tblsp sherry
Heat very carefully, blending all ingredients but do not let this dish boil!
Serves 4.

❖ ❖ ❖ ❖ ❖ ❖ ❖ ❖ ❖

CROCK POT ROAST BEEF   Scott Peters

3 lb. roast   1 Tblsp minced onion
1 bouillon cube   1 tsp caraway seeds
1 cup boiling water   2 tsp salt
1/4 cup catsup   1/2 tsp pepper
1 Tblsp Worcestershire sauce

Mix all these ingredients and pour over meat in crock pot. Cook all day on low. After meat is tender, drain off the juice and thicken with some flour. Add **1 can mushrooms** and **some sour cream** and pour back over the pot roast just before serving. Throw in a little red wine along the way.

FLEISCHLABALAN: _____ Gitte Peters

500 g ground beef
50 g bacon
50 g onions
3 garlic cloves
2 hard Kaiserrolls, white bread
1/2 Tblsp marjoram
1/2 Tblsp basil
1 tsp salt
1 dash nutmeg
1 Tblsp chopped parsley
1 egg
fresh ground pepper

oil to fry

Soak bread in water, squeeze dry, and mash it with a fork. Cut bacon and onions ino small pieces, brown, add garlic. Remove from stove and add bread, ground beef, herbs and egg. Mix all the ingredients together, form little patties (like hamburgers) and fry in oil til medium brown.
Serve with potato souffle and green salad. Guten Appetit!!!

❖ ❖ ❖ ❖ ❖ ❖ ❖ ❖ ❖

HAM MEAT LOAF _____ Dode Stroy

1 lb. each of ground beef, ground pork, and ground ham
1 small can Pet evaporated milk
1 can Campbell's tomato soup
1 cup crushed cracker crumbs
1/4 cup chopped green pepper
1 tsp dry mustard
3 egg yolks
1/2 cup chopped onion

Mix all ingredients together. Beat 4 egg whites until stiff and fold carefully into meat mixture. Place in baking pan and sprinkle top of meat with brown sugar. Bake at 400° for one hour.

PIROGI

A Russian engineer and his wife, a ballerina who danced with the Bolshoi defected to the United States in the late 70's and we entertained them at the Platte River in Fremont, Nebraska. Imagine the nerve! They brought pirogi's and I was so thrilled with them, I can't remember what we cooked. Anyway, these are delicious to just pop in your mouth while talking to fascinating guests, which is what we did.

10 oz. pkg. frozen patty shells	**2 Tblsp butter**
1/2 cup finely chopped onion	**2 Tblsp sour cream**
1 1/4 cups diced left over steak or beef roast	
2 hard boiled eggs, finely chopped	
1/2 tsp dill weed	**salt and pepper to taste**

Thaw frozen patty shells. Sauté onion in butter 3 minutes, add sour cream and stir in diced beef, egg, dill, salt and pepper. Preheat oven to 400°. On a floured board, roll each patty shell to a 1/8 inch circle. Cut as may circles as you can with a 3 1/2 inch biscuit cutter. Gather scraps and roll again to make more circles.

Spread a rounded Tblsp of meat on half of each circle, fold other half over filling and seal edges by pinching dough together. Cut a couple of slits to allow steam to escape. Place pies on buttered baking sheet and bake 20 minutes til golden brown.

OLDE TYME BARBEQUE BEEF BRISKET — Delores Borman

Start three days before serving day

6 lbs. of beef brisket	**1 1/2 tsp garlic salt**
1 1/2 tsp celery salt	**1 tsp onion powder**
1/2 tsp ground coriander	**1 bottle (3 oz.) liquid smoke**
water	**1 cup prepared barbecue sauce**
1/2 cup water	**1/2 cup packed brown sugar**
1 1/2 cups catsup	**1/2 tsp salt**

Rub both sides of beef with garlic salt, celery salt, onion powder and coriander. Place in flat glass dish. Pour half of liquid smoke on one side of meat and reminder on reverse side. Cover tightly with plastic wrap (not foil) and refrigerate at least 24 hours. Place glass dish containing meat in cold oven. Bake <u>uncovered</u> at 275° for 5 to 6 hours. Check every hour and add 1/2 cup of water as needed to keep dish from turning dry. Turn every hour. Cool meat and slice very thin. Combine barbecue sauce, water, brown sugar, catsup and salt and cook 15 to 20 minutes til sauce gets dark in color. Spoon sauce over meat and reheat. Do not leave in oven too long as this meat has a tendency to dry out. Can be served hot or cold.

TENDER LOVING CARE OF
NEBRASKA BEEF_____ Norris Swan

MEAT: Whole Top Sirloin cut 1 1/4" thick.
Fresh cut but hung for two plus weeks.
Best if never frozen but if frozen thaw completely at room temperature before use, then refrigerate.

FIRE: Start fire with electric starter at least one hour before cooking (cooking time 20 minutes)
Pile all charcoal in center and be sure all is burning. Charcoal Will burn down until about 1/2 size and become grey ash.
When charcoal is spread and shaken it becomes cherry red.

GRILL: Cast-iron is best as it holds the heat but stainless steel or whatever works.
Needs to be adjustable so chef can place grill no more than 2-3 inches from fire to obtain maximum heat.
When the grill is as hot as the fire and the fire is cherry red you are ready to cook.

Put the completely thawed meat on the grill with tongs. (trim the fat from the edges as it will "drip-and-flame" - it is the marbled fat within the meat that provides the flavor). Use a timer and sear the meat for 4 minutes. This seals the pores and retains the juice.

Turn the meat with TONGS and sear the other side for 4 minutes.
Turn the meat with tongs and cook for 5 minutes.
Turn again and cook for 5 minutes.

THEN - heavily shake on the cooked meat the following:
    GARLIC SALT
    ONION SALT
    COARSE GROUND PEPPER (fresh ground is best)
As soon as layered, turn meat with tongs and repeat on the other side.
Turn the meat with tongs and cook the 2nd seasoned side for one minute.

Time is a matter of trial and error. The fire, the breeze across the grill, the size and thickness of the meat, number of moves for "fat-drip-flame-ups" are all variables. You can test the meat by feel. Push the tongs onto the meat and the harder (firmer) the meat feels the more it is cooked. You want to catch the meat when it still is soft indicating juice.

The meat is placed on a cutting block and sliced into 1" servings. The individual will select rare, or well done, or in between. The meat will continue to cook, so again <u>undercook</u>.

Each time try your meat a little more rare than you did before and eventually you will arrive at the full appreciation of:

THE TENDER LOVING NEBRASKA BEEF

DO'S
Anticipate the meat so you don't try to cook frozen meat or force the thaw by Microwave. (Takes the moisture out and the result will be tough).

Start fire over 1 hour before you cook.

Plenty of charcoal, as you can not add more and keep uniform.
    (if fire is not correct i.e.: hot enough, meat will "drip-flame")

Have all supplies and utensils available.
    Tongs, timer, hot pad or gloves, towel, 3 seasonings.

Color code or mark so you can identify the seasonings.
    (garlic salt and onion salt appear the same)

Alert the Kitchen 5 minutes (or more) before the meat is ready to take off the fire as it must be served hot.

Under cook, as meat will continue to cook.

It is recommended the cook drinks while cooking.

DON'TS
Do not marinate meat as it breaks down the fiber and will be mushy and have an artificial taste.

Do not ever stick a fork in fresh meat as the juice will run out.

Do not season meat until after seared or the salt will open the pores and the juice will run out.

Do not economize on the seasoning as it is an outside crust and does not penetrate the meat. It provides the gourmet taste but can be scraped off before eating if excessive.

DO NOT OVERCOOK. The meat will continue to cook while being served and eaten. The rarer (juicier) the better texture (tender) and taste.

Do not squirt water on the fire as it covers the meat with ashes. (Move the meat with tongs away from the "fat-drip" flame)

Do not use lighter fluid, kerosene, etc. to start fire as all will leave a taste.

Four & Twenty Blackbird Pie...

Pies

PIES

Apple Pie 185
Bavarian Mint Pie 179
Black Bottom Pie 178
Buttermilk Pie Crust 181
Butterscotch Pie 186
Graham Cracker Pie Crust 179
Grasshopper Pie 179
Kennebunk Inn's Down East Apple Pie 180
Key Lime Pie 182
Lemon Pie with Meringue 178
Never Fail Pie Crust 180
Open Face Peach Pie 181
Perfect Pecan Pie 185
Pumpkin Pie No. 1 182
Pumpkin Pie No. 2 182
Sour Cream Raisin Pie 181

All of the Peters families have remembrances of the life style of Great-Grandmother Belle Snyder Hess, who was a consummate hostess. Beautiful silver, linens, and china are part of the treasures divided, used and loved by her descendants. I remember her Council Bluffs home of grand elegance and her enthusiasm for welcoming guests. Dinner at their house was a very special occasion.

❖ ❖ ❖ ❖ ❖ ❖ ❖ ❖ ❖

LAWYER:
"Now, sir, did you, or did you not, on the date in question, or at any other time, previously or subsequently say or even intimate to the defendant or anyone else, alone or with anyone, whether a friend or a mere acquaintance, or in fact, a stranger, that the statement imputed to you, whether just or unjust, and denied by the plaintiff, was a matter of no moment or otherwise? Answer me, yes or no."

WITNESS:
"Yes or no what?"

LEMON PIE WITH MERINGUE   Irene Dunnell

2 round Tblsp cornstarch   pinch of salt
1 1/2 cups water   1 cup sugar
3 Tblsp butter   3 egg yolks
juice and rind of one lemon

Combine sugar, cornstarch, water, salt and butter with the lemon and the rind and cook over double boiler until thick. Add egg yolks very slowly and blend until thick and hot. Pour into cooled baked pie shell when filling is cool.

MERINGUE:
3 egg whites
6 Tblsp sugar
1/4 tsp cream of tartar

Whip egg whites with beater and add cream of tartar and slowly add sugar til meringue stands up. Bake at 350° for about 15 minutes til golden brown.

BLACK BOTTOM PIE   Belle Hess

1 9" pie shell   1 tsp vanilla
1/4 cup butter   3 eggs
1/2 cup light corn syrup   1/2 cup sugar
1/3 cup unsweetened cocoa

In a medium saucepan, melt butter. Remove from heat and blend in syrup, vanilla and eggs. In a bowl, stir together sugar and cocoa and add to egg mixture and blend well. Pour into 9" pastry pie crust and bake at 350° for 30 to 40 minutes til center is set. Cool completely.

CUSTARD:
1/3 cup sugar   2 cups milk
2 Tblsp cornstarch   4 eggs
2 tsp Rum (Demarara)   Whipping cream and chocolate curls

In heavy saucepan, combine sugar and cornstarch. Add milk and eggs, mix well and cook over medium heat until mixture boils and thickens, stirring constantly. Remove from heat, stir in Rum and cover with plastic wrap and chill. Spoon over chocolate layer in pie shell, garnish with whipped cream and chocolate curls.

GRAHAM CRACKER PIE CRUST

Pulverize **20 graham crackers** in Cuisinart or with rolling pin.
Melt **5 Tblsp butter** and combine with crackers.
Press into 9" pie tin and refrigerate.

BAVARIAN MINT PIE   Steve Simmons

2 squares Bakers Chocolate chocolate
1/4 cup soft margarine
2 eggs
1 graham cracker pie crust

2 packets of liquid bitter
2 cups powdered sugar
1/2 tsp peppermint extract

Melt chocolate & butter in a double boiler. Add liquid chocolate. When thoroughly combined, add powdered sugar and combine. Beat 2 eggs in a small bowl and add slowly and carefully to heated chocolate mixture beating constantly until mixture begins to get fluffy. Add peppermint extract. Keep beating, until mixture cools. Pour into graham cracker pie shell. Put into fridge overnight and put lock on refrigerator door. This recipe just disappears!

GRASSHOPPER PIE   Momo

18 large chocolate wafers, crushed   1/3 cup of melted butter
Crush cookies and combine with butter and press into a 9" pie pan and chill in fridge.
24 large marshmallows   2/3 cup milk
Place marshmallows and milk in a double boiler and melt marshmallows. Then cool mixture.
1/2 pint heavy whipping cream   3 Tblsp green Creme De Menthe
3 Tblsp white Creme de Cocoa
Put whipping cream in bowl and whip until cream begins to hold together. Slowly add liqueurs and finish beating whip cream to stiff. Carefully fold cooled marshmallow mixture into whipped cream mixture and turn into pie crust. Chill - can make day before. Pretty with curled chocolate shavings over the top. Men love this!

KENNEBUNK INN'S DOWN EAST APPLE PIE

This is a 10-inch pie and won the Annual Great New England Food Festival First Prize.

Make a 2 pie crust recipe and put bottom crust in a 10-inch glass pie plate. Pour the following CRANBERRY BASE into the pie crust:

2 cups cranberries
1/2 cup orange juice
grated zest from 1 orange
1 cup sugar
1/2 cup water
dash of nutmeg

Combine all ingredients in a medium saucepan and cook over low heat until mixture is reduced by 1/3. You should have about 1 3/4 cups - cool this mixture. SLICE THIN 8 to 10 Courtland apples - Winesap apples are a good substitute.

1/3 cup flour
1 cup sugar
5 to 6 tsps buttermilk
Granulated sugar for topping
1 tsp cinnamon
3/4 tsp nutmeg
pinch of salt

Combine flour, sugar, cinnamon, nutmeg and salt and gently toss with apples til coated. Top the cranberry mixture with the apples and dot with butter. Place pie crust over top, brush with buttermilk and sprinkle with sugar. Cut steam vents. Bake at 400° for 50 minutes.

❖ ❖ ❖ ❖ ❖ ❖ ❖ ❖ ❖

NEVER FAIL PIE CRUST — Dottie Hohenstein
Perfect for flans and quiches. Makes five crusts.

Mix together:
1 egg
1 tsp vinegar and 5 Tblsp water
Add:
2 Tblsp sugar
1 tsp salt
Cut together
1 1/2 cups Crisco shortening and the liquid ingredients.
Add:
3 1/2 cups scant flour and mix dough. Chill overnight. Make pie crusts the following day from prepared dough.

OPEN FACE PEACH PIE — Dottie Naramore

1 cup sugar, scant
1/4 cup butter
1/2 cup flour

Cream together and put half in bottom of an unbaked pie shell. Place peach halves which have been peeled cavity-side up on mixture. Fill cavities with cream. Sprinkle the remaining half of above mixture over peaches. Sprinkle with cinnamon or nutmeg. Bake at 360° to 375° until peaches are tender, about 45 minutes.

BUTTERMILK PIE CRUST — Ruth Smith

5 cups flour
1 tsp salt
1 lb. room temperature lard
Mix above ingredients with hands to pea size
Add:
1 cup buttermilk
This makes 8 pie shells, is great to freeze and EASY to roll. Now you can go into business!

SOUR CREAM RAISIN PIE

1 cup raisins
1/2 cup water
2/3 cup plus 3 Tblsp sugar
1 Tblsp flour
1 cup sour cream
1 baked 9-inch pie shell

1/4 tsp cinnamon
1/4 scant tsp cloves
dash of salt
1/4 tsp cream of tartar
3 eggs, separated

Combine raisins and water and cook over medium heat for 5 minutes. Drain raisins reserving 1 Tblsp liquid. In a medium saucepan combine only 2/3 cup sugar, flour, spices and salt. Add sour cream, egg yolks, and raisin liquid. Cook until mixture boils, stirring constantly. Beat 3 egg whites til foamy and add cream of tartar and 3 Tblsp of sugar, one Tblsp at a time til egg whites are stiff. Put filling in pie crust, top with meringue and bake 12 to 15 minutes at 350° til top is golden.

PUMPKIN PIE NO. 1

**9 -inch pie shell
2 cups pumpkin puree
1 1/2 cups milk
3 eggs
1 cup sugar
2 Tblsp flour**

**1 1/2 tsp cinnamon
1/2 tsp salt
1/2 tsp ginger
1/4 tsp cloves**

Blend together, pour in unbaked pie shell and bake 450° for 20 minutes. Then bake 350° for about 30 minutes or until a silver knife inserted 1 inch from side of filling comes out clean.

PUMPKIN PIE NO. 2

**9-inch pie shell
1 1/2 cups pumpkin puree
1 cup brown sugar
1 tsp cinnamon
1/2 tsp ginger
1/2 tsp allspice**

**1/2 tsp salt
1 Tblsp flour
2 eggs
1 1/2 cup evaporated milk
1 tsp vanilla**

NOTE: If desired, use 3 eggs instead of 2 eggs and 1 Tblsp of flour.

To slightly beaten eggs add all ingredients and bake 10 minutes at 450°. Reduce oven to 325° and continue baking until firm.

KEY LIME PIE

**6 egg yolks
1/2 cup lime juice (hopefully Key limes, round and yellow)
1 cup sweetened condensed milk
1/2 tsp Cream of Tartar
6 egg whites
3/4 cup sugar**

Beat egg yolks until light! Blend in milk and lime juice slowly. Beat egg whites with the Cream of Tartar until foamy. Continue beating and slowly add sugar 1 Tblsp at a time until egg whites peak. Fold 6 Tblsp of meringue mixture into filling and put in a 9 inch pie shell. Pile the rest of the meringue on top of the pie and bake in a 325° oven until meringue is browned. Refrigerate.

George and Dorothy Naramore of Lake Plantagenet in Minnesota were responsible for a lot of hilarity in our lives. They owned the Red Squirrel resort near Bemidji, and for a week during the summer, we would rent cabins, usually with the Schenck family, at a larcenous rate. As a consequence, bills were made up during the week both by the hosts and the guests involving the quality of the fishing, the price of the minnows, the nature of the weather (gosh, you should have been here last week!), the condition of the cabins, and the temperament of the owners. These bills were presented at the end of the week with great glee.

Red Squirrel Resort, because of them, was a happy memory maker and George and Dottie are certainly assured of a place in Heaven at the behest of their many friends/guests. Dottie either had really good Indian friends or her own canoe, because whenever we yelled for wild rice, we were generously supplied. And could she ever make sweets hot out of the oven for pitiful sunburned vacationers. When she came shagging down the hill with a pan in her hand, people appeared out of the woods - literally!

1955
Young Resort Owners and
their first baby - Scott

1989 – STILL SMILING!!

OLD, OLD LADY

I want to be one of the spry ones,
The twinkling, spunky, sly ones –
The kind whose thoughts weave a pattern of lace
In a tatting of living all over my face.

I want to have lots of gray in my hair,
And a gingery tongue, and gumptiony air –
Just a frisky old dame with a jig in my toes
And a waggish tilt to the specs on my nose.
And when the kids whisper of wrinkles and such
I'll tell them they come from laughing so much;
And when they say, "Grandma, what big eyes you've got,"
I'll answer, "That's 'cause they've been opened alot!"

PERFECT PECAN PIE   Douglas Peters

1 cup pecan halves•
1/2 cup plus 1 Tblsp butter, melted and cooled •
1 unbaked 9" deep dish pie shell•
3/4 cup dark corn syrup •
3 eggs•
3/4 cup white sugar •
1 tsp vanilla•

Pre-heat oven to 350°. Combine pecans and 1 Tblsp of butter and spread on baking sheet. Bake til light golden, about 5 minutes. Cool. Maintain oven temperature. Place pecans in pie shell. Combine syrup and sugar in saucepan and bring to boil. Cook til syrup thickens about 5 minutes. Beat eggs to blend in bowl and add gradually add the syrup and then 1/2 cup melted butter. Stir in vanilla. Pour over pecans and bake til filling is firm and tester comes out clean, about 45 minutes.

APPLE PIE

12 large tart apples, peeled
Mix together:
3/4 to 1 cup of sugar •
1 tsp cinnamon •
1 pinch of nutmeg •
2 Tblsp cornstarch•
Toss apples with the **juice of 1/2 of a lemon** and then mix in rest of ingredients. Pile into 9-inch pie shell and cover with another crust. Brush crust with
1 egg, beaten
1 tsp water
a dash of salt
This will place a glaze on the pie and then refrigerate this pie for 2 hours or chill in the freezer for 1 hour before baking. Bake pie at 450° for 15 minutes and then reduce heat to 425° and bake until crust is brown and apples are tender when pierced with a skewer.

BUTTERSCOTCH PIE _____ Eileen Mathiasen

Make a baked 8-inch pie shell and set aside.
Make a paste of:
3 Tblsp flour
1/8 tsp salt
2/3 cup water
Then add:
2/3 cup milk•
2 egg yolks, slightly beaten with fork•
1/2 tsp vanilla•
Then set this mixture aside.

Melt in a saucepan:
2 Tblsp butter
Add:
1 cup brown sugar
Cook to the bubbly stage, about 3 minutes, over medium heat.
Then add the flour mixture to the butter/sugar mixture and cook until thick.
Pour into the baked pie shell.
Make meringue by beating
3 egg whites until frothy with
6 Tblsp of white sugar which is added slowly to the egg whites. Pile this meringue on top of pie filling and brown under a broiler.

❖ ❖ ❖ ❖ ❖ ❖ ❖ ❖ ❖

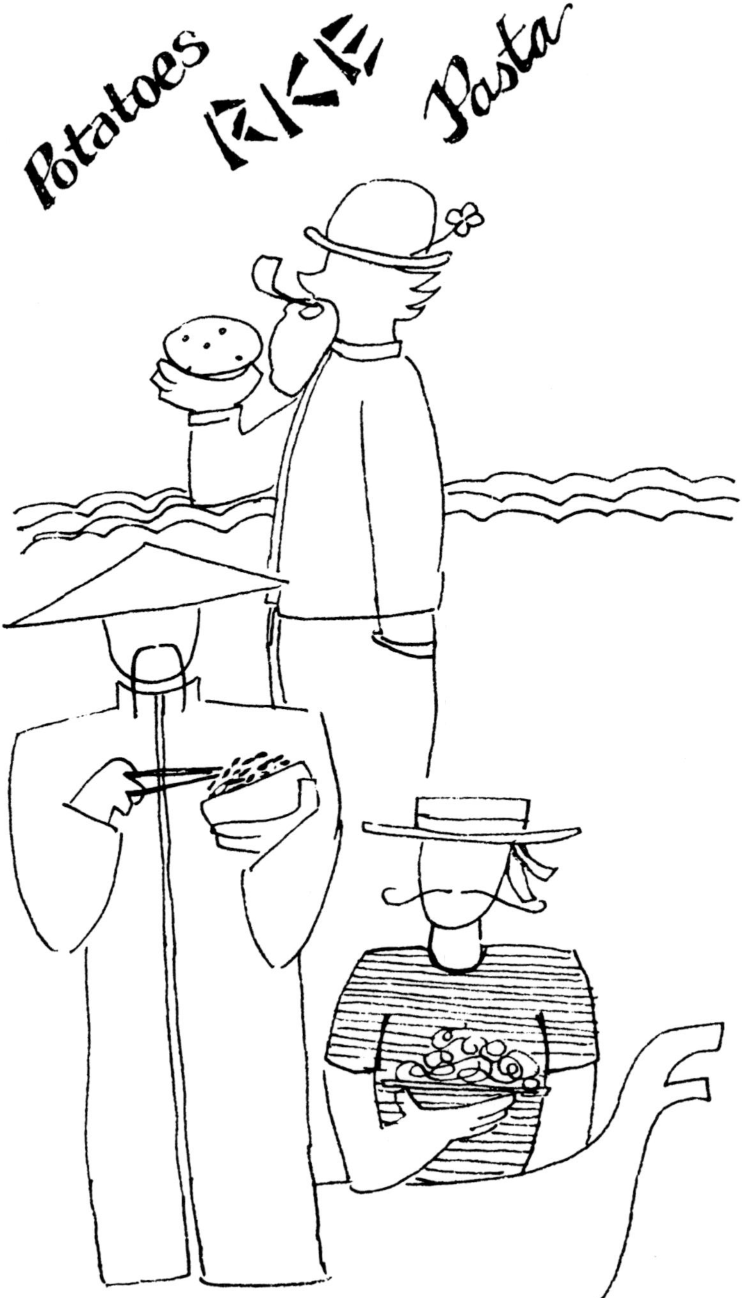
Potatoes
RICE
Pasta

POTATOES, PASTA, RICE

Cheese Grits 196
Erbsenreis 194
Farfel 197
Fried Rice 196
Green Rice 196
Green Spaghetti 195
Harvest Potatoes 197
Hungarian Noodles 189
Minnesota Wild Rice Casserole 193
Mushroom Spoon Bread 190
Mushroom-Almond Rice 190
Party Mashed Potatoes 195
Pasta Primavera 192
Peters Pork and Putt Potato Supreme 189
Potato Latkes 190
Potatoes Au Gratin 193
Pueblo Potatoes 194
Steamed Rice 193
Sweet Potato Casserole 194
Wild Rice Stuffing 197

About 8 years ago, Johnny and Mac Peters and wives started a yearly institution called PETERS PORK AND PUTT. There is always much hilarity as all male and female Peters and guests capable of swinging a golf club arrive for an 18-hole competition at the Fremont Golf Club. Rules for this Tournament are not known nor approved by the PGA. This outstanding contest is brought to a fever pitch each year by the attendance of all competitors plus non-competitors or even interested parties at a large BARBECUE, after the golf game, at the Peters cabin on the Platte River. Here, incredible awards are conceived for presentation to winners and losers alike and frivolity reigns. Some of the recipes for the food presented are herewith listed.

PETERS PORK AND PUTT POTATO SUPREME

2 lbs. frozen hashbrown potatoes
1 tsp salt and pepper
2 cups sour cream
1/2 cup chopped onion
1/3 cup melted butter
1 can Cream of Chicken soup
2 cups grated Cheddar cheese
1 clove of garlic

Defrost potatoes, combine all ingredients except the butter and put in a 9 x 13 casserole pan. Drizzle butter over the potatoes and top with crushed **potato chips**. Bake at 350° for 45 minutes.

HUNGARIAN NOODLES   Norris Swan
4 to 6 Servings

1 8 oz. pkg. fine noodles
1 cup sour cream
1/4 cup finely chopped onion
2 tsp Worcestershire sauce
1/2 tsp salt
3/4 cup Cheddar cheese, grated
1 cup cream style cottage cheese
2 eggs, lightly beaten
1 clove crushed garlic
Dash of Tabasco
Dash of pepper

Preheat oven to 350°. Grease 1 1/2 qt. casserole. Cook noodles according to package directions. Drain and rinse. In mixing bowl, blend cottage cheese, sour cream and eggs. Stir in onion, garlic, Worcestershire sauce, Tabasco, salt and pepper. Add noodles and 1/4 cup of the Cheddar cheese. Mix well. Turn into casserole. Set casserole in pan of hot water. Bake 30 minutes. Sprinkle remaining cheese on top. Bake for 10 minutes longer.

MUSHROOM SPOON BREAD
Instead of potatoes!

1 can Cream of Mushroom soup
1/2 cup corn meal
2 egg yolks, beaten
2 egg whites, stiffly beaten
3/4 cup milk
1 Tblsp butter
1/4 tsp salt

Combine soup and milk in a saucepan and stir in the corn meal and bring to a boil stirring constantly. Boil for 5 minutes. Add butter, yolks and salt. Mix well. Fold in egg whites and put in casserole to bake at 350° for 1 hour. Serve at once with gravy or butter.

MUSHROOM-ALMOND RICE   Irene Peters

1 cup chopped onions
4 Tblsp butter
1 cup uncooked rice
2 cups beef bouillon
1/4 tsp pepper
1/2 cup slivered almonds
1 cup sliced mushrooms

Saute onions in 2 Tblsp butter until soft and add rice and cook until rice is golden. Add the bouillon and pepper and stir and heat to boiling. Cover the rice, reduce heat and cook for 15 minutes or until rice has absorbed all the liquid. Sauté nuts and mushrooms in 2 Tblsp butter and add when the rice is tender.

POTATO LATKES

1 lb. potatoes, about 3 medium
1/4 cup Matzo meal
1/4 cup vegetable oil
3 beaten eggs
1/4 cup finely chopped onion

Peel and coarsely shred potatoes and as you work, place potatoes in a bowl of cold water to prevent darkening. Drain, rinse again and drain again. In a bowl stir together eggs, potatoes, matzo meal, onion, **1/4 tsp salt and 1/4 tsp pepper.** In a large skillet, heat oil to medium high and drop 1/4 cup mixture into hot oil. Press to flatten a little and fry 2 to 3 minutes til edges are crisp, turn, and fry two to three minutes more. Drain on paper towels and keep warm. Can serve with applesauce.

Doug and I were full of enthusiasm to go up in a hot air balloon in the Arizona desert. Each "flyer" received a logo hat, a signed certificate, and a little champagne lunch upon landing.
Standing in the basket, we ascended with the pilot blasting the air in the balloon with a gas flame burner. Otherwise, it is absolutely silent. Imagine our surprise when the balloon flying ahead of us hit high tension wires, fell to the ground and burned.
We got an extra long ride into a prohibited Indian reservation filled with balloon-ripping cactus because the ground winds were so high; the Captain feared to land until they abated!
I don't know - the thrill is gone for me.

PASTA PRIMAVERA — Jane T. Peters

1/2 cup butter	1 cup whipping cream
1 medium onion, minced	1/2 cup chicken stock
1 lb. asparagus, cut into 1/4" slices	2 Tblsp basil
1/2 lb. mushrooms, thinly sliced	5 green onions, chopped

1/2 cup cauliflower, broken into small florets
1 medium zucchini cut into 1/4" rounds   1 carrot, thinly sliced
1 lb. linguine, cooked   1 lb. cooked, peeled shrimp
1 cup freshly grated Parmesan cheese

In a large skillet add butter, onion and garlic. Sauté about 2 minutes. Mix in asparagus, mushrooms, cauliflower, zucchini and carrot. Cook for another 2 minutes. Increase heat to high. Add cream, stock and basil and boil about 3 minutes. Stir in green onion and shrimp, and cook 2 more minutes. Season with salt and pepper. Add pasta and cheese, tossing until thoroughly combined and pasta is heated through. Serve immediately!

SCOTT AND JANE PETERS

STEAMED RICE

1 tablespoon salt
2 cups unconverted long-grain rice

In a large saucepan bring 5 quarts water to a boil with the salt. Sprinkle in the rice, stirring until the water returns to a boil, and boil it for 10 minutes. Drain the rice in a large colander and rinse it. Set the colander over a saucepan of boiling water and steam the rice, covered with a dish towel and the lid, for 15 minutes, or until it is fluffy and dry. Makes about 6 cups.

POTATOES AU GRATIN   Jane S. Peters

4 potatoes
1/2 cup grated Swiss or Gruyere cheese
1/2 cup grated Parmesan cheese
4 Tblsp butter
1/4 cup heavy cream
salt and freshly ground pepper

Preheat oven to 375°. Peel potatoes and slice thinly, wash thoroughly with cold water to remove excess starch. Pat dry. Butter a baking dish and place layer of sliced potatoes on bottom. Cut butter in small pieces and put some on potatoes with salt and pepper. Sprinkle some of the cheeses over layer and continue in this fashion til ingredients are used. Pour heavy cream over all and cover with aluminum foil. Bake about one hour til they are soft. Remove foil 10 minutes before serving so the potatoes can brown. Serve immediately.

MINNESOTA WILD RICE CASSEROLE

Soak 1 cup wild rice in 2 cups of fresh water overnight.
Next day, wash and drain.
Cook rice in **3 cups chicken broth** til tender. Drain.
Add **sauteed mushrooms, green pepper and onion.**
Season with **butter, Lawry's Season Salt and pepper.**
Use lots of butter - maybe a little heavy cream to keep moist in casserole.

SWEET POTATO CASSEROLE

3 lbs. sweet potatoes, cooked
2 cups light cream
1/4 cup melted butter
1 1/2 tsp salt
1/4 tsp cloves

2 eggs, well beaten
1/2 cup sugar
1 tsp lemon zest
1 tsp nutmeg
2 Tblsp brown sugar

Beat until light and fluffy. Bake 30 minutes at 400°. Dot entire top with marshmallows, return to oven until marshmallows are just tan, about 5 minutes.

ERBSENREIS: Gitte Peters

1 cup rice
1 onion
1 cup green peas
salt

2 cups water
2 Tblsp butter
3 cloves

Chop onion small, melt butter and brown onion lightly; add rice, cloves and green peas; simmer til done.

The Havers and the Wilcoxson's of Pueblo, Colorado knew what they were doing when they suggested New Year's Eve in Taos, New Mexico. We and the Smiths packed our ear muffs and we all spent such a glorious time in that precious town that we did it again the next year. Who could resist gently falling snow, crisp mountain air flavored with pinon pine and our friend Ramon playing the guitar by the fireplace?

PUEBLO POTATOES Middy Haver Divelbiss

Boil **7 or 8 red potatoes** that are medium large until you can pierce with a knife; cool, peel and dice into a 9 x 13 glass casserole. Casserole should be about one-half full. Salt and pepper slightly. Mix together in a large bowl
1 pint carton commercial sour cream
2 small cans chopped green chilies, mild or medium hot
1 lb. of shredded Monterey Jack cheese
Put potatoes in with this mixture and coat them well. Return to casserole. Dot heavily with **one-half stick of butter** broken into pieces. Bake in 350° oven until hot, about 30 minutes or so. Dust with paprika. *Great with steaks.*

GREEN SPAGHETTI   Norris Swan

1 lg. clove garlic, chopped
1 Tblsp parsley flakes
1 1-lb. pkg. spaghetti
2 Tblsp sweet basil
1/4 lb. butter

Mash garlic, basil and parsley flakes together thoroughly with mortar and pestle. Melt butter and add remaining ingredients to it except for the spaghetti. Add mixture to cooked, drained and salted spaghetti. *Delicious with steaks!*

PARTY MASHED POTATOES   Sue MacElderry

8 to 10 mashed potatoes (large)
1/2 tsp garlic salt
8 oz. Cream Cheese
16 oz. Sour Cream

Let cream cheese soften and mix with sour cream. Then add potatoes and combine. You may top with cheddar cheese if you wish. Bake at 350° for 25 minutes. This is ideal for Thanksgiving, as potatoes can be prepared the night before and then heated while the turkey rests.

SUE MAC

CHEESE GRITS — Pat Burky

Cook: **1 cup grits in**
4 cups of boiling water with 1/2 tsp salt
Bring to a boil and cook til thick, about 3 minutes. Add:
1/2 lb. butter, cut up
1 roll of Kraft garlic cheese, cut up
Stir in butter and cheese to hot grits til they have melted. Add:
8 drops of Tabasco sauce
2 eggs beaten in a one cup measure. Then fill the one cup measure with **whole milk** and add to the grits. Mix thoroughly.
Put in large (9 x 12) greased shallow baking pan and top with **1/2 cup grated Cheddar cheese.** Bake at 350° for 30 minutes.
Serves 8.

Glenna Spetman is a marvelous cook and most of her recipes are so good we just keep cooking them over and over. And when it came to canning, she had no equal. And her flower gardens were just lovely too. What a talent. Here's a recipe for

GREEN RICE

This has always been a favorite with Supper Club and is a great accompaniment with any kind of meat dish.

Cook **2 cups of white rice** and drain.
Add **2 cups milk**   **3/4 cup melted butter**
2 cups grated American cheese   **1 cup chopped parsley**
1 chopped green pepper   **1 large clove garlic, chopped**
2 eggs, unbeaten
Mix above ingredients well and bake at 350° for about 1 hour and 20 minutes.

FRIED RICE — Fran Day

In frying pan melt:
3 Tblsp butter
2 cups of white rice that has been washed and drained
1/2 cup diced onion
Stirring constantly, brown the rice. When brown, add 3 cups of water and salt to taste. Cook for 20 minutes til water is absorbed and rice is fluffy, with saucepan covered but carefully watched.

WILD RICE STUFFING ____For Bob Wilcox's Thanksgiving turkey

2/3 cup wild rice
4 tsp beef bouillon
1 medium onion, chopped
1 tsp oregano
3 ribs celery chopped
salt and pepper to taste

3 cups water
4 slices bacon, cooked crisp & crumbled
1/2 lb. mushrooms, sliced
1/2 tsp sage
2 cups bread crumbs

Combine rice and water and bouillon in a pan and simmer about 50 minutes til rice is tender. Sauté onion and mushroom in bacon drippings. Add all to drained rice and combine in order to stuff a 10 to 14 pound turkey.

FARFEL ____Phyllis Weinberg

1 pkg. farfel
2 onions, diced
4 ribs celery, diced
1 Tblsp oil

1 4 oz. can sliced mushrooms
1 green pepper, diced
2 Tblsp chicken fat

Cook farfel in salted boiling water for 20 minutes. Sauté onions, celery, green pepper in oil. Drain farfel & combine with vegetables & chicken fat. Bake in greased casserole uncovered 40 minutes at 375°.

HARVEST POTATOES ____Glennice Carlson

1 pkg. (32 oz) frozen hash brown potatoes, thawed
1 can Cream of Chicken soup
1 cup sour cream
2 cups shredded Cheddar cheese
1/2 cup margarine or butter, melted
1 1/2 tsp salt
1 medium onion, diced

Mix all ingredients together and grease a 9 x 13 pan. Put potato casserole in pan and spoon on the following topping:
2 cups crushed corn flakes mixed with 1/4 cup melted butter
Bake 45 minutes in 350° oven. Serves 12.

SUMMERS AT LAKE OKOBOJI

LULU - CHAMPION DOG PADDLER

BILLY AND SALLY AT REST

Potpourri

Elephant Stew

POTPOURRI

Broiled Peach Halves	210
Caramel Popcorn	205
Chili Cheese Rellenos	211
Chili-Beef Rellenos	207
Cream Puffs	202
Curried Fruit	215
Eight Seasons Salt	206
French Custard Toast	203
Frosted Grapes Decoration	202
Glazed Cranberries	214
How to Make Tea	201
How to Stabilize Whipped Cream Frosting w/Gelatin	201
Irene's Fruit Pizza	212
Lemon Butter	215
Maid Rite Sandwiches	210
Mixed Vegetable Curry	206
Oh My Gosh Fritatta	202
Onion Stuffing for Turkeys or Chickens	204
Oooohh – Poppy Cock!	214
Play Dough Recipe	211
Reuben Sandwich	215
Ribbon Sandwich	209
Rink Tum Ditty	210
Rio Grande Swimmers	211
Sam's Favorite Dog Biscuits	208
Scrapple	205
Sopa Pilla	209
Sour Cream Waffles	214
Spicy Tomato Aspic	203
Welsh Rarebit	207
Yum Yums	207

ELEPHANT STEW

Take one elephant and cut into bite size pieces.
Add 4,000 tomatoes, peeled.
1,567 green peppers, diced fine. (Nice color with the grey).
Throw in 200 rabbits (if you don't mind some hare in your soup).
Get a fire going in an extinct volcano.
Cook ingredients in a trashed-out B-47 and stir constantly for 5 months.
Invite every single person in your town and call out the Reserves.
A Montrachet '74 is very nice with this entree.

❖ ❖ ❖ ❖ ❖ ❖ ❖ ❖ ❖

HOW TO MAKE TEA

1. Measure out the amount of water for the number of cups being made and bring to a boil in a kettle.
2. Meanwhile, pour hot water into the teapot and let it stand.
3. When the tea water has come to a boil, empty the teapot, then put in one rounded teaspoon of tea per cup and one extra for the pot.
4. Pour the boiling water into the pot and let it steep for five minutes. (If stronger tea is desired, increase the amount of tea rather than the steeping time, or the tea will become bitter.)
5. Serve with lemon or milk (not cream).

❖ ❖ ❖ ❖ ❖ ❖ ❖ ❖ ❖

HOW TO STABILIZE WHIPPED CREAM FROSTING WITH GELATIN

A teaspoon of unflavored gelatin will stabilize a 1/2 pint of whipping cream. Sprinkle gelatin over 1/4 cup cold water to soften. Heat on low heat, stirring constantly, until gelatin is dissolved. Cool to room temperature. Whip cream in chilled bowl with chilled beaters until stiff peaks form, scraping bowl occasionally. Fold in 2 Tblsp confectioners sugar and 1 tsp vanilla. Fold in gelatin mixture.

CREAM PUFFS

Every hostess has to make cream puffs either for filled appetizers or for luncheon containers for seafoods or chicken extravaganzas or especially as holders for ice cream or whipped cream, drizzled with chocolate, for dessert. Here's the recipe -

1/2 cup butter   **1/4 tsp salt**
1 cup boiling water   **4 eggs**
1 cup sifted flour

In a saucepan, melt the butter in boiling water. Add flour and salt all at once and stir constantly til mixture forms a ball that doesn't separate. Remove from heat and cool slightly and add eggs one at a time beating well after each addition.
Drop dough by heaping Tblsp 3 inches apart on greased cookie sheet. Bake at 450° for 15 minutes. Then bake at 325° for about 25 minutes. Remove puffs from oven and split. Turn off oven and put puffs back in oven to dry out about 20 minutes. Cool on rack. Fill just before serving.
Dough by <u>teaspoonful</u> will yield about 36 small puffs.

❖ ❖ ❖ ❖ ❖ ❖ ❖ ❖ ❖

Jane S. Peters suggests that when time has absolutely run out and 4 boys and a husband stand looking at a cold kitchen and a Mother who is breathing heavily from a fast dash home from a day out . . .

THE OH MY GOSH FRITATTA
is just the ticket!

Clean out the fridge, chop into bite size pieces, and scramble it with eggs. Maybe a little Hamburger Helper and possibly Cheez Whiz on top promise all kinds of excitement at the table.

❖ ❖ ❖ ❖ ❖ ❖ ❖ ❖ ❖

FROSTED GRAPES DECORATION

Beat egg whites til just foamy and coat a cluster of grapes with the egg white. Then dip and roll in granulated sugar until sugar coats grapes well. Refrigerate.

Barbara Heck served this delicious French toast for breakfast one beautiful late summer morning. We sat at the dining table with her and Mick in their summer home at Lake Hubert looking out through the trees across the water and listening to the Lake sounds. What a treasure to recollect that memory - good food, best of friends, and just another perfect Minnesota day.

FRENCH CUSTARD TOAST   Barbara Heck

Beat **3 eggs** slightly in a shallow pan and add **1 cup of milk and 1/2 tsp salt** Cut diagonally **4 slices day old French or Italian bread** about 1 1/2 inches thick. Put bread in egg mixture and soak at least 15 minutes on each side.

Heat **1/4 cup butter** in large skillet. Fry bread slowly about 5 minutes each side until browned. *Serve with real maple syrup.*

SPICY TOMATO ASPIC
Cut these into tasty gelatin shapes for decorations

Pour **1 envelope of plain gelatin over 1 1/2 cups tomato juice** and let rest for 3 minutes until gelatin softens.
Place tomato juice over heat and stir til gelatin dissolves. Add:
1 Tblsp sherry
1 tsp sugar
1/2 tsp powdered chicken bouillon
1/4 tsp fresh horseradish
Pour into an 8 x 8 pan and refrigerate til gelatin sets. Then cut into desired shapes and sizes.

HOW TO TELL WHEN YOU'RE OVER THE HILL

Everything hurts, and what doesn't hurt doesn't work.
You need your glasses to find your glasses.
Your back goes out more than you do.
Your little black book contains only names that end in "M.D."
You have too much room in the house & not enough in your medicine cabinet.
Your children begin to look middle-aged.
The policemen look too young to be policemen.
The little gray-haired woman you help across the street is your wife.
You can't take yes for an answer.

Great-Grandfather Jake Hess was well-loved, oft quoted, and a first-rate hunter, fisherman and gardener. The stories sworn to be true were that he walked a mile on a broken leg from a duck blind in the winter; and drove his Packard through the back of the garage one noon unscathed; and his passionate histrionics as legal counsel, defending or prosecuting, brought audiences from all over the County that filled the Courtroom.

ONION STUFFING FOR TURKEYS OR CHICKENS
From Lancaster County, Pennsylvania

6 cups dried bread cubes
1 Tblsp dried fresh sage, crumbled
1 onion, chopped
1 cup celery, chopped
Melt **3 Tblsp butter in 1 cup of chicken bouillon** made strong for flavoring
salt and pepper to taste
Stuff body and upper chest cavity and pin birds shut with skewers.

> Happiness is a perfume you cannot pour on others without getting a few drops on yourself.

CARAMEL POPCORN   Irene Peters

7 quarts of popped pop corn
Cook for 5 minutes:
2 cups brown sugar
1 cup margarine
1/2 cup white corn syrup
1 tsp salt
Then add:
1 tsp vanilla
1/2 tsp baking soda
Pour over the popcorn in a roaster pan and bake at 225° for one hour, stirring every 15 minutes.

❖ ❖ ❖ ❖ ❖ ❖ ❖ ❖ ❖

Great-Grandfather Jacob Hess' predecessors came from Switzerland in 1712 and settled in Lititz, Lancaster County, Pennsylvania. They were Mennonites and one of the great pleasures of Doug's and my life was to visit that unique settlement, the most productive agricultural county in the East. The countryside was perfectly groomed, foodstuffs were bounteous and delicious to eat and the people perfectly charming and wonderfully PLAIN. One of Jake's absolute favorite things to eat was Scrapple and if that isn't from Lancaster County, I don't know what is.

SCRAPPLE

Combine:
| **6 cups water** | **2 large onions, ground fine** |

1/2 lb. of pork, half fat - half lean, ground fine
Add:
| **1/2 tsp thyme** | **1/2 tsp sage** |
| **1/2 tsp pepper** | **1 1/2 tsp salt** |

Bring liquid slowly to a boil and simmer for 15 minutes, stirring with a fork to prevent meat from forming lumps. Add very slowly, in a thin trickle, **1/2 lb. of water-ground yellow corn meal,** stirring constantly. Continue to cook and stir until the mixture is very thick and smooth, about 10 minutes. Taste for seasoning and add more salt and pepper as needed. Pour scrapple into a square loaf pan to cool and set. To serve, unmold the loaf and cut into 1/2 inch slices. Brown the sliced scrapple on both sides on an ungreased griddle and serve with scrambled eggs, tart applesauce and toasted muffins. Some people like syrup on it.

EIGHT SEASONS SALT   Harris Golden
Makes 1 1/2 cups. Use this low-sodium salt as an alternative to your table salt and pepper.

1/2 cup dried parsley flakes   **2 Tblsp dried basil flakes**
2 Tblsp rosehips (for easy availability remove from rosehip tea bags)
2 Tblsp garlic salt   **1 Tblsp paprika**
1 Tblsp grated lemon rind   **1 tsp cayenne pepper**
1 tsp crushed saffron
Store in a jar with a tight fitting lid.

On a plane trip from London to the Cote d'Azure, Doug and I made friends with Hansa and Anyat Pandya, he a member of Parliament from Mombasa, Kenya. When they came to visit us in Fremont, their Moslem tastes necessitated a Vegetable Curry and Hansa said this was the way her cook prepared it for them.

MIXED VEGETABLE CURRY   East Indian

3/4 cup vegetable oil in a large and deep cooking vessel
4 cloves broken in half   **1 tsp cumin seed**
Scant tsp mustard seed   **1/2 bottle of curry powder**
1 tsp coriander
Cook these spices in oil about 5 minutes or so. Add:
1 large head of chopped garlic   **1 onion chopped**
1 bunch cut-up green onions   **3 leaves of mint**
1 hot green pepper cut up with some seeds
1 medium eggplant, cubed with skin intact
4 to 5 potatoes, peeled and cut up
1 box defrosted okra
(Also can add peas, beans, cauliflowerettes)
1 1/2 tsp paprika   **1/2 can tomato paste**
2 cups water   **1 to 2 tsp salt**
1 1/2 Tblsp sugar
Cook this all together for a while occasionally turning over the vegetables and spices. Then put in baking dish in a 350° oven and cook until vegetables are tender.
Plan on cooking 2 handfuls of rice for each person.   Wash and drain the rice and cook in boiling water. See rice preparation in another chapter of this book. Serve the rice with the vegetables, a bottle of Major Grey's Chutney and some shredded coconut.

CHILI-BEEF RELLENOS   Ruth Smith

1 4-oz. can green chilis, whole
1/2 medium onion, chopped
1 cup grated Monterey Jack cheese
1 cup milk
1 lb. hamburger
3 oz. grated Cheddar cheese
1 egg
2 Tblsp flour

Cover bottom of casserole with half of the seeded green chilis. Brown the hamburger and onion and add salt and pepper. Spread over chilis. Cover with the Monterey jack cheese and Cheddar cheese. Top with the rest of the green chilis. Beat egg, milk and flour together and pour over meat and cheese. Bake at 350° for 30 minutes til bubbly.

Our college crowd at the University of Nebraska loved bowling, dancing, movies, Cribs and Yum Yums. During the 1950's, Yum Yum's kept the campus from starving - all you had to do was find someone with a car that would be willing to drive to the Yum Yum Hut with an order for a couple of sacks full.

YUM YUMS!!

1 lb. ground beef
1/2 tsp salt
1/4 to 1/3 cup of catsup
1 tsp Worcestershire sauce
Sandwich buns, split
1 chopped onion
Water
2 tsp prepared mustard
a pinch of chili powder

Crumble beef. Combine with onion and salt. Cover with water and bring to a boil. Simmer until water is gone. Add catsup, mustard, Worcestershire and chili powder. Heat through and serve on split buns.

WELSH RAREBIT

1/4 lb. cream cheese
1/4 cup cream
1 tsp mustard
1/2 tsp salt
few grains of cayenne
1 egg
1 tsp butter
4 slices of toast

Grate cheese into double boiler and add cream, mustard, and salt and pepper. When cheese is melted, add beaten egg, butter and cook til rarebit thickens but does not curdle, about 2 minutes. Serve over toast points.

Sam, a Basset hound owned by the John Peters family, had almost better press releases than the family members. His shenanigans were published in the Council Bluffs Nonpareil regularly and he was well-known and beloved by the downtown merchants. He died from arthritis complications. Too much gallivanting, I guess.

SAM'S FAVORITE DOG BISCUITS – Microwaved

1 cup whole wheat flour   1/2 cup all-purpose flour
3/4 cup non-fat dry milk powder 1/2 cup yellow cornmeal
1 tsp sugar   1/3 cup shortening
1 egg, slightly beaten   1 Tblsp instant bouillon
1/2 cup hot water   1/2 cup quick-cooking oats

Combine dries, cut in shortening, stir in egg, stir in bouillon with hot water, form dough into ball and knead 5 minutes. Roll out to 1/2" thick. Cut shapes (preferably cats) or nuggets, arrange on plate and microwave at 50% 5 to 10 minutes until firm and dry. Shapes will crisp as they cool. Bark, Bark!!!

Altar boy to priest: "Why are all those names on that bronze plaque?"

Priest: "Oh, those people died in the service."

Altar Boy: "Wow! Was it the 8 o'clock or the 11?"

There never was a recipe in the world that struck terror into the heart of my dear friend, Kay Schenck. I don't remember eating the same thing twice at her house - she loved the adventure of surprise lurking on the unturned page of her cookbook. And it was GOURMET!

RIBBON SANDWICH   Kay Schenck

Order **1 Pullman loaf of bread** and have bakery remove the crusts. Slice loaf lengthwise into four sections. Butter these long slices.
1st layer: Chicken spread
2nd layer: Hardboiled eggs, bread and butter pickles, chopped fine with mayonnaise
3rd layer: Finely shredded lettuce, pimento, drained well and chopped fine, or marinated tomatoes, chopped fine
4th layer: Ham spread
Press layers gently together and frost with following:
1/2 lb. American cheese that has been melted in a double boiler with **1/2 cup cream.**
Lovely for luncheons and so pretty.

SOPA PILLA   Peachy Wilcoxson

4 cups flour	**3 tsp baking powder**
1 tsp salt	**3 Tblsp solid shortening**
water	

Sift flour, baking powder and salt. Cut in shortening adding enough water to make a stiff dough. Roll out dough to 1/4 inch. Cut in 2 inch squares and deep fry til golden brown. Serve with honey butter.

MAID RITE SANDWICHES   Cindy Schenck Kennedy

10 lbs finely ground beef
6 heaping tsp cream style horseradish
6 tsp Worcestershire sauce
2 cups warm water
2 tsp monosodium glutamate
Hamburger buns
7 heaping tsp prepared mustard
10 tsp salt
2 cups finely ground onions
1/2 tsp black pepper

Place beef in kettle. Combine everything but the buns and cook on low heat 15 minutes, stirring constantly. Increase heat slowly til mixture boils. Boil 25 minutes, stirring to avoid sticking. Use slotted spoon to pile meat on hamburger buns. Got to have dill pickles sliced THIN with this one! Does that bring back the memories of the 50's or what!

RINK TUM DITTY
A Sunday evening favorite of the Douglas Peters family on Ridgewood Road, Omaha

1/2 lb. American cheese
2 cups rich milk
2 Tblsp flour
1 tsp sugar
1 can tomato soup
a little scraped onion
pinch of soda
pinch of dry mustard

Mix together flour, sugar, onion, soda and mustard and slowly add milk to make cream sauce. Cook until hot and add soup and cheese cut in small pieces. Cook and blend until very hot, but DO NOT BOIL. Serve over English muffins that have been toasted and buttered.

BROILED PEACH HALVES
Here are 2 suggestions for filling and heating peach halves as a accompaniment to a main course - pretty and delicious.

I. Fill halves of canned peaches with prepared mincemeat. Place in a shallow pan and bake 30 minutes in a 350° oven, basting occasionally with juice from the peaches. Serve hot as a garnish.

II. Choose desired number of peach halves and fill with 1 tsp Major Grey's Chutney and 1/2 tsp brandy. Sprinkle lightly with ground cloves and put under broiler til browned.

CHILI CHEESE RELLENOS

2 7-oz. cans whole green chilis
5 large eggs
1 lb. Monterey Jack cheese, cut in fingers
1/4 cup flour
1/2 lb. sharp Cheddar cheese, grated
1 1/4 cup milk

Stuff fingers of Jack cheese in chilis. Make a paste of flour and milk, then carefully add rest of milk and eggs. Pour over chilis and top with grated Cheddar cheese. Cover casserole and bake 45 minutes at 350°. Let stand 10 minutes or so before cutting.

RIO GRANDE SWIMMERS   Peachy Wilcoxson
Serves 4 to 6

1 lb. ground round steak	1 chopped onion
1 clove garlic	1 Tblsp sugar
1 small can (8 oz) tomato sauce	1 small can (6 oz) tomato paste
1 small can water	

1 tsp oregano, chili powder, cumin, Accent and salt

Combine all ingredients and simmer 40 minutes. Serve by placing tortilla chips on individual plates and covering with meat sauce. Top with the following condiments which will be presented in individual bowls so that the guests may build their own:

Shredded lettuce	Chopped avocado
Chopped tomato	Sour cream
Grated Cheddar cheese	Chopped black olives
Chopped green onions	

PLAY DOUGH RECIPE
Caution: Hard to get out of carpet - use on hard surface floor

3 cups flour	1 1/2 cups salt
3 cups water	3 Tblsp cooking oil
	1 1/2 Tblsp Cream of Tartar

Mix all ingredients in a big pot and cook for a few minutes on medium heat. Turn out onto waxed paper. When cool enough to handle, divide dough into workable portions. Drop 1 or 2 drops of food coloring into a ball of dough and work the food coloring into the dough. You can add extract flavors to scent the play dough if desired. Store in airtight containers. Left out, the dough will air dry very hard in a few days.

My dear sister Irene - - - -
She has a joyous optimism for life that sustains us all! and is the best friend a sister could ask for. As my mentor through the process of this Cookbook, she will probably need an ear graft as we go to press.

IRENE'S FRUIT PIZZA

Pate Brisse:
1 1/3 cups all-purpose flour
1 stick cold butter, cut up
1 Tblsp sugar
1/4 cup ice water
Process this in the Cuisinart and spread in flan pan or quiche pan. Bake at 425° til golden.
Slice **kiwis, peaches, strawberries, blueberries, grapes, pears,** or whatever you find at the market. Arrange in a beautiful design. Cover with sauce and let set.
SAUCE:
1 cup sugar
2 Tblsp cornstarch
1/8 tsp salt
Add **1 3/4 cups boiling water, 1/4 cup orange Curacao, plus some orange rind.** Stir for 5 minutes or until thick and clear. Add **1/2 stick butter.** Pour over pizza. You may substitute fruit juice for the water.

This lovely little epitome was found in Olde Saint Paul's Church in Baltimore, Maryland and was dated 1692.

As one peruses these listed challenges, it becomes clear that there is a stability in the basic ethics of this world that transcends time and mortals. There is a comfort in that --- somehow knowing, by their listing, that we strive for those verities along with uncounted millions through the years.

GO PLACIDLY amid the noise and haste, & remember what peace there may be in silence. As far as possible without surrender be on good terms with all persons. Speak your Truth quietly and clearly; and listen to others, even the dull and ignorant; they too have their story. Avoid loud & aggressive persons; they are vexatious to the spirit. If you compare yourself with others, you may become vain and bitter, for always there will be greater & lesser persons than yourself.

Enjoy your achievements as well as your plans.

Keep interested in your own career, however humble; it is a real possession in the changing fortunes of time. Exercise caution in your business affairs; for the world is full of trickery. But let this not blind you to what virtue there is; many persons strive for high ideals; and everywhere life is full of heroism.

Be yourself. Especially, do not feign affection.

Neither be cynical about love; for in the face of all aridity & disenchantment it is perennial as the grass.

Take kindly the counsel of the years, gracefully surrendering the things of youth. Nurture strength of spirit to shield you in sudden misfortune. But do not distress yourself with imaginings. Many fears are born of fatigue & loneliness. Beyond a wholesome discipline, be gentle with yourself.

You are a Child of the Universe, no less than the trees and the stars; you have a Right to be here. And whether or not it is clear to you, no doubt the universe is unfolding as it should.

Therefore, be at peace with God, whatever you consider Him to be, and whatever your labors & aspirations, in the noisy confusion of life keep peace with your soul. With all its sham, drudgery & broken dreams, it is still a beautiful world. Be careful. Strive to be happy.

One cup ground coffee per 30 cups of water makes perfect coffee every time.

GLAZED CRANBERRIES　　　　　　　　　　Gladys Peters

4 cups cranberries
4 1/2 cups sugar
1/2 cup water

Stir gently while cooking in iron skillet very slowly for about 40 minutes. They should be deep red and kind of transparent.

SOUR CREAM WAFFLES

Separate **3 eggs** and beat the yolks in a bowl.
Beat in **3/4 cup milk**　　　　**1/2 cup melted butter**
3/4 cup sour cream
Combine and sift together:
1 1/2 cups flour　　　　**2 tsp baking powder**
1/2 tsp baking soda　　　　**1 Tblsp sugar**
Add to the mixture and beat well.
Beat the 3 egg whites until stiff and carefully fold into the batter.
Yields 8 waffles.

The best way to test a waffle iron to determine if it is hot enough to bake a waffle is to place the cold waffle iron on the shelf, raise the lid and place 1 tsp of cold water on the iron. Close the lid, plug in the iron and when the iron stops steaming, get ready to make the first waffle. Be sure to cook the first waffle the LONGEST time so that it WILL NOT STICK! It can produce agonizing groans and pitiful tears from little people who roll on the ground in death throes of hunger when not done properly.

OOOOOOOOH - POPPY COCK!

2 quarts of popped pop corn　　**1 1/3 cups pecan halves**
2/3 cup almonds　　　　　　　**1 1/3 cups sugar**
1 tsp vanilla　　　　　　　　　**1/2 cup light corn syrup**
1 cup margarine

Mix popped corn and nuts on a cookie sheet. Combine rest of ingredients in a 2 quart saucepan and bring to a boil over medium heat stirring constantly. Boil, stirring occasionally, 10 to 15 minutes or until mixture turns a light caramel color and looks thick and lightly foamy. Remove from heat and stir in vanilla. Pour over pop corn and nuts and mix to coat well. Spread out to dry. Break into smaller pieces and store in a tight container. Makes about 2 pounds.

REUBEN SANDWICH

One of the great sandwiches of all times is the famous REUBEN that we all learned to appreciate at the old Blackstone Hotel. High on the list of "Favorite Things to Do" was lunch at that Hotel with the waiter serving an ice-cold Coke, Suzi-Cues, and a Reuben sandwich with their terrific dill pickles. Here's my very best guess as to preparation.

Drain **1 can of sauerkraut** and mix with **Thousand Island Dressing**.
1 loaf of very good dark rye bread
sliced Kosher corned beef
sliced Swiss cheese

Butter slices of rye bread and lay unbutterd side up. Place Swiss cheese on <u>each piece</u>. On alternate slices lay corned beef and sauerkraut mixed with dressing. One sandwich will have 2 pieces cheese, corned beef and sauerkraut. Grill on buttered sides in skillet or sandwich grill until brown & cheese begins to melt. Slice & eat NOW!

CURRIED FRUIT   Jerry Dodson

1/4 cup butter	1 Tblsp plus 1 tsp powdered curry
1 can pineapple rings	1 can peach halves
1 can apricots, pitted	1/2 bottle maraschino cherries
3/4 cup brown sugar	1 pkg. slivered toasted almonds

Melt butter, add brown sugar and curry powder. Drain fruit thoroughly. Place in layers in low baking pan with cherries on top. Spread with butter mixture and bake at 350° for 1/2 hour adding the almonds shortly before the end of baking.

LEMON BUTTER   Irene Peters

Irene gave this to Glady and Daph every Christmas, and she was reminded in plenty of time so as not to forget!

3 egg yolks	2 lemons
1 cup sugar	3/4 stick butter (not oleo)

Grate lemon rind over sugar - add lemon juice. Mix. Beat egg yolks slightly, add melted butter. Cook all ingredients in a double boiler, stir til clear, like honey. Store in refrigerator for use on toast, muffins, waffles, pancakes.

BIRTHSTONES AND FLOWERS

Month	Stone	Flower
January	Garnet	Snowdrop
February	Amethyst	Primrose
March	Bloodstone	Violet
April	Diamond	Daisy
May	Emerald	Hawthorne
June	Pearl	Rose
July	Ruby	Water Lily
August	Sardonyx	Poppy
September	Sapphire	Goldenrod
October	Opal	Hops
November	Topaz	Chrysanthemum
December	Turquoise	Holly

WEDDING ANNIVERSARY GIFTS

Anniversary	Traditional	Modern
First	Paper	Clocks
Second	Cotton	China
Third	Leather	Crystal/Glass
Fourth	Fruit/Flowers	Appliances
Fifth	Wood	Silverware
Sixth	Candy/Iron	Wood
Seventh	Wool/Copper	Desk Sets
Eighth	Bronze/Pottery	Linens/Laces
Ninth	Pottery/Willow	Leather
Tenth	Tin/Aluminum	Diamond Jewelry
Eleventh	Steel	Fashion Jewelry
Twelfth	Silk/Linen	Pearls
Thirteenth	Lace	Textiles/Furs
Fourteenth	Ivory	Gold Jewelry
Fifteenth	Crystal	Watches
Twentieth	China	Platinum
Twenty-fifth	Silver	Silver
Thirtieth	Pearl	Diamond
Thirty-fifth	Coral	Jade
Fortieth	Ruby	Ruby
Forty-fifth	Sapphire	Sapphire
Fiftieth	Gold	Gold
Fifty-fifth	Emerald	Emerald
Sixtieth	Diamond	Diamond

Poultry & Game

POULTRY & GAME

Bec-Figues	225
Bird Cleaning Made Easy	225
Chicken a la King	230
Chicken Cannelloni for 4	234
Chicken Elegante	235
Chicken Hawaiian	223
Chicken Newburg	232
Chicken Strata	232
Deluxe Duck	226
Favorite Chicken	223
Favorite Party Casserole	231
Fried Chicken	236
Gabe's Easy Grilled Ducks	220
Hot Chicken Soufflé Sandwich	235
Kappa Kappa Gamma Chicken	231
Olde Pheasant Revival	220
Ortolan a la Perigourdine	220
Polynesian Chicken Salad	231
Pressed Duck	229
Quail Morengo	223
Teal Duck	224
Wild Turkey	219
Yorkshire Chicken Pudding	236

Doug Peters loved to go to O'Neill, Nebraska to hunt wild turkeys with his friend Virgil Laursen. Turkeys are so big that, if trained, they could take the place of your hunting dog. Try to get one of those babies in your oven! Also, unless the turkey is young, it is hard to keep the meat moist when you roast the bird. But the quills and beards really tickle the children and how FANCY to have WILD turkey for Thanksgiving.

After cooking more than my share of the wiley bird, this is the definitive recipe reducing the pain and strain of cooking . . .

WILD TURKEY _____ Mary Peters

Remove the two breasts from the turkey and also the thigh and drum stick if duty demands. Dredge all meat in flour, salt and pepper. Sauté the meat in 1/2 butter and 1/2 bacon grease til brown and remove to a covered dutch oven for baking in the oven. In fry pan, in which turkey has been browned, remove all but 2 Tblsp of fat, pour in 1/2 cup water and deglaze pan scraping up all the goodies. Pour over breasts along with 1 ½ cups of sherry. Bake covered in a 325° oven until tender. It depends on the age of the bird. When tender, remove meat and stir into pan 1 to 2 tsp Kitchen Bouquet or BV sauce and one or so cups of sour cream. Do not boil this gravy - just heat. Do this recipe ahead. It just gets better as the meat sits in the gravy.

OLDE PHEASANT REVIVAL   Johnny Peters

1 pheasant cut in serving size pieces
1 1/2 cups chicken broth
1 cup sliced mushrooms
1 cup white wine
Parsley
Butter

Brown pheasant pieces in butter and remove to baking dish. Add remaining ingredients to pan drippings and mix well. Pour over pheasant and cover tightly. Bake at 325° for three hours. This recipe makes that tough, old rooster extra moist!

GABE'S EASY GRILLED DUCKS   Johnny Peters

1 large duck per person (or 2 teal)
1 cup BBQ sauce
4 Tblsp soy sauce
salt and pepper

Cut whole birds up the back and lay flat. Rub both sides with salt and pepper. Mix BBQ and soy sauce. Place birds breast side up on grill and brush with sauce. Cover with foil tent. Cook for 15 minutes basting frequently with sauce. Turn after 15 min. and cook breast side down for 5 min. Turn again and cook 10 min. more. Hickory or mesquite chips thrown on the coals add a great smokey flavor.

ORTOLAN A LA PERIGOURDINE

The great Alexis Soyer was once asked to prepare Ortolan stuffed with truffles. He replied "An Ortolan cannot be stuffed with truffles, but l will gladly stuff a truffle with an Ortolan!"

Sort out truffles slightly larger than the Ortolans, scoop out the center of the truffle to form a case for the tiny bird. Chop the scooped truffle finely and form a well on circles of toast. Stand the truffle case on the toast and slip in the Ortolan. Put in a pea-size bit of butter and roast for 20 minutes. Allow one bird per person which will be entirely consumed.

After leaving academia which was my vocation for 16 years, I embraced a new profession called wifeing. I had never been a wife before, & it takes 40 years before you get fairly comfortable with it. It is the most challenging of all professions outside of mothering, simply because it involves getting expert at figuring out another person's deep desires which do not always happen to coincide with your deep desires. But it soon becomes apparent that if the other person nods his head and smiles alot, your job becomes most pleasant also.

At my husband's behest, I agreed, the first year of marriage, to shoot a shotgun. I cut my teeth on Turtle Doves, a difficult shot at best; but with proficiency (he insisted) comes ease at larger game; plus, it gave him such pleasure to see me score, he began nodding his head and smiling. To the female, scoring apparently compares in pleasure to the purchase of the most incredible label dress on sale for practically nothing.

Doug's fraternity brother had married my sorority sister and their new life included running the family ranch at Lakeside, Nebraska as the young Land Lords. One fall, they asked us to come for a long weekend duckshoot which was all pass shooting in blinds set between sloughs. What an opportunity; the car was packed before the glue on the reply envelope was dry.

We arrived early enough for a few pleasant hours of pass shooting in perfect Bluebird weather. I scored, knocking myself flat one time, by following a duck to zenith position and firing my 16 gauge, a trick I did not repeat. I also could not touch my shoulder after an afternoon in the blind.

Much frivolity followed back at the ranch house. Celebration drinks were in order for such a great days' shoot, then we all bathed, changed, and were off for the Country Club, about 25 miles away. Out-state people invented hospitality and after a full day's drive, pass shooting, drinking, eating, non-stop talking, dancing and another 25-mile drive home, I was almost comatose. At 2:30 a.m. my head touched the pillow and it seemed I was immediately awakened by Doug whispering in my ear in our dark room, "Come on, honey, we've got to get to the slough before daybreak." I wanted to pull his tongue out by the roots, but did not have the strength.

Struggling into clothes at that satanic hour, Doug, our host and I headed around the house and got into a jeep, I in the back seat with a

*large German Draughthair that had, in his excitement to be included, run through a pond and was simply filthy. The odor was incredible. No one spoke as we catapulted off cross-country in the blackness jouncing every bone unmercifully until I yelled -
"Stop the damn car - the dog has vomited all over me!"*

As Doug helped to clean out the car & wipe off my clothes, he threw up; and finally, it was too much for our host, so he followed suit. As I surveyed this scene in the headlights of the jeep, disbelief was my paramount sensation. Who drew up this day's plan? It was not going well.

Back into the jeep and another half-hour of monstrous jolting. Finally the car stopped in total darkness. The dog was leashed, guns and shells were claimed and in a low crouch, three hunters crept through the black pre-dawn to I knew not. Finally, a heavy hand pushed me to the ground and we then crawled in heavy silence up a rise to lay on the crest of a hill.

It was not long before a soft gentle light began to appear on the horizon and as we lay there, it finally became apparent that there was a great large lake before us and the surface was totally black.

As dawn began to brighten, the black covering on the water started to swirl in a circular fashion, and as if on command, to rise. I found it impossible to speak as thousands of birds flew into the air to greet the sunrise. The magnificence of that sight must have made the angels sing. The euphoria of that moment, watching the ducks, has stayed with me in perfect clarity. It is one of my greatest gifts. It compares with saying my prayers in the early dawn on an Andean mountaintop at MachuPicchu.

Keep within your heart a place for dreams.

CHICKEN HAWAIIAN   Ninette Beaver

Ninette Beaver and I have eaten chicken all over the United States and keep begging for more. Now HERE'S a new one she found and the sauce can be substituted on chicken drumettes for fantastic appetizers!

Mix together:
1 small bottle of Wishbone Russian salad dressing•
1 pkg. dry onion soup mix •
1 10 oz. jar of apricot preserves or peach-pineapple preserves•

Pour this mixture over a chicken that has been cut up, or thighs and breast, or chicken drumettes. Bake at 350° for about 1 hour.

QUAIL MORENGO   John Peters, Jr.

1/2 cup flour	1 cup dry white wine•
1 tsp salt	2 cups canned tomatoes•
1 clove garlic, finely chopped	1/2 tsp fresh ground black pepper•
1 tsp tarragon	8 to 10 mushrooms, sliced•
l/4 cup olive oil	chopped parsley •
1/2 cup butter	12 quail •

Preheat oven to 350°. Mix flour, salt, pepper and tarragon. Dredge quail in seasoned flour. Heat olive oil and butter in heavy skillet and brown quail on all sides. Remove to casserole. Add reserved flour to fat in skillet and gradually stir in the wine. Add tomatoes, garlic, and mushrooms. When sauce is thickened and smooth, pour over quail. Cover with heavy lid and bake 40 to 50 minutes until fork tender. Just before serving, sprinkle with chopped parsley.

FAVORITE CHICKEN   Melvin Laird

2 chickens cut up and placed in baking dish
Mix **1 pint sour cream** with **1 cup Sauterne wine and 2 cans Campbell's Cream of Mushroom soup.** Pour over chickens and dredge dish HEAVILY with paprika. Bake 350° for 1 1/2 hours. Let chicken stand overnight in the fridge and reheat til bubbly to serve at 350°, about 1/2 hour.

TEAL DUCK   Momo

Take one bird for each guest, if you can bear to share. I make very sure those guests love duck as much as I do. Pluck, clean, wash and drain birds. When ready to roast, sprinkle a little Lawry's Seasoned Salt inside each dry bird. Then stuff with chopped onion and tart apple combination. Place birds in roasting pan and rub breasts with butter. Stir together:

1 cup brown sugar•
1/8 cup of frozen orange juice concentrate•

Pour over ducks' breasts and cover each duck completely with strips of uncooked bacon. Baste occasionally with drippings and fresh orange juice after you have placed them in a 325° oven and in about 2 hours these birds will be done.

SAUCE:
Pour off all grease from duck pan and add to drippings:

1/4 cup sherry	**1/2 stick butter**
2/3 cup CURRANT jelly	**1 tsp lemon juice**
1 lg. pinch salt	

Cook this mixture down til a nice viscous sauce forms to spoon over each duck. Serve a bowl of currant jelly also with the birds.

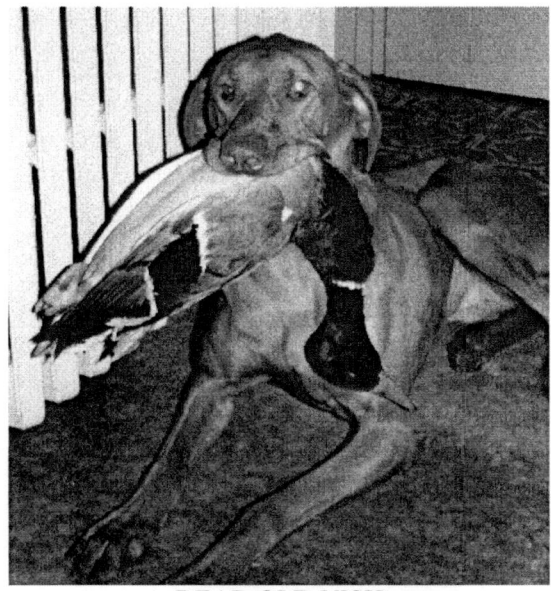

DEAR OLD VISH

BIRD CLEANING MADE EASY   Johnny Peters

Here's a trick that makes removing the entrails from your game birds quick, clean and easy.

After picking and singeing your birds, remove the head, wings, feet and tail with shears. Holding bird, breast side down in the palm of your hand, cut along both sides of the backbone. With the tips slightly open, slide the shears along the breast plate with a lifting motion.

With a little practice, you'll be able to completely clean your bird in one pass. No more punctured fingers from broken rib bones or birds that are not fully cleaned because of limited access, as is often the case with quail or teal.

BEC-FIGUES, BEGUINETTE (Fig-pecker Lucullus)

Brillat-Savarin put the fig-pecker first among small birds, for it has always moved gastronomes to rhapsody. They and the Ortolans, though small and very rare, are much esteemed by epicures for the delicacy of their flesh. They prefer Southern climes where they feed upon figs and grapes. The birds at one time were netted in great numbers in Europe. They were then kept alive in darkened rooms and fattened on oats and millet in preparation for the epicures palate.

Pluck but do not, on any account, draw the birds, for the trails are held in high esteem. Dip each bird in melted butter. Cover with a fresh vine leaf. Wrap in a piece of bacon, skewer and roast in front of a hickory log fire for 25 minutes, basting the while, being careful to catch the drippings from the trails on a piece of toast.

When cooked, remove bacon and vine leaf and serve with the toast and fresh cut watercress.

ARTHRITIS
Nancy Milliken suggests that this remedy ameliorates the nagging pain of arthritis. Whether it does or not, it seems like it would be such an agreeable way to begin the day, simulating an automotive jump-start.

Into a pint jar, place **Golden raisins** to within 1 inch from the top
Fill to the top of the jar with **White Rum**

DOSAGE: 1 teaspoon a day, raisins and rum
PROGNOSIS: Active participation in the Boston Marathon

JOHN M. PETERS, JR.
I'm very nice to this handsome nephew. He is a great duckhunter and has heretofore been most generous with his game

DELUXE DUCK _____ John Peters, Jr.

2 ducks, cleaned
1/2 cup red wine
Potatoes, celery, onion

1 cup orange juice
orange slices
Salt and pepper

Rub ducks inside and out with salt and pepper. Fill ducks with pieces of potato, onion & celery. Place in baking dish breast side up. Cover breasts with orange slices. Pour half of orange juice/wine mixture over birds and cover tightly with foil. Bake 45 minutes at 350°. Uncover and remove orange slices. Bake til breasts are browned, basting with remainder of o.j./wine mixture. About 25 minutes.

Bill Schenck's Dad and Mother owned and ran the 3-story Royal Hotel in Red Cloud, Nebraska for many years. Their private apartment there was a treasure trove of lovely antiques. They also ran the restaurant in the Hotel. Gertrude rose early every day and made all the pies - and Bill, Sr. owned the liquor store on the other side of the Hotel. Gertrude also ran a Flower shop down the street. They were well known and loved.

Gertrude was a world class cook and had a kitchen built adjacent to a large dining room in the Hotel that turned out private luncheons and dinners that are still being talked about. She has her own cook book published called MOM'S Cook Book. It's fabulous! The young Schencks and the Peters would load all their kids in cars and head for Red Cloud, famous in the early fall for pheasant and quail hunting, for a weekend of shooting and eating and general merriment. One weekend, a popular Red Cloud citizen had died and Gertrude needed emergency help at the Florist shop making wreaths for the funeral that afternoon. Kay and I sent the kids off to the movie house and tore down to the shop to help out - boy, was that fun! Bill and Doug hung around in their hunting gear loading wreaths in the Station Wagon and finally were off to deliver them. When they arrived at the little Church in the country, they helped some men unload the casket from the hearse, placed the wreaths in the Church, bade adieu, and went on to the finest quail shoot they ever had in their whole lives. They've been looking for funerals to assist ever since.

❖ ❖ ❖ ❖ ❖ ❖ ❖ ❖ ❖

Another time, the boys were hunting in Red Cloud out on a lonely country road and they came upon a beautiful covey of quail standing near the road and refusing to move. So the boys took 'em. The only problem was, as they left the area, they realized they were in a Preserve! The agony they suffered coming back with the birds to the Hotel is famous; also we girls were sure the Wardens would walk in on us in the kitchen cleaning them and who would take care of the children while we were all in jail ? So, I hid them under my blouse, sneaked up to our room in the Hotel, locked the door, jumped into the bath tub and cleaned them out. We never had anything that tasted that good.

Marilyn and Tracy Diers were the only people in the whole world we knew that owned a duck press! So we met one evening at their house with ducks in hand and, in the ensuing effort, realized that the press should be bolted to the floor. But with a lot of grunting and groaning & a bottle of red wine, we got the ducks pressed & had such a good time, we gave several dinner parties & were pronounced incredible chefs.

TRACY DIERS

PRESSED DUCK

Clean and draw three ducks and save the livers. Roast in a 475° oven for 15 minutes. Carve the roasted ducks in thin slices and send the legs to the broiler to finish cooking.

Mash the 3 livers with an equal amount of butter in a frying pan over heat. Add:
6 ounces of port
4 ounces of Madiera

Crush all the duck bones in a duck press and add the resultant blood and juices to the livers. Rinse the duck press well by pouring through **it 1/2 cup strong chicken stock.**

Add duck slices to liver sauce with **the juice of 1 lemon.**
Pour over **1/4 cup warmed brandy** and set aflame. Throughout these preparations, the sauce must be stirred constantly until it becomes thick and the color of melted chocolate. Season with salt and pepper and serve very hot. The broiled legs are served as second helping.

There are a million recipes for ducks, but the best EATING in the world are blue and green wing teal. It is worth ANY disgusting display of emotion or ingratiating promises of eternal reward in order to avail yourself of these fowl. I, Mary Peters, have committed this degrading act but, as I place a morsel of Teal in my mouth, the remembrance of my undesirable behavior is obscured by the pleasure of eating THE INCREDIBLE -- TEAL--.

Lakeside Ranch Largesse

The Victorious Hunters
Jake, Jimmy and Mark Peters

CHICKEN A LA KING

What is nicer than creamed chicken in Patty shells or on Toast points for a luncheon?

3 Tblsp butter	**1 green pepper, shredded**
1/2 cup celery, chopped	**1 small can mushrooms**

Melt butter in pan and add pepper, celery and mushrooms. Cook about 4 minutes
Then add:

1 small onion, grated	**1/4 tsp dry mustard**
3 Tblsp flour	**2 cubes chicken bouillon**

1 cup milk and 1 cup cream

Add grated onion and flour made into a paste with part of the milk and then diluted in the rest of the milk and cream. Stir into the vegetables and keep stirring until thickened. Add

2 cups diced chicken
2 Tblsp dry sherry
1 pimento, drained and chopped
2 egg yolks beaten and stirred into the cream mixture.

Stir constantly. Add a **few drops of lemon juice, salt, pepper** and **1 cup frozen peas.**
Stir til hot but DO NOT BOIL! Serve in patty shells.
Serves 8.

KAPPA KAPPA GAMMA CHICKEN   Joani Mitten
Great dish for wedding showers

4 whole chicken breasts, cut in 1/2
1 to 2 cans artichoke hearts
1 cup Hellman's mayonnaise
1 can Cream of Mushroom soup
1 can Cream of Chicken soup
1 tsp curry powder

Simmer breasts in chicken broth with a little carrot, celery and onion for 40 minutes. Line bottom of buttered casserole with quartered artichoke hearts and top with chicken breasts. Combine soups and mayonnaise and curry. Spread over chicken. Top with grated Parmesan cheese. Bake for 30 minutes at 350°. Serves 8.

POLYNESIAN CHICKEN SALAD

4 cups cooked and diced chicken breasts
Mix Well:
1 cup mayonnaise   **1 cup sour cream**
1/4 cup Major Grey's chutney **1/2 tsp curry**
Stir mayonnaise sauce into chicken, **add 1 large can pineapple chunks,** well drained **and one 8 1/2 oz. can sliced water chestnuts, drained,** & toss to cover. Place in fridge overnight. JUST BEFORE SERVING ADD
1/4 cup fresh coconut   **1 cup chow mein noodles**
Serve on lettuce - VERY nice for a luncheon in summer!

FAVORITE PARTY CASSEROLE   Irene Peters

1 cup uncooked rice   **1/2 cup milk**
1 can Cream of Mushroom soup **1 can Cream of Celery soup**
1 package onion soup mix
1 chicken cut in serving size pieces

Butter 9 x 12 inch baking dish and sprinkle rice over bottom of pan. Mix soups together with milk and pour over rice. Place pieces of uncooked chicken (I like skin removed) on top and sprinkle with onion soup mixture. Cover tightly with foil and bake at 325° for 2 1/4 hours. Serves 6.

CHICKEN STRATA

6 slices white bread
4 cups cooked chicken, cut in bite size pieces
8 oz. mushrooms, sliced
2 Tblsp butter or margarine
1 8 oz. can water chestnuts, drained and chopped
1/2 cup mayonnaise
6 oz. sliced Monterey Jack cheese
4 oz. sliced American cheese
3 beaten eggs
1 1/2 cups milk
1 can Cream of Mushroom soup
1 can Cream of Chicken soup
1/4 cup melted butter with 2/3 cup dry bread crumbs

Butter 9 x 13 baking dish. Line with bread slices. Sprinkle chicken over bread. In saucepan, cook mushrooms in 2 Tblsp butter, and put over chicken. Combine water chestnuts and mayonnaise, put over chicken, and top with cheese. Combine milk and eggs, pour into dish. Combine soups and spread over the cheeses. Cover and chill overnight. Bake uncovered in 350° oven for 1 1/4 hrs. Combine melted butter and crumbs, sprinkle on casserole and bake 10 minutes.

CHICKEN NEWBURG   Kitty Lemen

2 cups diced cooked chicken
Make a roux of:

4 Tblsp butter	6 Tblsp flour
2 1/2 cups milk	1/2 tsp salt
1/4 tsp paprika	1/4 tsp celery salt

2 Tblsp chopped pimento
Add very carefully a little sauce to
3 beaten egg yolks
Add rest of sauce as yolks warm and then flavor with
2 Tblsp sherry
1/2 cup grated cheese
Add chicken, warm chicken in sauce and serve newburg on toast points or melba toast baskets.

ODE TO DUFF, MAC AND STEVE
In alphabetical order

And here's fair warning to all of you out there ---

Don't even start to suggest that my three boys aren't the dearest, sweetest, most thoughtful, kindest, cleverest, most lovable, just all-around perfect boys that ever were . . .
Or I'll come out of my den with fangs bared and claw's glistening - - -
They are all a mother could hope for!

DUFF with Mary

MAC with Maggie

STEVE with Gere

233

CHICKEN CANNELLONI FOR 4   Dr. Alexander Harvey

SAUCE: Make a white sauce of

4 Tblsp flour	**1/2 tsp salt**
4 Tblsp butter	**1/8 tsp white pepper**
2 cups hot milk	**1/8 tsp nutmeg**

Cook over low heat for 5 minutes after it has thickened.

FILLING: In a skillet cook for about 10 minutes until vegetables are tender in **2 Tblsp of olive oil**

3 Tblsp onion, minced	**3 Tblsp celery, minced**
2 Tblsp carrot, minced	**1 Tblsp minced parsley**

ADD:

3/4 tsp salt	**1/4 tsp oregano**
1/4 tsp basil	**1/2 tsp white pepper**

2 cups chicken, turkey or veal, minced fine
3/4 cup dry vermouth
Simmer til wine is reduced by half, then stir in 1/2 cup of white sauce.

CANNELLONI: Preheat oven to 450° and then cook **8 cannelloni** in boiling salted water for 8 minutes and then rinse in cold water. Stuff each cannelloni with 2 Tblsp of filling. Arrange in a buttered au gratin dish. To remaining sauce add:
4 Tblsp tomato sauce
1/4 cup cream
Pour this over cannelloni and top with grated Parmesan cheese.
Bake in a very hot oven for 10 minutes til top browns.

Major R.A. Forrest
Commander
Tour of Black Watch

PITY HE'S
NOT A MACDONALD

HOT CHICKEN SOUFFLE SANDWICH

Lovely luncheon or brunch dish as you can prepare ahead and pop in oven!

Cut crusts off **12 slices of grocery store white bread**. Spread 6 sides of bread with a chicken salad made of **3 cooked chicken breasts minced and seasoned with mayonnaise**. Place a thin slice of sharp cheddar cheese on each. Top each with a plain slice of bread. These 6 sandwiches will fit exactly in a 12 x 7 casserole.
Pour over sandwiches the following mixture:

4 well beaten eggs	**2 1/2 cups whole milk**
1/2 tsp onion salt	**1/2 tsp celery salt**
1 Tblsp powdered mustard	**Salt and pepper to taste**

Cover the sandwiches with the liquid and refrigerate the casserole overnight. The next day sprinkle well with **grated Parmesan cheese**. Bake at 300° for 1 hour and 15 minutes. Let rest before cutting and serving. This is a rich casserole and you should be able to serve 12 people 1/2 sandwich each unless, of course, they have come in from a 6-mile marathon.

❖ ❖ ❖ ❖ ❖ ❖ ❖ ❖ ❖

CHICKEN ELEGANTE_____Fran Day

Wouldn't you know that Victorian Canadians would come up with a chicken recipe with a name like Chicken Elegante . . .can you see that little hen going to the chopping block with her little breast all puffed out, joyful in knowing that her epitaph will include the word ELEGANTE. Well, Frances assures me that she shall not have died in vain - that this is one of the best of her "fowl" recipes, pun intended.

Put chicken pieces in baking dish and cover with the following which as been mixed in a bowl:

1/2 pint sour cream	**1 pkg. dried onion soup mix**
1 can Mushroom soup	**1 Tblsp plus 2 tsp lemon juice**
1/2 cup white wine (Vermouth)	**2 Tblsp dill weed**

Put sautéed mushrooms all over the chickens and pour over the soup mixture. Bake 3/4 of an hour covered and 3/4 of an hour uncovered in a 350° oven.

YORKSHIRE CHICKEN PUDDING — Florence Hatt

Florence Hatt is Joe Smith's sister and when she came to visit in Council Bluffs she brought this back from Washington, D.C. A dear friend had prepared this from a recipe she had found in the Portland, Maine newspaper. This serves 4 people.

2 chicken breasts, skinned, boned and halved
1/4 cup oil

Pour oil in a baking dish and place into the dish chicken breasts that have been coated in the following mixture:

1/3 cup flour   **1/4 tsp pepper**
1/2 tsp sage   **dash of Garlic powder**

Turn chicken pieces in the oil so all are well coated with oil. Bake at 400° for 30 minutes. Prepare pudding while chicken is cooking.

1 cup flour   **3 eggs**
1 tsp salt   **1 tsp baking powder**
1 1/2 cups milk   **1/4 cup chopped parsley**

Mix flour, salt, and baking powder in bowl. In another bowl mix milk, eggs and parsley. Pour liquid into dry ingredients and lightly blend with a fork. Pour over the hot chicken. Place baking dish on a cookie sheet and return to oven for 20 to 25 minutes.

FRIED CHICKEN — Momo

Cut chickens into serving pieces, wash in cold water and drain on paper towels. In a plastic baggie put:

2/3 cup flour
1/4 tsp Lawry Season salt
1/8 tsp ground pepper

Toss chicken pieces individually in flour mixture and shake off excess. Brown in iron skillet that has **had 2 Tblsp bacon fat and 2 Tblsp butter** brought to high heat. Fry til golden brown on both sides. Put fried chicken in cake pan in one layer and then add 1/4 cup water to pan drippings and deglaze pan. Pour over chickens.

Seal chicken in cake pan with heavy foil and bake in a 325° oven until tender - usually about 1 hour.

Preserves, Jellies & Pickles

PRESERVES

Apricot Jam 239
Bread and Butter Pickles 240
Chili Sauce 241
Freezing Fresh Cherries for Desserts 242
Jalapeno Jelly 240
Pickled Peaches 241
Red Pepper Jelly 239
Simple Simon Pickles 241
Watermelon Rind Pickles 239

RED PEPPER JELLY

Makes 4 pints of jelly

3 large red peppers, seeded
1 1/2 cups WHITE vinegar
6 1/2 cups sugar
1/4 cup fresh hot peppers or
2 - 3 tsp crushed dried red peppers (hot)
1 bottle Certo
3 to 4 drops red food coloring

Put hot peppers and chopped red peppers in blender with a little vinegar and blend. Pour into pot, and add sugar and rest of vinegar. Bring to boil and add Certo. Stir in and boil again. Skim foam. After it boils for 1 minute, add food coloring. Skim once again. Put in jelly jars and seal. This is good poured over a block of cream cheese and served with crackers for hors d'oeuvres.

WATERMELON RIND PICKLES

Rind from 1 large watermelon (about 7 pounds of rind)
Lime water (1 cup lime juice to 2 gallons water)
3 3/4 lbs of sugar
1 quart of vinegar
1 pkg. cinnamon sticks
cloves

Pick out a melon that has a good thick rind. Remove the green skin and red meat. Cut into 1 inch squares. Soak overnight in limewater. Drain and put in preserving kettle. Cover with water and boil til easily pierced, about 2 hours. Drain, cool rind, and put a clove in each piece. Boil sugar, vinegar and cinnamon for 10 minutes. Add fruit and cook til rind is spotted, about 2 hours. Place in hot jars and seal. 9 to 10 jars.

APRICOT JAM   Mom Schenck

1 lb. dried apricots

Grind and soak apricots in 3 cups water overnight. Add
One large can crushed pineapple, juice and all, together with
4 1/2 cups sugar. Boil for 30 minutes and put in jars and refrigerate.

BREAD AND BUTTER PICKLES   Nancy Jenkins
These are the Best!

4 quarts of small cucumbers (about 32), thinly sliced
6 medium onions, thinly sliced
1 large green pepper, thinly sliced
1 large red pepper, thinly sliced
3 cloves minced garlic

Place all ingredients in a canning kettle and sprinkle with **1/3 cup canning** salt. Place contents of **2 trays of ice cubes** over pickles and let stand for 3 hours. Drain. In a separate pan, mix:
3 cups WHITE vinegar
5 cups sugar
1 1/2 tsp turmeric
1 1/2 tsp celery seed
2 Tblsp mustard seed

Warm the contents, but do not boil. Pour over the pickle slices and heat to boiling. Put in sterilized glass jars and seal.

❖ ❖ ❖ ❖ ❖ ❖ ❖ ❖ ❖

JALAPENO JELLY   Frances Weaver

5 medium size canned Jalapeno peppers
1 cup green bell peppers, cut in chunks
6 cups sugar
2 1/2 cups cider vinegar
1 bottle (6 oz.) liquid pectin
3 or 4 drops green food coloring

Rinse Jalapenos, discarding stem ends, any blackened skin, and about 1/2 the seeds. Place in blender with bell pepper chunks and vinegar. Blend to chop fine. Add to 6 cups sugar in large kettle and mix thoroughly. Bring to a rolling boil over high heat stirring constantly. Pour in food coloring and pectin. Return to boil and boil for ONE MINUTE, stirring constantly. Remove from heat and pour into boiled jelly glasses and seal. Makes 7 half-pints.

CHILI SAUCE — Glenna Spetman

This is a wonderful sauce that I make religiously every year. With mayonnaise, it makes marvelous 1000 Island dressing. But it is principally to use on meat loaves or hamburgers. Try it on cottage cheese!

1 heaping market basket of tomatoes
Drop in boiling water, skin, quarter and grind in Cuisinart or meat grinder.

8 medium onions, chopped   **6 green peppers, chopped**
5 sticks of celery, chopped   **4 Tblsp salt**
12 to 15 whole cloves   **1 tsp mace**
1 tsp nutmeg   **4 cups sugar**
3 cups cider vinegar

Grind so that vegetables are not TOO fine. You will be cooking the sauce around six hours and it should make about 12 pints. Bew careful not to burn. Stir frequently.

SIMPLE SIMON PICKLES — Carol Sue Spetman

5 cups cucumbers, unpeeled and sliced
1 large onion, thinly sliced
1/3 tsp turmeric   **1/3 tsp celery seed**
1/3 tsp mustard seed   **1 1/3 cups sugar**
1 1/3 cups vinegar   **2 tsp NON-IODIZED salt**

In large glass jar put cucumbers and onions. Mix rest of ingredients and pour over cucumbers. Cover and refrigerate. Stir occasionally. These will keep indefinitely in the fridge.

PICKLED PEACHES — Mrs. Thomas Norris

From the 1933 Junior League Cookbook

1 pt. vinegar   **5 pts. sugar**
2 Tblsp whole cloves   **3 sticks cinnamon**

Let this syrup come to a boil. Then add **7 lbs of peaches**. There are 4 medium peaches to a pound.
Add the peeled peaches to the syrup. When fruit is cooked, remove it and boil syrup until thick. Return fruit to syrup, heat thoroughly and "bottle".

FREEZING FRESH CHERRIES FOR DESSERTS

Pit cherries and put in quart plastic containers with **1/2 cup sugar**. Freeze til ready for use. Then boil on medium high flame to cook, about 15 minutes. Skim.

KATHLEEN
at the celebration of her
BAPTISMAL
1984

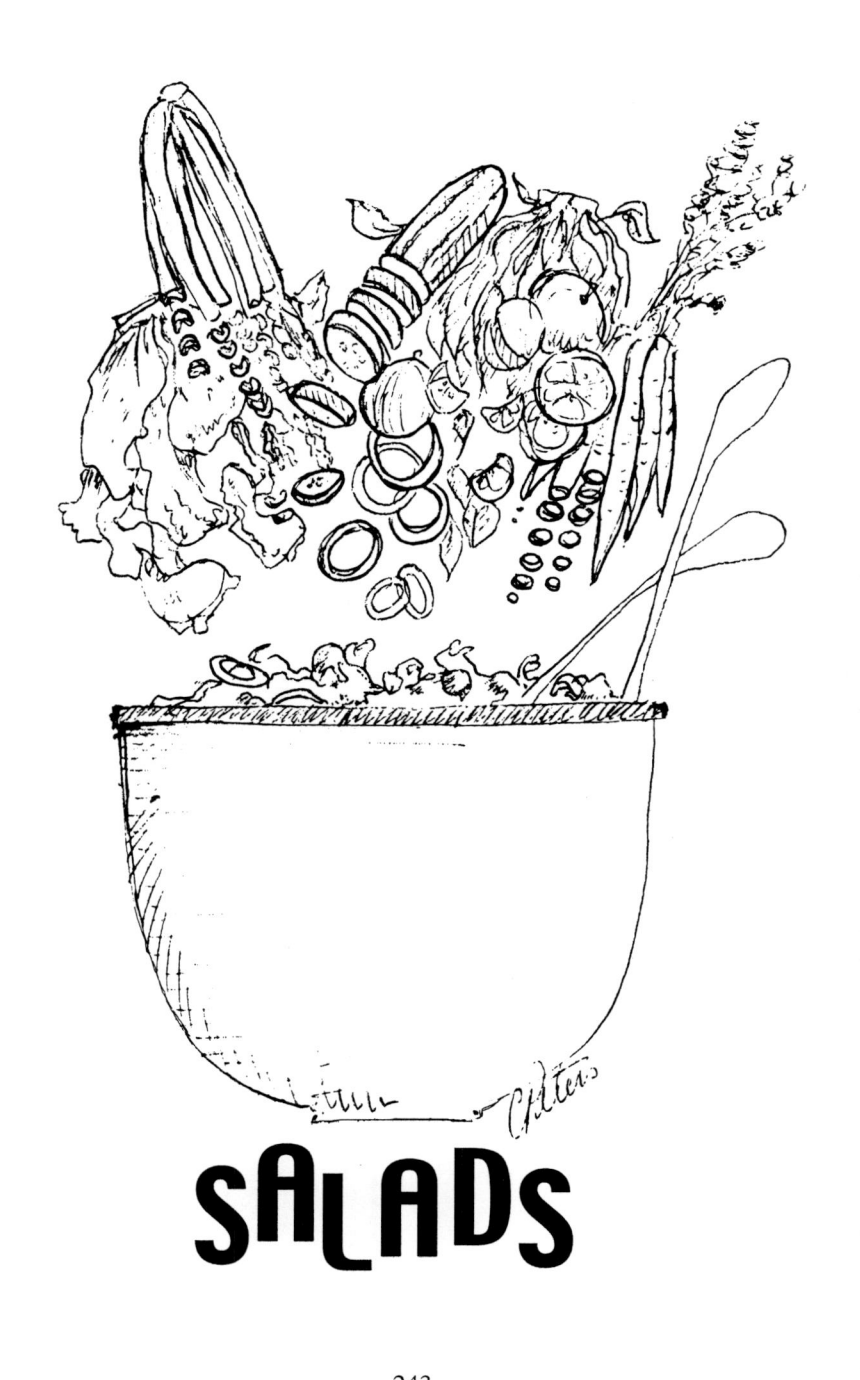

SALADS

SALADS

Cauliflower Salad and Dressing	253
Caesar Salad	245
Chasen's Spinach Salad	258
Cottage Cheese Jubilee	255
Cranberry Jello	248
"Different" Salad	247
Fourth of July Cole Slaw	247
Fourth of July Potato Salad	256
Frozen Cherry Cream Salad	250
Frozen Fruit Salad	254
Homemade Croutons by Malcolm	245
Layered Salad	248
Lemon-Orange Jello Salad	246
Lime Fruit Jello	257
Linguine Salad	251
Macaroni Salad	255
Marinated Vegetable Salad	253
Molded Tunafish Salad	252
Orange and Almond Salad	255
Orange Gelatin	245
Party Salad	254
Peas and Cheese Salad	256
Pretty Christmas Cinnamon-Cheese Gelatin Salad	251
Summertime Fruit Salad	257
Three Bean Salad	253
Tomato Aspic I	249
Tomato Aspic II	258
Tuna-Cream Cheese Fish Mold	250

CEASAR SALAD — Malcolm Peters

Season the bottom of a wooden salad bowl with **3 to 4 buds of garlic split and rubbed into wood.** Add
6 hearty twists of gound pepper
A big splotch of anchovy paste
6 garlic buds through the garlic press
1 egg
1 heaping tsp Dijon mustard
2 squirts of Worcestershire sauce
3 glugs of cider vinegar
Juice of 1/2 lemon
6 squirts of tarragon vinegar
4 glugs of oil
1 heaping tsp sugar
Stir and stir and taste. If too tart, add more sugar to smooth.
Add **1 head of Romaine lettuce** and sprinkle heavily with **Parmesan cheese fresh ground**
Add homemade croutons
Toss gaily and serve at once!

* Sal at Arnauds' Restaurant also adds a bit of horseradish

HOMEMADE CROUTONS BY MALCOLM

Cube 1 loaf of French bread
Place on cookie sheet and drizzle with garlic butter and sprinkle with Parmesan cheese. Bake in oven anywhere from 300 to 450° depending on how late you're running. Turn to brown evenly.
Please note that you dirty very few measuring utensils with this recipe. Isn't that special!

ORANGE GELATIN — Daphne Peters

Wonderful when nothing else will go down.

2 Tblsp plain gelatin dissolved in 1/2 cup water
When soft turn into
1 cup of boiling water and stir til dissolved.
Add **1 cup sugar**
1/4 cup real lemon juice
2 cups of real orange juice
the zest of one orange
Mix all together and chill til set in refrigerator.

When Douglas Peters wanted to bring home the dining room table and 8 chairs from the estate of Aunt Daphne and Aunt Gladys Peters, I strenuously resisted. Doug's grandfather, Milton C. Peters, father to Daphne and Gladys, had commissioned the Honduran mahogany colossus for the old manse at 206 So. 32nd Street in Omaha. It was rococo Victorian and had 12 extension leaves. Under deep pressure, I succumbed.

When an entire family of 26 is couched at one board enjoying a Festive feast, it is difficult not to be grateful to prevailing judiciousness. Even though the furniture does not measure up to my aesthetic tastes, its radiant utility now makes me rejoice. (I never won a judgment with The Lawyer, anyway - he is most persuasive).

MATTHEW'S FIRST EASTER BASKET

LEMON-ORANGE JELLO SALAD

Dissolve 1 package of lemon jello in 1 cup hot apple sauce.
Add the juice and zest of 1 orange
Add 1 cup of Seven-Up.
Refrigerate til set.

FOURTH OF JULY COLE SLAW   Mary Peters

1 medium head of cabbage
3 large ribs of celery
1 large green pepper
1/2 small onion - yellow

This is not a shredded cole slaw. Gladys Peters taught me how to chop the cabbage with a sharp knife into tiny pieces as with the rest of the vegetables. Plan on chopping alot, as it takes a little time. It is worth it as the vegetables do not bleed and this keeps well in the refrigerator for several days!

Add **half Mayonnaise and half Salad Dressing** along with
Lawry's Season Salt
Ground pepper
Salad Herbs
about 1 tsp sugar
about 1 Tblsp lemon juice

It is impossible to give precision measurements for this salad as the proportions of the cabbage are always different. Suffice it to say that this slaw should say HELLO! because you will be serving it with baked beans and fried chicken that are rather bland. So experiment with the seasonings and your good sense will garner the rave notices, trust me. Just be sure the salad is moist with enough salad dressing.

"DIFFERENT" SALAD   Glenna Spetman

1 large head of broccoli, separated into little flowerets
1 cup cashew nuts, split
1 cup raisins
1 red onion, chopped
1 lb. of bacon cooked crisp and chopped in bits

DRESSING
1 cup mayonnaise
1/2 cup sugar
2 Tblsp vinegar

Do not mix SALAD with DRESSING until just before serving.

CRANBERRY JELLO — Belle Hess

2 packages cherry jello dissolved in 1 1/2 cups boiling water. Then grind
1 pkg. cranberries, washed and picked over
1 whole orange including rind
2 or 3 apples, skin included
nuts if desired

You really need an old fashioned grinder to process the fruit properly. It is delicious with turkey dinner. Put in mold and refrigerate for 24 hours. Kids love to turn the grinder and help at holiday!

❖ ❖ ❖ ❖ ❖ ❖ ❖ ❖ ❖

LAYERED SALAD — Delores Borman

4 cups chopped lettuce
2 1/2 cups grated Monterey Jack cheese
5 hard boiled eggs, sliced
1 lb. frozen green peas, thawed and drained
6 green onions, chopped
3 cups torn fresh spinach
1 lb. bacon cooked crisp and crumbled
1/2 lb. fresh mushrooms sliced
1/2 tsp sugar
salt and pepper

DRESSING
1 1/4 cups sour cream
1/2 cup mayonnaise
1/2 pkg. Italian dressing mix

Use a large glass bowl. Dry lettuce and spinach well. Layer lettuce in bottom of bowl. Sprinkle with salt and pepper and sugar. Place some of egg slices around sides of bowl, chop remaining eggs and sprinkle over lettuce. Sprinkle 1 cup cheese next, then peas, then spinach, green onions, mushrooms, 3/4 of the bacon and remaining cheese. Mix together dressing and spread over top of salad sealing top completely. Cover and refrigerate overnight. Garnish with remaining bacon, green onions and a sprinkle of paprika. Toss at serving.
Serves 10

Maybelle & Bob Bridge
Playa de Cortez - Mexico
Put a little more fertilizer on that bougainvillea . . .

> I keep three wishes ready,
> Lest I should chance to meet
> Any day a fairy
> Coming down the street.

TOMATO ASPIC _____ Gertrude "MOM" Schenck

Soften **2 envelopes of plain gelatin in 1/2 cold water**
heat 4 cups of tomato juice with
1/2 cup celery leaves
1 bay leaf
2 Tblsp minced onion
2 Tblsp vinegar
1/2 tsp salt
2 tsp sugar
1 tsp chili powder and simmer for 5 minutes.
Strain the liquid from the vegetables and add the softened gelatin stirring till it is dissolved. Pour in mold and chill. Unmold on bed of lettuce and decorate with sliced cucumbers that have been marinated in French dressing arranged overlapping around aspic mold. Garnish plate with ripe olives, cold artichoke hearts quartered and celery bits stuffed with sharp cheese.

As young marrieds, we were invited to a dinner buffet where this was presented as a salad. It had been molded in a fish mold and I thought it just about the fanciest dish ever. Present the mold on curly endive and use lots of pimento stuffed olives for eyes and decoration and VERY thinly sliced cucumber for scales.

TUNA-CREAM CHEESE FISH MOLD

Heat **1 can tomato soup in double boiler**
Add **2 envelopes of Knox gelatin** after having been dissolved in 1/2 cup cold water
Add **3 small squares of Philadelphia brand cream cheese**
    1 pinch salt
Mix and cool. Then add: **1 cup Miracle Whip dressing**
    1/2 green pepper, chopped
    1 cup celery, chopped
    1 can drained tuna or you can use crab meat
    1 Tblsp grated onion

Combine all ingredients and put in fish mold that has been rinsed out in cold water. (Easy to unmold!)

FROZEN CHERRY CREAM SALAD
A white salad with Royal Ann Cherries

3 egg yolks
1 Tblsp powdered sugar
3 Tblsp cream
Juice of one lemon
Place ingredients in a double boiler and cook about 15 minutes until it forms a soft custard. Cool.
1 pint whipping cream
1/2 lb. marshmallows, chopped
1 20 oz. can pineapple, small chunks
1 20 oz. can pitted Royal Anne cherries
1/2 cup broken nut meats - pecans, preferably
Whip cream and carefully turn into the cooled custard. Stir in carefully the rest of the ingredients, place in a glass casserole and store in refrigerator at least 12 hours.
Serves 10 to 12 persons.

The best wedding I ever attended were the nuptials of Joanne McDonnell, a theatre choreographer who married Jim Cady, a great wit and graphic artist. After some years in New York, the two of them came back to the Midwest to brighten our lives. All the bridesmaids and girl friends, after the garden reception, wound up in Joanne's bedroom to help her change into her Going Away outfit. It was girliedom at its best!

PRETTY CHRISTMAS CINNAMON-CHEESE GELATIN SALAD _____ Joanne Cady

1/2 cup cinnamon red hots (cinnamon candies)
2 cups of boiling water

Put red hots in 2 cups of boiling water and stir until the candies dissolve. Add

1 6-oz. pkg Cherry Jell-O

Stir until Jello dissolves and then add

2 1/2 cups applesauce

After applesauce is mixed into Jello mixture, pour in HALF of gelatin mixture into 8 x 8 pan. Chill until set.

1 8-oz. pkg cream cheese at room temperature
1 cup nuts, chopped
1/2 cup finely chopped celery
1/2 cup mayonnaise

Blend together cream cheese, nuts and celery. Mix in salad dressing. Spread this layer over the firm jello mixture. Pour over the remaining jello mixture and chill until all of salad is firm. You may have to keep the remaining jello soft over a double boiler while first layer of jello is setting up. *This serves 9.*

LINGUINE SALAD _____ Jane T. Peters

1 1-lb. can artichoke hearts quartered - pat dry
1/2 cup black olives
1/4 cup olive oil
3 Tblsp fresh lemon juice
2 garlic cloves
1/8 tsp crushed red pepper

Combine above ingredients and marinate overnight or at least a couple of hours. Make linguine - cooked al dente.
Toss - serve with meat or fish dish.

MOLDED TUNAFISH SALAD — Grandma Esther Wilcox

2 6-oz. cans tuna fish, drained
2 hardboiled eggs, chopped
1/2 cup chopped stuffed olives
2 Tblsp capers
1 Tblsp chopped chives or onions
1 envelope gelatin
1/4 cup cold water
2 cups mayonnaise

Combine first 5 ingredients. Soak gelatin in water 3 minutes, then dissolve over hot water. Add gradually to mayonnaise while stirring. Fold into fish and vegetable mixture and turn into 10 inch ring mold or individual molds, that have been rinsed with water. *Serves 8.*

FOOD CONNECTION

Because the act of eating necessarily sustains us, great memories are often connected with certain foods and wines. Wine, bread and cheese recall a morning in 1979 in an open market in Vienna, Austria near a train station, as Doug and I, together with Mac, Duff and Mary, made our selections before boarding a train bound for Budapest.
As we approached Hungary, I vividly recall the soldiers stationed at the border of the Iron Curtain standing at the ready with guns and bullets - a frightening novelty for the citizens of the United States. Our trip through Austria had depleted the cheese and wine, as we had shared with fellow travelers, so the train conductor suggested our boys hop off the train at the border and buy a local bottle called Heuringer. This adventure of procurement, because of the incipient danger, was just what Mac and Duff needed. So, we all lined the train windows and watched the heroes buy the biggest jeroboam they could get. The train whistle blew, the soldiers were laughing and yelling, the crowd of people were cheering, and the boys jumped back on the moving train - enough to give a Mother a downright heart attack.

MARINATED VEGETABLE SALAD — Middy Divelbiss

1 can white shoepeg corn
1 large can tiny baby peas
1 medium green pepper chopped
1 cup onion chopped
1 can French style green beans
1 jar pimento chopped
1 cup celery chopped

Drain vegetables in colander well.
Mix the following dressing and pour over vegetables and marinate overnight.

1 tsp salt
3/4 cup sugar
3/4 cup white vinegar
1 tsp pepper
1/2 cup salad oil
1 Tblsp water

CAULIFLOWER SALAD AND DRESSING — Ginny Wilcox

1 cup mayonnaise
1 Tblsp lemon juice
1/8 tsp Accent
1/4 tsp garlic salt
1/8 tsp fresh ground pepper
2 Tblsp Parmesan cheese

Enough cream to thin the above ingredients so that this will coat the lettuce nicely

Into a salad bowl, grate **4 or 5 large florets of fresh cauliflower** and add **a head of romaine or greens of your choice.** Then add dressing and toasted bread croutons and toss well.

THREE BEAN SALAD

1 cup Kraft's Apple jelly
1/3 cup cider vinegar
4 tsp cornstarch
1 tsp salt
1 16 oz. can cut green beans, drained
1 16 oz. can cut wax beans, drained
1 16 oz. can kidney beans, drained
2 cups sliced celery
1 cup sliced green onions

Combine jelly, vinegar, cornstarch and salt and cook in a small sauce pan until slightly thickened. Wash kidney beans and drain well. Pour over hot dressing and chill overnight. Then add celery and onions before serving. Keeps well.

PARTY SALAD — Irene Peters

6 cups chopped lettuce
salt and pepper
2 tsp sugar
6 hard boiled eggs, sliced
1 10 oz. pkg. frozen peas, thawed
1 lb. bacon, cooked crisp and crumbled
8 oz. shredded Swiss cheese
1 cup of mayonnaise or salad dressing
1/4 cup sliced green onions
paprika

Put 3 cups of lettuce in bottom of large ceramic bowl. Sprinkle with salt and pepper and 1 tsp sugar.
Arrange 3 of the sliced hard boiled eggs over the lettuce and sprinkle with more salt,
then half the box of peas, half the pound of bacon, and 4 oz. of the shredded Swiss cheese.
Start over again and repeat the process.
Then take the cup of mayonnaise and spread it over the top of the salad, sealing to the edge of the bowl.
Cover with foil and chill for 24 hours.
Before serving, toss the salad to mix all ingredients and garnish with green onions and paprika.

FROZEN FRUIT SALAD

1 3-oz. pkg. cream cheese
2 Tblsp lemon juice
1 Tblsp Maraschino cherry juice
Mix until smooth and set aside.
16 large marshmallows
2/3 cup evaporated milk (1 small can)
Melt the marshmallows and evaporated milk over heat and when melted and blended add cream cheese mixture.
1 can fruit cocktail (1 lb) juice and fruit
1/4 cup cut up maraschino cherries
Then blend in the cherries and fruit cocktail
Fill 12 paper fluted cups that have been inserted in a muffin tin and put in freezer, after covering with plastic wrap.

MACARONI SALAD   Kay Schenck

1 1/2 cups small macaroni, cooked following directions on package in salt water.
Blanche with cold water and drain and marinate in **1/3 cup vinegar.** Then chop

6 hardboiled eggs	**1/2 green pepper, chopped**
1 Tblsp chopped onion	**1 cup chopped celery**
6 sweet pickles, chopped	**15 stuffed olives, sliced**

Pour off vinegar and mix all the above together binding with half mayonnaise, half salad dressing, to make a moist salad.

ORANGE AND ALMOND SALAD

This is a recipe of Harris Golden - the wonderful chef at <u>Maine Chance</u> *which is a health spa that I was privileged to enjoy in Arizona. A week at that marvelous place was just as close to perfection as anything I can possibly think of. I was Doug Peters' guest for many years and can remember every minute of my special time in January when I was the Princess and the World had to go on without me. Ah - bliss...*

2 Tblsp safflower oil	**1/4 cup tarragon vinegar**
1/2 cup fresh orange juice	**1 Tblsp fresh chopped parsley**
1/8 tsp black pepper	**1/8 tsp salt**

pinch of dry mustard
honey (add if necessary depending on sweetness of orange)

Use this dressing on:
12 cups of mixed greens
1 1/2 cups mandarin orange slices
1/2 cup slivered <u>toasted almonds</u>

COTTAGE CHEESE JUBILEE

1 large container cottage cheese
Mix into cottage cheese the following vegetables

1 large rib of chopped celery	**2 green onions w/ green stems, chopped**
1 large chopped carrot	**1/2 chopped green pepper**
1 tsp Salad Herbs	**ground fresh pepper**
1/2 tsp Lawry's season salt	

FOURTH OF JULY POTATO SALAD

8 red potatoes boiled, peeled and diced
6 to 7 hard boiled eggs, diced
5 large ribs of celery, diced
1/2 small onion or 4 to 5 green onions, chopped
You may add green pepper if you like.

Marinate diced potatoes in **1/2 cup cider vinegar** for a few hours in the refrigerator. When ready to mix salad, drain off vinegar and add eggs and vegetables. Add **1/2 mayonnaise and 1/2 salad dressing** to salad, mixing well and seasoning with lots of **ground pepper** and **Lawry's Seasoning Salt**. Salad must be real moist with mayonnaise to be good, so add 1/2 cup at a time.

PEAS AND CHEESE SALAD

6 Tblsp mayonnaise	1/4 cup lemon juice
1/2 cup minced green onions	2 cups frozen green peas

1 cup cubed Cheddar cheese, about 4 oz.

1/8 tsp pepper	1/8 tsp salt

2 cups lettuce torn in bite size pieces
8 slices bacon fried crisp and crumbled

Day before combine all ingredients except lettuce and bacon. Refrigerate overnight. Just before serving, add bacon and lettuce.

TRIUMPHS WE HAVE KNOWN AND LOVED

RAINBOW LAYERED SALAD
JANE S. PETERS

Momo's favorite picture – Grandchildren in Florida

SUMMERTIME FRUIT SALAD _____ Mary W. Peters

1 fresh pineapple cut into chunks. Reserve juice or one 20 oz. can chunk pineapple, reserve juice.
2 oranges, peeled and cut into chunks
1/2 cup sugar
Combine pineapple, oranges, juice and sugar in bowl and let stand in refrigerator overnight.
Drain next day and add water to make one cup.
Blend liquid, **2 Tblsp cornstarch and juice of 1/2 to 1 lemon** depending on your taste for tartness.
Heat to boiling. When cool, mix with pineapple, oranges, and **6 cups of fresh fruit including raspberries, strawberries, blueberries, melons, peaches, pears, apples, grapes and bananas.** Cover and refrigerate.
Serves 8.

LIME FRUIT JELLO

A pretty and tasty jello salad is made from **1 pkg. of lime jello** using **Gingerale** for the second cup of liquid. Into this mixture, put **honeydew melon balls and green grapes.** A favorite of Googah the Clown!

TOMATO ASPIC   Jerry Dodson

2 pkgs lemon Jello dissolved in
2 cups hot Tomato or Vegemato juice
Add 2 more cups of tomato juice when gelatin is dissolved and spice with the following ingredients:
1 or 2 dashes of Worcestershire sauce
4 dashes of Louisiana hot sauce
salt and pepper
The juice of 1/2 a lemon. (Taste to correct flavor)
Pour into a ring mold that has been rinsed with cold water and add to the tomato aspic the following vegetables, about 2 cups combined:
diced green pepper
diced green onion
diced celery
diced cucumber, seeded. Then add
3 hard cooked eggs, sliced
1/2 cup sliced stuffed olives
When the mold is set, put in a sink full of hot water VERY BRIEFLY and unmold on a platter. Decorate with fresh greens and fill the center of the aspic with Cottage Cheese Jubilee (listed in this chapter). Offer mayonnaise and French dressing in a divided dish with ladles.

CHASEN'S SPINACH SALAD   Ruth Smith

| 1 lb. fresh spinach | 3/4 lb. bacon |

Wash spinach and remove stems and tear into bite size pieces and chill in refrigerator. Cut sliced bacon into 1/2 inch pieces and fry til crisp. Drain.

Make dressing of the following ingredients:

2 Tblsp bacon drippings	2/3 cup salad oil or olive oil
1/4 cup red wine vinegar	2 small cloves of garlic crushed
1 Tblsp Worcestershire sauce	1 tsp sugar
1/2 tsp salt	3/4 tsp pepper, fresh ground

Put all ingredients in jar and shake until combined. Do not refrigerate.

Combine spinach, bacon bits, **sliced pickled beets, very thin slices of red onion, thin sliced fresh mushrooms** and enough dressing to coat salad lightly.

Salad Dressings

SALAD DRESSING

Addie Mae's Salad Dressing 265
Cooked French Dressing 265
French Dressing 262
French Dressing 265
Fruit Salad Dressing 262
Green Goddess Dressing 264
Maple Syrup Salad Dressing 264
Mayonnaise Dressing 261
Maytag Blue Cheese 263
Mock Caesar Salad Dressing 262
Perfect Mayonnaise 263
Peters Dressing 263
Piccadilly Dressing 264
Sour Cream Dressing 264

If you have any predisposition toward claustrophobia, forget about traveling in a Dogsled. The layers of clothing, the plethora of blankets coupled with the cramped seating design are enough to give even the most audacious a case of the heebie jeebies. After being seated and tucked into the sled air-tight, the snarling, snapping beasts are lashed into harness and whipped into action.

These powerful Huskies have been tethered to their dog houses for a full day, are full of digested dry dog food, and the effluvium that hits the sled as the dogs step smartly out at a trot makes your eyes glaze over. What mountains? What snow? What scenery?

You are at ground level, tucked up to your eyeballs, rocketing along in the freezing cold, eyes watering. No thanks, I'll take my Chrysler LeBaron TurboJet. The wine at the end of the trip was first rate.

MAYONNAISE DRESSING

1 cup mayonnaise
1 Tblsp lemon juice
1/8 tsp Accent
1/2 cup grated cauliflower

2 Tblsp Parmesan cheese
1/8 tsp Garlic salt
1/4 tsp ground pepper

Croutons fried in fresh pressed garlic and olive oil

Combine all ingredients except cauliflower and croutons and thin with **milk** til it is like a heavy sauce. Place **lettuce** in bowl, add croutons and cauliflower and mix with dressing.

MOCK CESAR SALAD DRESSING

Can use on spinach, romaine, and endive. I made quarts of this to sell at a Church Bazaar and it was very successful.

In a Blender put:

1 stalk celery	3 egg yolks
1 medium onion	1/2 tsp pepper
2 small cloves garlic	1 cup good olive oil
1 cup Mazola corn oil	2 Tblsp prepared mustard
1 oz. Accent	1 can flat anchovies, drained
2 oz. wine vinegar	a dash of Tabasco

As you toss salad, you can add croutons and Romano cheese for the ultimate deception.

FRENCH DRESSING   Harris Golden

This makes 1 112 cups dressing, is delicious and has only 32 calories per serving. A mainstay at MAINE CHANCE.

1 cup strong flavored chicken stock
1/2 cup red wine vinegar
1/2 cup safflower oil
2 cloves garlic, minced
2 Tblsp chopped parsley
1 tsp sugar
pinch of dry mustard
1/2 tsp pepper and 1/2 tsp salt

Put all in pint jar and shake well. Refrigerate.

FRUIT SALAD DRESSING   Jane S. Peters

1 1/2 cups sugar	**2 tsp dry mustard**
2 tsp salt	**2/3 cup good vinegar**

Mix all dry ingredients in a saucepan, add the vinegar and bring to a boil on the stove. Let stand until cold. Put in a Waring Blender and add VERY slowly:

2 cups of Wesson oil   **3 Tblsp onion juice**
Just a few drops of green food coloring

Remove from the blender and stir in **3 Tblsp poppy seeds**

This dressing stores in the refrigerator for a long time and is lovely on grapefruit and avocado salad, dressed with pomegranate seeds.

PERFECT MAYONNAISE
Made in a Waring Blender! Easy and Fast.

1 egg	1/2 tsp prepared mustard
3/4 tsp salt	1/2 tsp sugar
dash of black pepper	dash of cayenne
1/3 cup salad oil	2/3 cup of salad oil

3 Tblsp vinegar or lemon juice, or half of each

Place all ingredients EXCEPT 2/3 cup of oil, in Blender. Cover and blend at medium speed for 5 seconds. Remove cover insert and quickly pour 2/3 cup oil in center of egg mixture in a steady stream while blending at medium speed. Blend til mixture is thick and smooth. VOILA!!

PETERS DRESSING
For mixed greens, in a large wooden salad bowl

1 clove of garlic, pureed with a fork in wooden bowl
1/4 tsp salt and lots of ground pepper
1 tsp Honey mustard or Prepared mustard with a large pinch of sugar
1 tsp capers, crushed in a bowl
2 inches of Anchovy paste
1 tsp Balsamic vinegar
1/3 cup combination olive and vegetable oil
1 Tblsp Tarragon vinegar poured slowly into oil while mixing with the fork
Fresh lemon juice to taste
Fresh buttered croutons are a must while mixing, **and fresh tarragon leaves** are a pleasant diversion.

MAYTAG BLUE CHEESE
Chef's Special Salad Dressing

4 oz. or 3/4 cup of crumbled blue cheese
1 cup mayonnaise	1/2 cup sour cream
1 clove of garlic, minced	2 Tblsp green onions & tops, minced
1 Tblsp wine vinegar	1 Tblsp lemon juice
1 tsp sugar	

Makes 2 cups and stores well in refrigerator.

PICCADILLY DRESSING
from Inn on the Park - London

1 cup vinegar
1 cup olive oil
1/4 cup sesame oil
2 garlic buds, crushed
1/4 tsp pepper
1 Tblsp chopped parsley
1/2 tsp dry mustard
1/4 tsp onion powder
1 tsp salt
pinch of tarragon, basil, and rosemary

MAPLE SYRUP SALAD DRESSING

1 cup salad oil
1/2 cup catsup
1/2 cup maple syrup
2 Tblsp vinegar
1 Tblsp Worcestershire sauce
garlic salt

SOUR CREAM DRESSING   Daphy and Glady Peters

1 cup commercial sour cream
1/4 cup minced raw onion
3 Tblsp wine vinegar
1 tsp salt
2 tsp sugar
1 tsp prepared mustard
dash Tabasco

Blend thoroughly and chill at least 1 hour.

GREEN GODDESS DRESSING   Cory Loucks

1 cup mayonnaise
1/2 cup cream
2 Tblsp lemon juice
1/2 cup chopped parsley
1/2 tsp pepper
2 Tblsp tarragon vinegar
2 Tblsp garlic vinegar
2 Tblsp grated onion
1/2 tsp salt

Whirl in blender.

ADDIE MAE'S SALAD DRESSING

1 tsp dry mustard
1 tsp salt
Paprika up to 1 tsp
1 Tblsp sugar
1 Tblsp lemon juice
1 Tblsp olive oil

Beat all this smooth with a wire whisk and then add:
2 Tblsp olive oil
2 Tblsp lemon juice

Beat with a whisk and then add slowly:
3 Tblsp olive oil
2 Tblsp vinegar

Beat til thick and then add the following:
2 buds garlic, cut in half
2 hard boiled eggs, chopped
1 large package Roquefort cheese, mashed

Place dressing on mixed greens pulled apart in chunks and crumble **crisp fried bacon** over all.

COOKED FRENCH DRESSING   Judge Charles Roe

1 cup salad oil
1/2 cup sugar
1/2 cup vinegar
2 tsp salt
1/2 tsp paprika
1 can condensed tomato soup

Mix together and bring to boil in saucepan. Grate into mixture **1 small onion**. Pour into glass jar and refrigerate. Will keep indefinitely. Shake well before using.

FRENGH DRESSING   Mrs. Wohlers

1 Tblsp mustard powder
1 tsp salt
1/2 tsp paprika
1/4 cup sugar
1 Tblsp Worcestershire sauce
1/2 cup Mazola oil
1 can tomato soup
1 tsp onion juice
3/4 cup vinegar

Put in a quart jar and shake thoroughly. Can be kept indefinitely.

This is my Mother with her first granddaughter, Gere Peters. I now know the great jubilation she felt holding that child; there is nothing that is quite so profound. Being a grandmother is bliss.

SAUCES

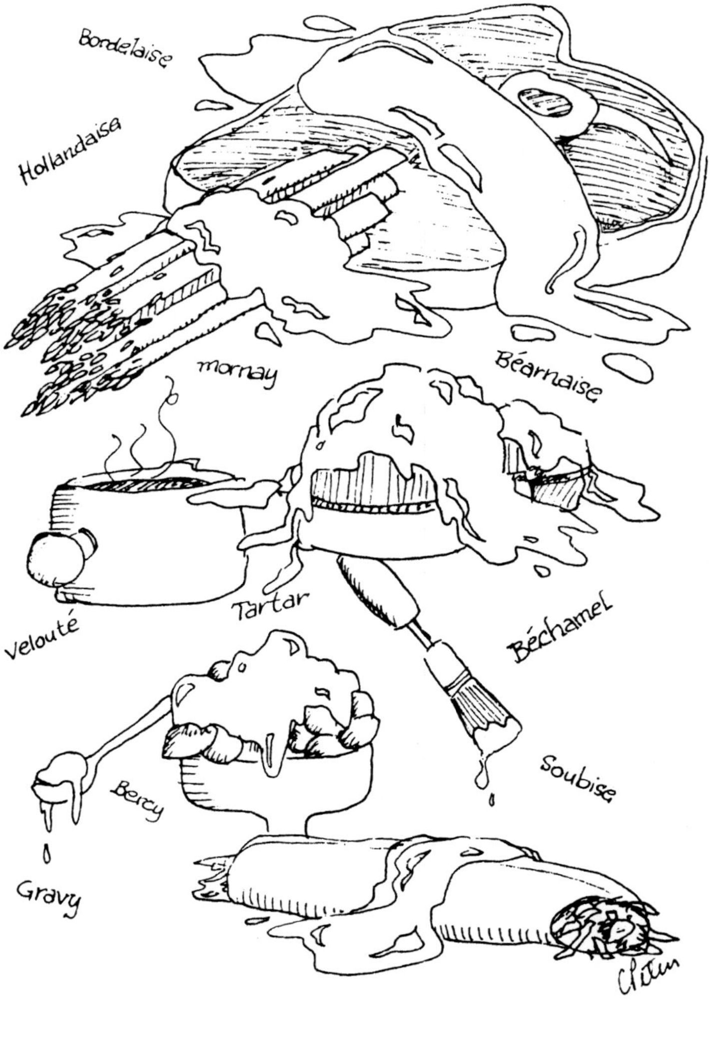
Bordelaise
Hollandaise
mornay
Béarnaise
Velouté
Tartar
Béchamel
Soubise
Bercy
Gravy

SAUCES

Béarnaise Sauce for Steaks 269
Black Bing Cherry Sauce for Fowl 269
Blender Hollandaise Sauce 274
Chateaubrainde Sauce 275
Come Back Barbeque Sauce 276
Deeevine Chocolate Sauce 276
Duff's Chocolate Sauce 273
Fluffy Hard Sauce 272
Foamy Sauce for Plum Pudding 273
Ham Sauce 274
Hollandaise Sauce 275
Horseradish Sauce for Ham 276
Joe's Mustard Sauce 270
Mint Sauce for Lamb 272
Mornay sauce 269
Oriental Marinade for chicken 271
Philadelphia Dunker Sauce 273
Remoulade Sauce 270
Sauce for Fish 270
Sauce for Game Birds 269
Tartar Sauce 270

BLACK BING CHERRY SAUCE for
Cornish Game Hens or other Fowl

1 - # 2 1/2 can Black Bing cherries
2 Tblsp sugar
2 tsp cornstarch
1/2 cup good burgundy
1/4 tsp salt

Drain juice from berries and combine with cornstarch, wine, sugar and salt. Bring to a boil and add drained cherries. Pour over hot baked chicken.

SAUCE FOR GAME BIRDS

1/2 lb. butter
5 Tblsp currant jelly
2 Tblsp prepared mustard
1/2 tsp garlic salt
2 tsp lemon juice
1/2 cup dry sherry
pepper & salt

Combine in sauce pan and cook til well blended. Serve hot.

BEARNAISE SAUCE FOR STEAKS

1 Tblsp Tarragon vinegar
1 Tblsp water
1/2 Tblsp chopped onion, very fine
Heat and let cool. To above mixture add in double boiler:
4 egg yolks
Heat and stir constantly until smooth.
Add 5 Tblsp consommé
4 Tblsp butter, all the while stirring
Add 1/2 Tblsp chopped parsley; also salt, pepper and paprika, stirring until smooth.

MORNAY SAUCE   Jane T. Peters

2 Tblsp butter
1 1/2 cups milk
1/2 tsp Dijon mustard
2 Tblsp flour
1/2 cup Parmesan cheese

Melt butter in sauce pan, stir in flour and when foaming, remove from heat and stir in milk. Bring to boil, stirring til sauce thickens. Simmer 2-3 minutes. Remove from heat, stir in cheese and mustard.

TARTAR SAUCE

Into 1 cup of mayonnaise stir 2 teaspoons each of the following herbs that have been chopped:
Parsley • Capers • Chives • 1 tsp. Tarragon
1 Tblsp chopped Gherkins (small SWEET pickles with a tang)
Add a tsp or two of lemon juice and a little lemon rind that has been grated.

SAUCE FOR FISH

1 cup mayonnaise
1 Tblsp parsley, chopped
1 Tblsp chervil, chopped
1 Tblsp capers, chopped
1 Tblsp chives, chopped
1 Tblsp tarragon, chopped
1 small chopped SOUR pickle

Combine ahead and let flavors combine. Makes 1 1/4 cups

REMOULADE SAUCE
This sauce is served with iced peeled shrimp as a luncheon dish on a hot day

2 chopped hard boiled eggs
2 Tblsp chopped celery
1 Tblsp pickle relish
1 tsp anchovy paste
1 tsp chopped fresh parsley
1 cup mayonnaise
1 tsp horseradish
1 Tblsp Dijon mustard
dash of cayenne
1/4 tsp tarragon, chopped
1 Tblsp chopped capers
1 tsp chopped onion

This sauce should be made the day before using, for flavors to meld.

JOE'S MUSTARD SAUCE
This is the famous sauce from Joe's Stone Crab in Miami, Florida. It goes on cold or hot stone crab claws. It is good on everything. I use it as toothpaste.

3 1/2 tsp dry mustard
1 cup mayonnaise
2 tsp Worcestershire sauce
1 tsp A-1 sauce
1 1/2 tsp light cream
1/8 tsp salt

Beat all ingredients 3 full minutes. Chill and serve.

FATHER MOSES OIYANLADE FROM NIGERIA
Suffers Christmas culture shock in Fremont
"NO SPIRITS PLEASE"

Speaking of an Improved Ecology
Irene Peters says:

An economical way to avoid commercial pesticides on your vegetable garden is to make your own bug spray. In a blender, liquefy one clove of garlic, one quart water, two tablespoons cayenne pepper and four medium onions. To this mixture add one tablespoon of soap flakes. Put the mixture into an empty spray container and you're all set to de-bug. Keeps away the pests but it won't harm bees or other useful insects.

ORIENTAL MARINADE FOR CHICKEN

1/2 tsp soy sauce
1 tsp sesame oil
1/3 cup Hoisin sauce
1/2 tsp salt
1/2 cup water

I'D LIKE TO THINK

I'd like to think when life is done, that I had filled a needed post;
And here and there had paid my fare with more than idle talk and boast.
That I had taken gifts divine, the breath of life and manhood fine,
And tried to use them now and then, in service for my fellow men.
I'd hate to think when life is through that I had lived my round of years
A useless kind that leaves behind no record in this vale of tears.
That I had wasted all my days by treading only selfish ways,
And that this world would be the same, if it had never known my name.
I'd like to think that here and there when I am gone, there shall remain
A happier spot that might have not existed had I toiled for gain.
That someone's cheery voice and smile shall prove that I had been worthwhile,
That I had paid with something fine, my debt to God for a life divine.

MINT SAUCE FOR LAMB

Serve warm in a pipkin

2 cups sugar **1/2 cup water**
1/2 cup vinegar **a pinch of salt**
about 20 sprigs of mint, 5 to 6" tall

Remove the leaves of the mint from the stalks and put in liquid mixture. Bring to a boil and reduce heat to low bubbling and cook about 20 to 30 minutes until sauce has some viscosity. If it gets too thick, add a little hot water. Can keep in a jar in the fridge for months. This also is a wonderful dressing to pour over fresh fruit compote.

FLUFFY HARD SAUCE

1/2 cup butter or margarine
1 1/2 cups confectioners' sugar
2-3 Tblsp brandy

Beat butter til soft and fluffy with an electric beater. Add sugar little at a time til thick and glossy. Stir in brandy and serve with Mincemeat pie or Apple streusel or Plum Pudding.

FOAMY SAUCE for Plum Pudding

2 eggs, separated
1 cup powdered sugar
3 Tblsp brandy

Beat egg yolks lightly. Add sugar and beat again. Add stiffly beaten egg whites and brandy. Pour over Plum Pudding.

DUFF'S CHOCOLATE SAUCE   Douglas Peters, III

1 cup sugar   1 Tblsp Karo syrup
1/3 cup milk   1 large Tblsp butter
1 square Baker's chocolate   1 tsp vanilla
pinch of salt

Boil this sugar, milk, chocolate, salt & Karo syrup until chocolate has melted and sauce has reached the soft ball stage (240°). If you don't have a candy thermometer, drop a little sauce in a cup of cold water, and stir with finger until soft ball forms. Remove from stove. Add butter and vanilla.

This sauce can also be beaten with a spoon and then poured into a pie pan, refrigerated and voila!   FUDGE!

DEP III

PHILADELPHIA DUNKER SAUCE
Great for Cold Shrimp

1 cup mayonnaise   2 Tblsp tarragon vinegar
2 Tblsp catsup   1 tsp lemon juice
2 Tblsp chili sauce   1 tsp minced onion
1/4 tsp Worcestershire sauce

Combine and chill and serve.

RECIPE FOR DEEVINE CHOCOLATE FUDGE SAUCE
Jere Mitten

1/2 cup butter
2 1/4 cups powdered sugar
2/3 cups evaporated milk or 1 small can
6 squares of Baker's chocolate

Mix butter and sugar in top of a double boiler. Add the chocolate and the milk. Cook over hot water for 30 minutes. DO NOT STIR!!
After cooking for 30 minutes, remove from heat and beat sauce til it is medium consistency. Store in refrigerator. When ready to serve, warm slightly and add cream if too thick.

BLENDER HOLLANDAISE SAUCE

3 egg yolks
1 stick of butter, not oleo
2 Tblsp lemon juice
3 drops of Tabasco

Place egg yolks, lemon juice and Tabasco in blender and whir on high for 30 seconds. Heat butter in small pan til bubbling hot but not burned. Remove small opening in lid of blender and VERY SLOWLY pour in hot butter while blender is on high. As you finish pouring, the sauce will be thick. Pour at once into a large drinking glass and cover loosely with a piece of wax paper. This sauce can be warmed by setting in a pan of medium hot water so you can make a large quantity ahead if you're serving Eggs Benedict to a big crowd.

This is great on fresh broccoli or green beans. Don't forget the paprika! If it gets too thick, add a little hot water and stir. Paprika dusted on top of Hollandaise is a must for eye appeal.

HAM SAUCE   Marge Spomer
To serve with Ham Loaf

1/2 cup tomato soup
1/2 cup prepared mustard
1/2 cup vinegar
1/2 cup sugar
1/2 cup butter
3 beaten egg yolks

Cook in double boiler until thickened and serve with ham loaf.

HOLLANDAISE SAUCE — Jane S. Peters

4 egg yolks
2 Tblsp lemon juice
salt and pepper
2 Tblsp heavy cream
dash of cayenne pepper
1 stick of cold butter

Put all ingredients except butter in top of a double boiler. Make sure the water in the bottom is simmering slowly. Stir the mixture with a wire whisk constantly until the eggs begin to thicken. Then add the butter a tablespoon at a time, melting each one before adding the next. When the butter is all absorbed, remove sauce from heat and serve. Makes 1 cup.

CHATEAUBRIANDE SAUCE — Grandma Wilcox

Cook together:
1 cup brown gravy or sauce Espagnole
1 cup white wine
When thick, add:
1/4 lb. of butter
3 Tblsp minced parsley
salt and pepper to taste
Beat well and serve when the butter is melted.

Doing our favorite thing -
SCHENCKS AND PETERS

LORD, Thou knowest that I am growing older.
Keep me from becoming talkative and possessed with the idea that I must express myself on every subject.
Release me from the craving to straighten out every one's affairs.
Keep my mind free from the recital of endless detail.
Give me wings to get to the point.
Seal my lips when I am inclined to tell of my aches and pains. They are increasing with the years and my love to speak of them grows sweeter as time goes by.
Teach me the glorious lesson that occasionally I may be wrong.
Make me thoughtful but not nosey -- helpful but not bossy.
Thou knowest, LORD, that I want a few friends at the end.

COME BACK BARBEQUE SAUCE

1 cup cider vinegar	3/4 cup catsup
1/2 cup water	1 tsp salt
3 Tblsp brown sugar	2 tsp paprika
2 Tblsp Worcestershire sauce	1 tsp dry mustard
2 cloves crushed garlic	1 cup red wine

Bring to a boil, stirring well.
Brown spare ribs in 450° oven, basting with of the sauce frequently. When brown, pour on the rest of the sauce, turn oven to 300° and cook ribs til tender.

HORSERADISH SAUCE for Ham

1/2 cup whipping cream	1/2 tsp lemon juice
1/4 cup mayonnaise	1/4 tsp seasoned salt
2 Tblsp prepared mustard	1/8 tsp salt
1 heaping Tblsp horseradish	1/8 tsp pepper
1/2 tsp Worcestershire sauce	

Beat cream til stiff and fold in rest of ingredients. Chill.

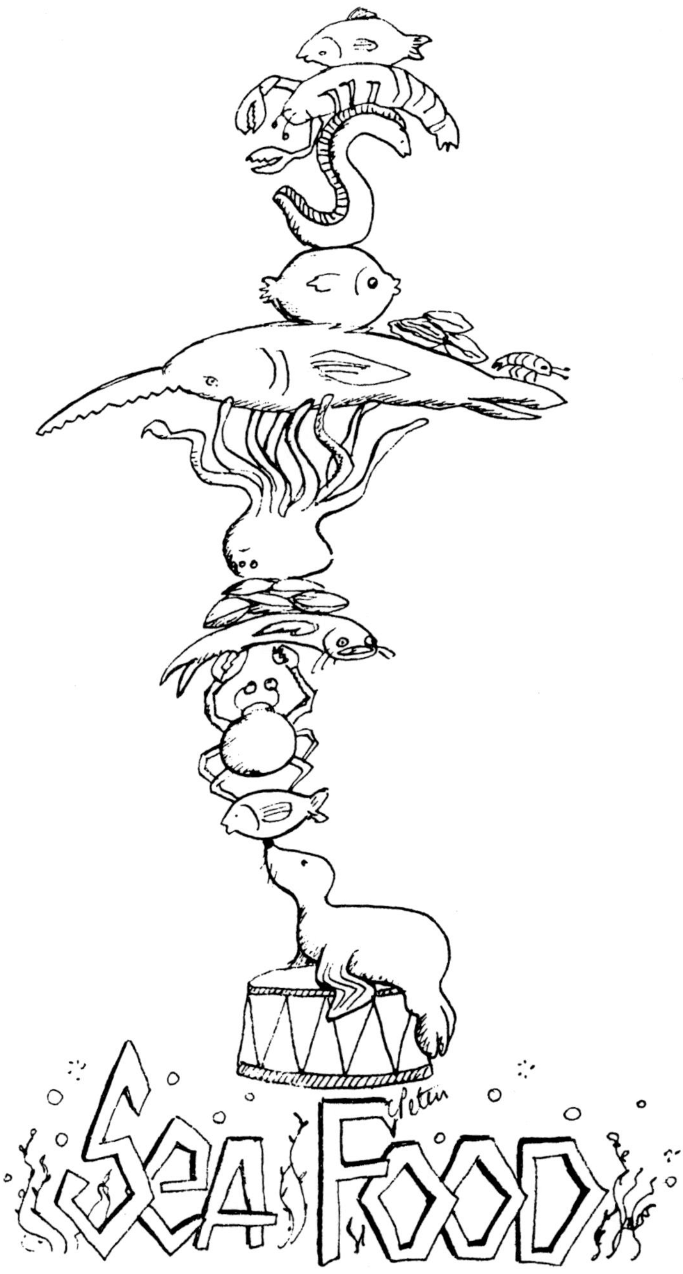
Sea Food
Peter

SEAFOOD

Beer Batter for Cubed Fish 285
Caribbean Lobster in Rum Cream Sauce... 279
Cold Crab Salad.. 280
Crispy Walleye Fillets.. 284
Fish Chowder.. 287
Gramma Dunnell's Crabmeat or Shrimp Soufflé 287
Lobster Newburg 287
Mousseline Poisson a la Marchal 280
Oysters Rockefeller.. 282
Paella.. 279
Plantagenet Fried Walleye 287
Real Maine Crab Cakes 285
Salmon Loaf 280
Scalloped Oysters 284
Seviche 281
Shrimp Creole... 288
Shrimp Creole without File'.. 285
Shrimp Jambalaya.. 286
Walnut-Stuffed Lemon Sole 288
White Fish Stock.. 287

CARRIBBEAN LOBSTER IN RUM CREAM SAUCE

12 oz. of lobster tail medallions, raw 2 oz. diced shallots
4 oz. sliced mushrooms   2 oz. melted butter
2 oz. whole butter   2 oz. GOOD Rum, golden
1/2 tsp of lemon juice, chopped parsley, salt, ground pepper
10 oz. heavy cream

Heat 2 oz. butter in pan and sear lobster. Remove from pan. Add shallots and mushrooms, sauté and deglaze with rum. Reduce to 1/2 oz. liquid. Add cream and reduce til creamy and smooth. Finish with lemon, butter, parsley, salt and pepper to taste.

❖ ❖ ❖ ❖ ❖ ❖ ❖ ❖ ❖

PAELLA   Louise Filbert

Mash **1 tsp oregano**
2 peppercorns
1 clove garlic
1/2 tsp salt
In **2 Tblsp olive oil** and **1 tsp vinegar**
After combining, rub into **1 or 1 1/2 chickens, cut into serving pieces.**
Then brown the chicken in
4 Tblsp olive oil
Add **2 oz. cooked ham, large chunks**
1 hot sausage, large chunks   **1 onion cut up**
1 green pepper, cut up   **1/2 tsp coriander**
Cook on low for 10 minutes and then add
3 Tblsp tomato sauce   **2 1/4 cup raw rice**
Cook this for 5 minutes and then add
1 tsp saffron and 4 cups boiling water
1 pound of shrimp, whole & shelled
Mix well and cook rapidly until liquid is absorbed. This takes about 20 minutes. Turn rice from top to bottom. Then **add 1 cup lobster meat** and **1 cup frozen green peas** and cook another 5 minutes.
Steam: **1 dozen clams**
Use the clams and a bottle of stuffed olives as garni. All you need is bread and salad.

COLD CRAB SALAD

2 cups canned crab meat
3/4 cup diced celery
4 green onions, chopped
1 Tblsp prepared mustard
1/4 cup sour cream
1/4 cup minced parsley
1/4 cup mayonnaise
1 Tblsp lemon juice
seasoned salt to taste
2 Tblsp toasted slivered almonds

Fold mayonnaise, mustard, lemon juice and sour cream together and toss lightly with the rest of the ingredients. Serve on a bed of lettuce greens with slender lemon zest curls. Sippets are very nice with this.

❖ ❖ ❖ ❖ ❖ ❖ ❖ ❖ ❖

SALMON LOAF

Combine in order given:
1/2 cup buttered bread crumbs
1 one pound can of salmon, bone and skin removed and drained
Dash of pepper
2 eggs, beaten
1/2 tsp sage
1/2 cup milk
2 tsp chopped onion
1 Tblsp chopped parsley
1 tsp lemon juice
1 Tblsp melted butter
1/2 tsp salt

Mix together and place in buttered loaf pan. Cook in 350° oven for 30 to 40 minutes.

❖ ❖ ❖ ❖ ❖ ❖ ❖ ❖ ❖

MOUSSELINE POISSON A LA MARCHAL

1 1/2 cups of ground fish, about 6 medium filets of pike or flounder or whiting
1 egg white, beaten
6 Tblsp of heavy cream
salt and pepper
1/8 tsp fresh nutmeg

Grind fish in Cuisinart and add egg white and cream until mixed. Roll patties of prepared raw fish in buttered bread crumbs and fry slowly in butter until light brown and moist. Simply delicious and a different way to serve fish.

FISH CHOWDER   Jane T. Peters

2 lbs. of fish (we use cod, haddock, roughy. Especially good with 1 lb. fish and 1 lb. scallops)

2 cups water	2 oz. salt pork, diced
2 onions, sliced	4 large potatoes, peeled and diced
1 cup celery, chopped	1 bay leaf, crumbled
1 quart whole milk	2 Tblsp butter
Salt, pepper to taste	

Simmer fish in water for 15 minutes. Drain and reserve broth. Remove bones from fish and cut into small chunks. Sauté salt pork until crisp. Sauté onions in pork fat. Add this to broth. Also add fish, potatoes, celery, bay leaf, salt and pepper, milk and butter. Simmer about 30 minutes. Garnish with diced salt pork. *6 Servings.*

SEVICHE

1 lb. raw scallops	2 tsp prepared mustard
1/3 cup fresh lime juice	1/2 cup chopped onion
1/2 tsp salt	1 hot red pepper, chopped
1/2 tsp Accent	

Put raw scallops in colander and pour boiling water over them and then drain on paper towels well. Put scallops in bowl and add rest of ingredients. Let stand 4 hours but stir occasionally to marinate. Drain well and serve as first course.

LOBSTER NEWBURG

Give me this and a glass of champagne and I'll say yes to anything - this is a New England recipe and is perfect.

2 cups cold boiled lobster meat, cut into chunky pieces.
Melt 1/4 cup butter, add lobster and sauté for 1 minute, tossing lightly.
Pour **over 1/4 cup dry sherry**
Let stand while making heavy cream sauce in a large double boiler.

3 Tblsp flour	1 cup heavy cream
1/2 tsp salt	pinch of cayenne
1/4 tsp paprika	

Add lobster to cream sauce and cook in double boiler 10 to 15 minutes. Cool. Chill in refrigerator for 24 hours. Heat before serving. WOW!

Aunt Jane and Uncle Pete Peters came home from New Orleans with this recipe. They prepared OYSTERS ROCKEFELLER for Easter dinner for all the adults, while the little children had Shoe Box lunches. In fact, little Mark met Gere at the front door when we arrived and boasted, "We have BOX LUNCHES, and we get to take them down to the creek WITHOUT OUR MOMS!"

I thought is was one of the really great Easter parties. The recipe for the oysters is perfect and none other will do.

Jane's mother, Irene Savidge was a great cook and it is obviously genetic in the family. Jane's gift also lies in presentation, plus the knack of organization. This art allows her to be with her guests - a feat that needs to be mastered by all hostesses.

OYSTERS ROCKEFELLER

1 cup chopped shallots
1/2 cup chopped parsley
1/4 cup minced anchovy
1/2 tsp salt
1 cup oyster liquor
1/4 cup flour
4 oz. PERNOD liqueur

1 1/2 cup chopped spinach (you may use frozen spinach, but drain WELL)
2 cloves chopped garlic
1/4 tsp cayenne
3 to 4 dozen oysters
1 cup melted butter

Fill a jelly roll pan with a layer of rock salt to preheat in a 400° oven. Stir flour into butter and cook CAREFULLY for five minutes - do not brown this mixture. Then add all the rest of the ingredients EXCEPT the Pernod and the Oysters. Simmer covered for 20 minutes. Stir in the Pernod & cook til thickened. Place 3 to 4 oysters on scallop shells & cover with spinach sauce. Place on the rock salt pan & bake in 400° oven for about 5 minutes or until bubbly. Serve with French Bread.

GRANDPA REPLIES
(in response to an article entitled "Never Strike Your Child in Anger")
by Tom Byrnes

Never strike your child in anger,
Never hit him when irate,
But save it for some happy time,
When both are feeling great.
Save it for some pleasant bedtime,
And as you tuck him in his crib,
Clench your fist and let him have it,
Or better, choke him with his bib.
Or wait until a Sunday morning,
Try to catch him at his prayers,
And as he whispers, "Dod bwess Dada,"
Kick him neatly down the stairs.
Or how about a Happy Birthday,
When friends and laughter fill the house,
Then bash him with a cake you've lettered,
"Greetings to a little louse."
Or how about a family outing,
A Sunday morning at the zoo,
And when it's time to feed the lions,
Supplement with you-know-who.
Or take him with you on an airplane,
The family plan's the cheapest way,
And when it reaches cruising level,
Tell him, "Go outside and play."
Although he breaks a Wedgwood platter,
Spills your bourbon on the floor,
Never strike your child in anger,
It isn't civilized anymore.
It makes the child feel insecure,
When parents strike or even shove,
But you can do him in completely,
As long as it is done with love.

Your temper is one of the few things that will improve the longer you keep it!

SCALLOPED OYSTERS   Irene Peters

1 quart of oysters, drained	3/4 cup of oyster liquor
1/2 cup butter	2 Tblsp flour
1 tsp salt, scant	1/8 tsp pepper
2 Tblsp minced green pepper	2 Tblsp minced onion
small clove of garlic, pressed	1 Tblsp lemon juice

1 tsp Worcestershire sauce
1 1/4 cup finely crushed soda cracker crumbs

Warm oysters in liquor over low heat. Then melt butter, blend in flour and add remaining ingredients except for 1/4 cup of cracker crumbs. Turn into the mixture the oysters and the liquor. Put in greased shallow baking dish, sprinkle with 1/4 cup cracker crumbs, bake at 375° for 20 minutes or so til golden brown and bubbly.

day's catch of Walleyes from Lake of the Woods in Canada -- Peters family with Grandma Jer and Raymond Eaglefeather

CRISPY WALLEYE FILLETS   John Peters, Jr.

Cut walleye fillets into smaller pieces.
Beat 2 eggs and a small amount of beer in a bowl. Dry filets with paper towels and coat with egg mixture.
In a plastic bag, combine
1 cup pancake mix   **1/4 cup cornmeal**
lemon pepper to taste
Dredge fillets in flour mixture and fry in hot oil til brown.

SHRIMP CREOLE without File´

2 lbs peeled shrimp	1 bay leaf
1/4 cup butter	1/2 cup chopped onion
1/2 cup chopped celery	1 large sprig parsley
1/3 cup chopped green pepper	1 1/2 tsp salt
2 1/2 cups canned chopped tomatoes	1 tsp sugar
3/4 tsp Worcestershire sauce	1/4 tsp fresh ground pepper
3 drops Tabasco sauce	2 Tblsp flour

Melt butter in skillet and add onion, celery and green pepper, cooking until tender. Blend in flour and add tomatoes, stirring constantly. Add rest of ingredients EXCEPT shrimp, and simmer 30 minutes. Remove bay leaf and parsley and add shrimp and cook over low heat until heated thoroughly and shrimp are firm. Serve over hot rice. *Serves 6.*

BEER BATTER FOR CUBED FISH

Mix with a beater

3/4 cup flour	1 egg
1/2 tsp baking powder	1/2 can of beer
1/2 tsp salt	

Cut fish in 1 1/2" cubes, DO NOT SALT FISH, dip in batter and fry in deep fat at 375° til brown.

REAL MAINE CRAB CAKES
Get your scallop shells out

2 cups fresh crab meat	2 hard boiled eggs, chopped well
1 tsp grated onion	1 tsp chopped parsley
2 tsp lemon juice	1/2 tsp dry mustard
3 tsp sherry (dry, not sweet)	1 cup buttered bread crumbs (Leave some for topping)

Mix all ingredients together and place in scallop shells that have been greased. Top with bread crumbs and bake at 400° for 15 minutes.

❖ ❖ ❖ ❖ ❖ ❖ ❖ ❖ ❖

SHRIMP JAMBALAYA

Doug and I were in New Orleans and went to a fish market so that we could bring home 10 pounds of frozen shrimp on the airplane. What a terrible time at security in the airport! Though we insisted they were shrimp for a dinner party, guards began to unwrap the box until the smell hit their nostrils. We made it home just in time to prepare this great shrimp dish for our guests (whew!).

To prepare frozen or fresh shrimp in their shells: In a large pan add the following:

4 cups water   **1 1/2 lbs fresh shrimp in shells**
1 tsp seafood seasoning   **2 tsp salt**
1 slice of onion   **1/2 cup celery leaves**
2 Tblsp vinegar

Bring to boiling, add shrimp and return to boiling. Cook about 3 minutes until shrimp turn pink. Drain and peel under cold water.
In another large pot, cook the following:

1/2 cup chopped onion   **1/2 cup chopped celery**
1 clove garlic, chopped   **1/4 cup butter**
1 16 oz. can tomatoes, cut up   **One 1 oz. can tomato paste**
1 tsp sugar   **1 tsp Worcestershire sauce**
1/2 tsp seafood seasoning
Several dashes of Tabasco
1 cup sliced mushrooms, fresh
1 tsp file' powder - you can usually find this in a seafood market. It is crushed sassafras leaves and its thickening and flavor is very essential to a good gumbo or jambalaya. ADD JUST BEFORE SERVING!
Cook raw vegetables in butter til tender and then add rest of ingredients plus **1 1/2 cups water**   **1/2 tsp salt**
Simmer covered for 30 minutes. Add shrimp and heat all thoroughly. Serve over rice.

FROZEN LEMON JUICE: Buy lemons on sale, usually a little overripe; squeeze the juice out of them and freeze in ice cube trays. After freezing, empty the cubes into a freezer bag for fast use when you need them.

TO LIGHT CANDLES IN DEEP CONTAINERS:
Use a long piece of lit spaghetti

WHITE FISH STOCK

1 lb. bones and trimmings of any white fish such as sole, flounder, or whiting, chopped
1 cup sliced onion
2 Tblsp fresh lemon juice
12 parsley sprigs
1/2 cup dry white wine
1/2 tsp salt

In a well-buttered heavy saucepan, combine the fish bones and trimmings, the onion, the parsley, the lemon juice, and the salt and steam the mixture, covered, over moderately high heat for 5 minutes. Add 3 1/2 cups cold water and the wine, bring the liquid to a boil, skimming the froth, and cook the stock over moderate heat for 25 minutes. Strain the stock through a fine sieve into a bowl, pressing hard on the solids, and let it cool. The stock may be frozen. Makes about 3 cups.

PLANTAGENET FRIED WALLEYE

Cut walleye fillets into serving size pieces, wash and pat dry. On medium high heat, melt **1/4 cup bacon grease and 1/2 stick butter** in skillet. Crush **1/2 box of real soda crackers** to fine ground and put into pie tin. **Beat 2 eggs with 1 Tblsp water** in another pie tin. Dip dried fish in egg wash and coat on both sides. Then dip fish into soda crackers crumbs and put in hot grease.

Fry til nicely browned on both sides and serve quickly with Fish sauce, the recipe for which you will find in another chapter. You will need to add more butter and bacon grease as you continue to fry the fillets.

GRAMMA DUNNELL'S CRABMEAT OR SHRIMP SOUFFLE

8 slices of bread, cubed
1/2 cup mayonnaise
2 cans of crabmeat, drained and picked over
1 cup chopped onion
1 can Cream of Mushroom soup
1 cup chopped celery
grated Cheddar cheese
1 cup chopped green pepper
Paprika
3 cups whole milk
4 eggs
1 tsp salt

Put 1/2 of bread in greased 9 x 13 baking dish. Mix crab, mayonnaise, onion, pepper, and celery and spread over bread. Put remaining cubed bread over mixture. Beat eggs and milk and pour over mixture and place in refrigerator overnight. Bake in preheated 325° oven for 15 minutes. Remove from oven and pour over 1 can mushroom soup, add plenty of cheese and sprinkle with paprika. Bake 1 hour at 325°.
Serves 8

Don and Dode Stroy and Doug and I gave a series of dinner parties. This was the main course and they are very pretty and just delicious. Be sure that the sole is THIN so that the fillets roll well.

WALNUT-STUFFED LEMON SOLE

2 Tblsp butter or margarine	1 1/2 cups chopped mushrooms
2 Tblsp chopped onion	1/2 cup chopped toasted walnuts
1/4 cup parsley chopped	1/4 tsp salt & 1/8 tsp scant pepper
1/8 tsp dill weed	6 fillets of sole
juice of 1 lemon	Mornay sauce (See Sauces section)

Brown mushrooms and onion in butter and add walnuts, parsley & salt. Drizzle sole with lemon juice, dill, and pepper. Put spoonful of mushroom mixture on skin side of fish and roll up, put in greased baking dish and brush with butter. Bake 350° for 25 to 30 minutes. Top with Mornay sauce and a walnut half. (see sauce section).

SHRIMP CREOLE

Here's a recipe that will serve 40 and make a hero of the host

**12 lbs raw shrimp, cleaned
18 cups canned tomatoes, juice & pulp
8 green peppers, chopped
12 large onions, chopped
1 cup salad oil or preferably bacon drippings
12 cloves garlic, chopped
1 cup chopped parsley
1 Tblsp chili powder
6 cups chopped celery
6 Tblsp Worcestershire sauce
6 bay leaves
1 Tblsp sugar
salt and pepper to taste
3 tsp file´ powder - ADD JUST BEFORE SERVING**

Sauté onions, celery, garlic, peppers, and parsley in bacon drippings til tender. Add paste, tomatoes and 6 cups water and stir. Add remaining ingredients (EXCEPT SHRIMP AND FILE´) and let simmer slowly for one hour, stirring occasionally. Add shrimp and simmer for 20 minutes more. Remove from heat & stir in file powder. Serve on steamed rice.

SOUPS

SOUPS

Black Bean Soup...300
Bouillabaisse...298
Candlelight Bisque..298
Chasen's Famous Chili...300
Chicken Soup..295
Chilled Broccoli Soup...296
Cream of Peanut Soup 294
Easy Chili 295
Erdaepfelsuppe 293
Fourth of July Soup..299
Health Food Chili 291
Kansas City Steak Soup 292
Leek and Potato Soup 294
Mikey's Killer Chili..299
New England Clam Chowder...296
Onion Soup...291
Vichyssoise...297
U.S. Senate Bean Soup 292
Wild Rice Soup...297

ONION SOUP — Dr. A. T. Harvey

In a 4 quart saucepan place
5 cups thin sliced yellow onions   3 Tblsp butter
1 Tblsp oil
Cover and cook slowly for 15 minutes. Then stir in
1 tsp salt   1 tsp sugar
Cook uncovered for 30 to 40 minutes stirring frequently til onions have turned a deep golden brown. Then sprinkle in **3 Tblsp flour**, cook 3 minutes. Then add
1 quart boiling water
1 quart canned beef bouillon
1 cup Port wine
3 Tblsp cognac and simmer covered for 40 minutes.
Put rounds of hard toasted French bread in soup bowls. Pour in soup and pass **grated Swiss or Parmesan cheese.**

HEALTH FOOD CHILI — Warren A. Connell

2 lbs ground turkey   1 12 oz. can tomato sauce
4 #303 cans Kidney beans   4 tsp cumin
2 small green peppers, diced   6 tsp chili powder
2 cups white onions, diced   1/4 tsp black pepper
1 8 oz. can tomato paste   2 cans tomatoes, quartered
3/4 cup ground & pureed red chili peppers

Buy red chilies and deseed and destem them. Soak in warm water about 1 hour. Puree in blender and freeze leftovers.
Sauté turkey in Dutch oven with a little olive oil along with onion and green peppers. Drain and add beans and all the rest. Simmer over low heat about 1 1/2 hrs. Add a little water if too thick. Add black pepper. Spoon should stand upright in mixture. Serve with Tabasco sauce and chopped onions. Serves 8 people.

HARD BOILED EGGS THAT PEEL EASILY!
Set eggs into kettle and cover with cold water. Add a tsp of vinegar to water, and set pan on stove to boil. When eggs boil, remove pan from heat and cover tightly; let sit for at least 15 minutes. After 15 minutes, drain water from eggs and shake eggs in pan to crack shells. Run cold water over eggs, let cool and peel.

KANSAS CITY STEAK SOUP   Irene Peters

Make a roux of
1 stick butter or margarine
1 cup of flour and cook until tan.
Add **2 quarts of water** and blend.
Cook **1 lb. of ground beef** in a separate pan, drain grease from beef well, and add to liquid. In **one cup of water** parboil together:
1 cup diced onion
1 cup diced carrot
1 cup diced celery
When vegetables are cooked, puree in a Food Processor or Blender and return to the soup. Then add the following:

1 Tblsp MSG	**2 cups frozen Mixed Vegetables**
1 2 1/2 lb. can of tomatoes	**1 Tblsp Kitchen Bouquet**
1 tsp pepper	**Salt to taste**
1 Tblsp BV or Beef Concentrate	

Bring to a boil, then simmer.

This soup is better the second day. Serves 15.

❖ ❖ ❖ ❖ ❖ ❖ ❖ ❖ ❖

A good soup combination for a cold winter's day is Campbell's canned Chicken Gumbo & Clam Chowder

❖ ❖ ❖ ❖ ❖ ❖ ❖ ❖ ❖

U.S. SENATE BEAN SOUP
as served daily in the
U.S. Senate Cafeteria

Soak 1 pound white beans overnight in cold water and cover. Drain the beans and put them in a soup kettle with a ham bone that still has some meat on it and 3 quarts water. Bring the water to a boil and simmer the mixture for about 2 hours. Stir in 1 cup cooked mashed potatoes and add 3 onions, 1 small bunch of celery including the tops, and 2 garlic cloves, all finely chopped, and 1/4 cup chopped parsley. Simmer the soup for 1 hour longer, until the beans are thoroughly cooked. Remove the ham bone from the kettle, dice the meat on it, and return the meat to the soup.
Serves 6

ERDAEPFELSUPPE   Gitte Peters

50 g leeks
50 g celery   1/2 Tblsp thyme
50 g parsley roots   1/2 Tblsp caraway seeds
50 g carrots   2-4 bay leaves
1/2 Tblsp basil   3/4 liter water
1/2 Tblsp marjoram   200 g potatoes
40 g butter   1 Tblsp vinegar
30 g flour   1 tsp salt

Cut vegetables into small cubes, add herbs and water and simmer for 1/2 hour. Then add the potatoes, cut into cubes. Brown butter and flour and add to soup. Let cook for one more hour - low heat. Before serving add vinegar and salt.

This soup is served as a main course in Austria, with pumpernickel bread. Usually followed by apfelstrudel. Strange customs, eh???

Jim & Gitte on their Home Turf

> Ask, and it shall be given to you
> Seek, and ye shall find
> Knock and it shall be opened unto you.
> For every one that asketh, receiveth
> And he that seeketh, findeth
> And to him that knocketh
> It shall be opened!
> These are the words of Jesus Christ.
> Could anything inspire more HOPE?

The Good Doctor and Wife
A. T. & Carol Harvey

LEEK AND POTATO SOUP _____ Jane T. Peters

8 leeks - white & light green parts only
1 stick butter   **1 qt. water**
4 medium potatoes, peeled, diced **1 cup milk**
1 carrot, sliced thin   **salt & white pepper**
4 cups chicken broth   **chopped parsley**

Cut leeks in half lengthwise & then crosswise in 1 inch pieces. Simmer in butter about 10 minutes. Add potatoes, carrot, chicken broth and water. Season with salt & pepper. Cook over low heat until potatoes can be mashed easily against sides of pan. Let cool slightly and put through blender. Return to stove. Stir in scant cup of milk. Taste. Garnish with chopped parsley.

CREAM OF PEANUT SOUP _____ Williamsburg, VA

1 Tblsp butter   **3 Tblsp peanut butter**
1 tsp minced onion   **2 Tblsp flour**
2 cups scalded milk OR 2 cups milk & 1 cup chicken stock
salt & pepper to taste

Cook onions in butter & peanut butter for 5 minutes. Add flour & stir until smooth. Add milk and season. Cook over a double boiler for 15 to 20 minutes. You may add chopped peanuts also.

❖ ❖ ❖ ❖ ❖ ❖ ❖ ❖ ❖

A smile is a light in the window of your face to
show your heart is at home.

CHICKEN SOUP   Mary Peters

If anyone is "under the weather," a quart of this elixir is as welcome as a large bouquet. It is guaranteed to cure the difficult cases.

5 or 6 pounds of Chicken, cut up	1 stalk celery
2 or 3 Veal bones	1 carrot
6 to 7 cups of water	2 to 3 sprigs parsley
1 onion	A pinch of thyme and nutmeg

Put all ingredients in a soup pot and cook three hours. Remove chicken and cook soup 1 1/2 hours longer. Strain soup and you can add chopped chicken, rice or noodles; whatever the patient can stand. ADD THE SALT TO TASTE AT THE END, keeping in mind the condition of the afflicted.

TRIUMPHS WE HAVE KNOWN & LOVED

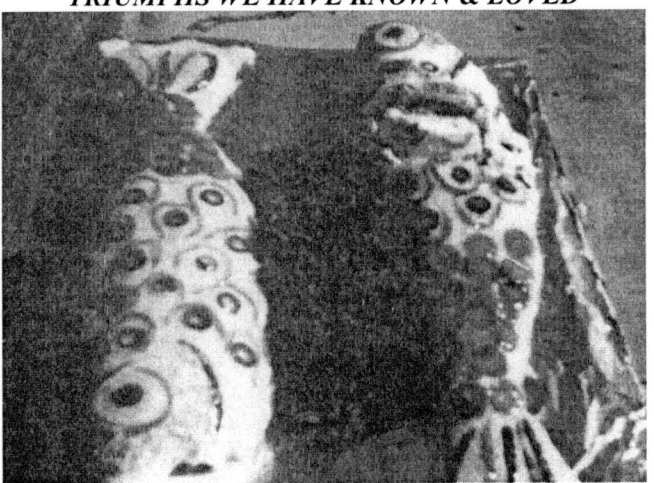

Salmon Chaud-froid

EASY CHILI   Johnny Peters

1 lb. ground beef	2 tsp chili powder
3/4 cup chopped green pepper	1 bay leaf
1 lb. can stewed tomatoes	1 tsp salt
1 cup chopped onion	1 lb. can chili beans in sauce
1 8-oz. can tomato sauce	Picante sauce if desired

Brown meat with onions, green pepper. Stir in remaining ingredients, cover and simmer one hour.

NEW ENGLAND CLAM CHOWDER
Makes 1 gallon

8 thin slices of salt pork
1 stick of butter
3 cups diced onions
6 cups cubed peeled potatoes
4 cups clam juice (bottled)
3 cups chopped clams
1 pint light cream
1/2 cup flour

In a large pot gently sauté salt pork til rendered. Remove pork and add butter over low heat. When bubbly, add onions; sauté til transparent. Add potatoes; cook about 5 minutes, stirring. Add flour, stirring well for 3 minutes. Add clam juice and cook till potatoes are tender. Add clams and cream and heat through; DO NOT BOIL.

CHILLED BROCCOLI SOUP   Irene Peters

1/3 cup margarine
1 cup sliced green onions
1 clove garlic, minced
3 cups sliced broccoli
1 cup water
1/2 tsp salt and fresh ground pepper
4 cups whole milk
2 Tblsp cornstarch
1/4 cup dry vermouth
2 cubes chicken bouillon

1/2 cup finely chopped green onion for garnish

In a 3 quart saucepan, melt butter. Sauté onion and garlic 5 minutes. Add broccoli and sauté for 10 minutes, or til soft. Add water, bouillon, salt and pepper. Cover and simmer for 15 minutes. Then put in a blender a little at a time and blend about 30 seconds. Return all to saucepan. Stir milk into cornstarch and add to saucepan. Stir constantly and bring to a boil. Stir in wine. Chill in refrigerator several hours. Serve with chopped onion garnee. Can make this same soup using zucchini instead.

WILD RICE SOUP   Dorothy Naramore

Fry **6 slices of bacon** til crisp; cool and crumble.
In **1/4 lb of butter,**
sauté **1 medium onion, chopped**
1/2 lb mushrooms sliced thin
1/2 cup celery sliced thin
Mix in **1/2 cup of flour** to vegetables and gradually add
6 cups of chicken broth
Stir 5 to 8 minutes til slightly thickened. Then add
2 cups COOKED wild rice

1/2 tsp salt	**1/2 tsp curry powder**
1/2 tsp dry mustard	**1/4 cup butter**
1/2 tsp chervil	**1/4 tsp pepper**
2 cups half & half cream	**2/3 cup dry sherry**

Simmer on low heat about 1/2 hour and DO NOT BOIL.
Add bacon, and parsley or chives before serving.

❖ ❖ ❖ ❖ ❖ ❖ ❖ ❖ ❖

VICCHYSSOISE_____ from the famous SARDI'S in New York

1 medium onion, chopped	**1/4 tsp white pepper**
1 cup of leeks, washed carefully	**2 Tblsp salt**
** and sliced fine**	**4 cups chicken broth**
5 large potatoes washed, peeled	**1/2 bay leaf**
** and sliced fine**	

Put vegetables in a large saucepan with all the spices and broth and bring to a boil, simmer for 15 minutes covered and 30 minutes uncovered.
Remove from stove and beat contents til fairly smooth. Cool this in the refrigerator overnight.

1/2 cup dry sherry wine	**2 1/2 cups light cream**
1/4 tsp celery salt	**1 tsp monosodium glutamate**
1/4 tsp salt, additional	**Chopped chives**

Boil the sherry with the celery salt, salt, and msg. Cool this liquid quickly and stir into cold potato mixture. Add 2 1/2 cups light cream and whirl this all in the blender. Serve cold with a sprinkling of chopped chives.

BOULLIBAISE _____ Doug Peters

1/2 cup olive oil	1/2 tsp thyme
4 cups sliced onion	1 piece of orange peel 2" x 1"

Cook onion 5 minutes in olive oil, covered. Add:

6 cups tomatoes, chopped coarse	4 to 5 garlic cloves
1 Tblsp fennel seeds	2 pinches of saffron
2 1/2 quarts of water	1 Tblsp salt
1 quart clam juice	2 Tblsp fresh parsley

Cook together for 40 to 50 minutes uncovered in a large soup kettle. One half hour before serving, put all trimmings from the fish (head, body bones, etc.) into stock and cook. After 1/2 hour, strain the stock and add fish as here listed:
1st: Bass, halibut and lobster - cook 5 minutes
2nd: Scallops, shrimp, flounder, pollack, striped bass and cook another 5 min.
Count on cooking a frozen lobster tail 1/2 hour. If scallops and shrimp are frozen, count on cooking for 20 minutes.
Serve in large bowls with crunchy hot French bread and a nice bottle of Reisling.

CANDLELIGHT BISQUE _____ Mynn Peterson

For 6 bowls of soup; mix and heat

2 cans Mushroom soup	1 chopped onion
2 cans Tomato soup	1 pound crab or lobster meat
1 1/2 soup cans of whole milk	1/3 cup sherry or lemon juice
2 Tblsp chopped parsley	

Just before serving, top with a dollop of sour cream.

❖ ❖ ❖ ❖ ❖ ❖ ❖ ❖ ❖

*The secret of life is not to do what one likes -
But to try to LIKE what one has to do*

FOURTH OF JULY SOUP
Malcolm D. Peters
for lots and lots of people at the Platte River

Take 1 large wash tub of water.
Add friendly advice of cousins and brothers on how to make a Surprise Soup none will forget.
Add advise of Poppo "NOT TO WRECK NEW TUB!!!"
Add "Mr. Gullible" Jimmy with wax-covered M-80 soup helper.
Put soup helper into water and light fuse.
Let soup cook 15 seconds.
After soup helper splits seams of new tub and thorough mixing occurs, let Poppo find spoon and test fast-moving soup.
After soup runs from tub to ground, try to find other helpers than Chef Jimmy to share in the joy!
Alas, no one wants to steal the limelight from the Chef. Isn't that special! What a great group of cook's helpers.
Then let Jimmy and Poppo discuss NEW ways to cook soup other than in new wash tub.
Maybe yelling and hollering DOES make soup taste better.
I guess Poppo thinks so.

❖ ❖ ❖ ❖ ❖ ❖ ❖ ❖ ❖

MIKEY'S KILLER CHILI
Johnny Peters

3 lbs pork cubed
3 lbs beef cubed
6 oz tomato paste
2 cans chili beans with sauce

1 cup chopped green pepper
3 cup onion, chopped
20 oz stewed tomatoes
Mushrooms, if desired

In sauce pan mix together:
2 cups water
1 Tblsp sugar
2 Tblsp cumin
1 Tblsp celery salt
2 Tblsp M S G
1 tsp garlic powder

1 beef bouillon cube
2 tsp oregano
2 Tblsp paprika
5 Tblsp chili powder
1 tsp cayenne pepper
1/2 tsp cocoa

BROWN: Beef, pork, onion and green pepper. Add remaining ingredients and mixture from sauce pan. Makes 6 quarts. KEEP ICE WATER HANDY!!

BLACK BEAN SOUP _____ Jane T. Peters

- 1 cup dried black beans
- 1/2 tsp baking soda
- 4 pints water
- 2 Tblsp BV concentrate
- 2 stalks chopped celery
- 1/2 lb. cubed ham
- 1 Tblsp chopped parsley
- 1 tsp coarse ground pepper
- 1 tsp paprika
- 2 med. onion chopped
- 1 green pepper chopped
- 1 clove garlic crushed
- 1/3 lb. salt pork
- 1 c. Chianti/or dry red wine
- 6 - 8 lemon slices
- 2 hard boiled eggs
- 1 bay leaf

Wash beans!!! Soak overnight in water with baking soda added. Wash beans AGAIN!!! Drain. In large pot put beans, water, BV, celery, ham, parsley, pepper and paprika. Brown onion, green pepper, garlic and salt pork over low heat. Empty these ingredients into pot with beans, etc. Simmer about 4 hours. Cool to luke warm and put through blender in batches. Return to stove and add wine - heat but do not boil. Garnish with lemon slice & grated egg. Even better on 2nd - 3rd day. *Feeds 6 - 8 regular people.*

CHASEN'S FAMOUS CHILI _____

From Chasen's Restaurant in Los Angeles, this tasty chili was flown across country to please the palate of movie queen Elizabeth Taylor.

8 oz. pinto beans

Place in a pan with water two inches above surface of beans to soak overnight. Simmer until tender next day.

5 cups canned tomatoes

Add tomatoes to beans and simmer for 5 more minutes.

1 pound of green peppers, chopped   **1 1/2 pounds onion, chopped**
2 buds garlic, pressed   **1/2 cup chopped parsley**
1 1/2 Tblsp salad oil

In oil, sauté garlic, green peppers and onion til soft and add parsley. Vegetables are then added to beans and tomatoes.

1/2 cup butter   **2 1/2 pounds hamburger**
1 pound pork, ground

Sauté meats in butter until cooked and add

1/3 cup chili powder   **2 Tblsp salt**
1 1/2 tsp pepper   **1 1/2 tsp cumin seed**
1 1/2 tsp monosodium glutamate

Add meat and spice mixture to vegetables and beans and simmer the chili for 1 hour covered and for 30 minutes uncovered. Skim fat. Makes about 4 quarts.

VEGETABLES

good ones

mushroom kids · mr. onion · mr. broccoli · miss green pepper · mr. celery · mrs. pea · mr. corn · miss carrot · mr. potato · mrs. bean

maybe...

the zucchini

bad ones

mr. eggplant · mr. brussels sprout · mrs. rutabaga

VEGETABLES

Baked Cauliflower	311
Baked Lima Beans	307
Broccoli Cheese Casserole	306
Cantonese Vegetables	303
Carrot Cauliflower Pie	303
Carrot Soufflé	304
Cold Green Beans	314
Egg Plant Parmigiana	314
Famous Corn Casserole	313
Garlic Spinach	304
Herbed Spinach Bake	306
Karfiol Gratiniert	305
Minted Carrots	315
Party Broccoli Casserole	307
Party Green Bean Casserole	310
Peppy Lima Beans	312
Simple Cabbage	307
Spinach Stuffed Zucchini	310
Spinach-Mushroom	312
Three Vegetables Latkes	306
Tomato Pudding	309
Twice Baked Potatoes	311
Vegetable Casserole Mendenhall	305
Zucchini Patties	304
Zucchini with Shrimps	312

CANTONESE VEGETABLES   Joyce Pogge

1 can water chestnuts
1 box frozen Italian green beans
1 lb. fresh mushrooms, sliced
1 cup celery, cut on diagonal 1"
1 green pepper, sliced
1 jar pimento, sliced

1 cup chicken stock
1/4 cup cooking oil
2 Tblsp cornstarch
1/4 tsp garlic salt
1 1/2 tsp salt
1 package SLICED almonds

Simmer thawed beans in oil with celery & green pepper, covered, for 10 minutes. Add seasonings, mushrooms, water chestnuts, pimento, 1/2 the almonds and chicken stock into which has been stirred the cornstarch; cook til hot. Turn into greased casserole and heat at 350 degrees. When ready to serve, top with other 1/2 of almonds.

❖ ❖ ❖ ❖ ❖ ❖ ❖ ❖ ❖

CARROT CAULIFLOWER PIE

Pulverize **2 cups of Herb Seasoned Croutons** and mix with **1/4 cup melted butter** and press into a 9 inch pie plate. Bake at 375° for 8 to 10 minutes.
In a sauté pan cook for 5 minutes:
1 cup chopped onion
1 clove garlic, chopped
2 Tblsp butter
Then add the following ingredients:
1/2 tsp savory
1/2 tsp oregano
1/4 tsp salt and fresh ground pepper
4 cups of cauliflower florets
1/2 cup sliced carrots
Cook low for 10 or 15 minutes
Then sprinkle on cooled pie shell **3/4 cup grated cheddar cheese.** Add the vegetables.
Beat **2 eggs** with **1/4 cup milk** and add to vegetables. Add **3/4 cup additional cheddar cheese** over the top of casserole. Bake at 375° for 15 minutes more or til set.
Serves 6 to 8

ZUCCHINI PATTIES — Irene Peters

3 1/2 cups grated zucchini
3 Tblsp onion, grated
2 Tblsp parsley, minced
1/3 cup grated Parmesan cheese
1 cup soft bread crumbs
2 eggs, well beaten
1/4 tsp pepper
3/4 tsp salt

After grating zucchini, squeeze as much liquid out as possible with hands. Combine all ingredients and shape into patties.
Coat with additional bread crumbs and brush with melted butter. Bake at 350° for 30 to 40 minutes or you can fry them in a skillet with butter if you prefer.

CARROT SOUFFLE — Grandma Esther Wilcox

2 bunches of carrots (about 10)
4 egg yolks
4 egg whites
5 tblsp butter
5 tblsp flour
5 tblsp milk
fresh ground nutmeg

Wash and cook carrots until soft and grind fine in a cuisinart. Mix the 4 egg yolks with the ground carrots and salt to taste. Beat well.
Carefully make a cream sauce of the butter, flour and milk. Fold into the carrot-egg mixture. Fold in the 4 beaten egg whites. Rinse the mold with water before turning in the soufflé mixture and place mold in a pan of warm water in the oven. Bake 3/4 of an hour at 300° oven. Remove from mold immediately.

GARLIC SPINACH

1 cup chopped onion
1/4 cup margarine
5 packages thawed chopped spinach, squeezed dry
1 cup milk
1/2 cup grated Parmesan cheese
1 tsp crushed marjoram
2 cloves chopped garlic
1 cup heavy cream
1 tsp salt
1/4 tsp pepper
1/2 cup bread crumbs

Sauté garlic & onion in margarine and combine all ingredients except for 1/4 cup of Parmesan. Place in 2 quart baking dish, greased, and sprinkle with 1/4 cup Parmesan and bake 30 minutes at 350° until cheese browns on top.

KARFIOL GRATINIERT   Gitte Peters

1 cauliflower
20 dkg butter
breadcrumbs, plain

Clean, separate and cook cauliflower in light saltwater; drain, pour melted butter over cauliflower and sprinkle breadcrumbs on top. Bake 4 - 7 minutes in oven.

Usually served with any kind of meat dish as vegetable. I always ate it as my main course with green tomato and cucumber salad.

❖ ❖ ❖ ❖ ❖ ❖ ❖ ❖ ❖

VEGETABLE CASSEROLE MENDENHALL

This is a great recipe that you must use in July when the following vegetables are in all the fresh-air markets and are jumping with color and flavor. Almost like a fritatta, it can be used as a one-dish meal with hot bread. Simply delicious.

Slice **6 unpeeled zucchini (cucumber size).** Brown in a bit of **olive oil** and set aside.
Peel and slice **2 small eggplants** and parboil for 4 minutes. Pat dry with paper towels.

In a greased 9 x 13 casserole, alternate **two** layers of the following:
Zucchini
Onion rings - 2 medium, sliced thin
Eggplant
Green Pepper - 2 medium, sliced thin
Tomatoes - 6 medium, sliced and skin removed
Salt each layer and sprinkle with **Parmesan or Romano cheese** very generously.
Beat together **3 eggs** and pour over casserole. Sprinkle with **buttered bread crumbs** and dot with butter. Bake for 40 minutes at 350° with casserole covered for the first half of the baking period.

HERBED SPINACH BAKE   Jane S. Peters

Cook and drain **1 10 oz. package of frozen, chopped spinach.** Mix with **1 cup cooked rice, 1 cup shredded sharp process American cheese, 2 slightly beaten eggs, 2 Tblsp soft butter or margarine, 1/3 cup milk, 2 Tblsp chopped onion, 1/2 tsp Worcestershire sauce, 1 tsp salt and 1/4 tsp rosemary or thyme, crushed.**
Pour mixture into 10 x 6 x 2 baking dish. Bake in 350° oven for 20 to 25 minutes til knife comes out clean. Cut into squares.
Makes 6 servings

THREE VEGETABLES LATKES

1 cup of potatoes, peeled and shredded
(immerse in water to keep from discoloring)
2 1/2 cup shredded & peeled zucchini
1/2 tsp salt
1 cup carrots, shredded & peeled
1/8 tsp pepper
1/2 cup onion, chopped or shredded
3/4 cup Matzo meal
1/2 cup chopped parsley

Take potatoes from water, pat dry, mix with all other ingredients. Shape into 2 Tblsp cakes and fry for 1 1/2 minutes per side in oil in frying pan.
Can do ahead and warm latkes at 350° for 8 to 10 minutes.

BROCCOLI CHEESE CASSEROLE

Line a 12 x 7 casserole with one layer of **broccoli spears** that have been pre-cooked until just barely tender - about 1 1/2 pounds.
Mix together:

2 eggs	**2 Tblsp chopped onion**
3/4 cup cottage cheese	**1 tsp Worcestershire sauce**
1/2 cup grated cheddar	**1/2 tsp salt**
1/8 tsp pepper	

Pour this mixture over the broccoli spears and top with **1/3 cup bread crumbs** that have been mixed with **2 Tblsp melted butter.** Bake at 350° for 20 minutes or longer, until mixture is set.

SIMPLE CABBAGE

1 small head of cabbage, sliced
1 medium onion, sliced
Stir fry this in oil over low heat in fry pan til limp and translucent.
Add **salt, pepper, about 1 Tblsp sugar and 1 tsp of caraway seed**
At the end, add **1/3 cup of heavy cream** and heat through.

BAKED LIMA BEANS   Jane T. Peters

4 cup dried lima beans	1 Tblsp salt
1 lb. thickly sliced bacon, diced	1 tsp pepper
6 Tblsp brown sugar	1 1/4 cup boiling water
1 Tblsp dry mustard	6 Tblsp molasses

Cover beans with cold water. Soak overnight. Drain well. Cover again with cold water and bring to a boil. Reduce heat and simmer until tender, about 40 minutes. Drain well.
Preheat oven to 250°. Transfer beans to 3 qt. pot, add bacon and stir gently. Combine next 5 ingredients with 1/4 cup boiling water and blend well. Stir in molasses. Pour over beans & then add 1 cup boiling water. Cover and bake 2 - 3 hours. Stir thoroughly several times. Increase heat to 300° & bake about 1 more hour. Add more boiling water if beans seem dry.

PARTY BROCCOLI CASSEROLE

This is for a big bunch of people - think about this one when it's your turn to take the vegetable to Thanksgiving dinner.

Sauté **2 large, chopped onions** in
1 stick of butter
Add **6 packages of unfrozen chopped broccoli** and cook until tender.
Add **4 cans Cream of Mushroom soup**
3 rolls garlic cheese, chopped in pieces
1 large can mushrooms
2 tsp MSG
3/4 cup sliced or slivered almonds
Put all ingredients in a large buttered casserole and sprinkle over top:
1/4 cup sliced almonds
1 cup bread crumbs
Bake about 45 minutes at 350° until bubbly.
Serves 15

NEW SICK LEAVE POLICY

Sickness: No excuse. We will no longer accept your doctor's statement as proof, as we believe that if you are able to go to the doctor, you are able to come to work.

Leave of Absence (For an Operation): We are no longer allowing this practice. We wish to discourage any thought that you may have about needing an operation. We believe that as long as you are employed here, you will need all of whatever you have and should not consider having anything removed. We hired you as you are and to have anything removed would certainly make you less than we bargained for.

Rest Rooms: Too much time is being spent in the Rest Room. In the future, we will follow the practice of going to the Rest Room in alphabetical order. For instance, those whose names begin with 'A' will go from 8:00 a.m. to 8:05 a.m., 'B' will go from 8:05 a.m. to 8:10 a.m., and so on. If you are unable to go at your time, it will be necessary to wait until the day when your turn comes again.

Death (Other Than Your Own): This is no excuse. There is nothing you can do for them, and we are sure that someone else in a lesser position can attend to the arrangements. However, if the funeral can be held in late afternoon, we will be glad to let you off one hour early, provided that your share of work is ahead enough to keep the job going in your absence.

Death (Your Own): This will be accepted as an excuse, but we would like a two-week notice, as we feel it is your duty to teach someone else your job.

JEFF, ANDY AND JAKE

I notice that as the recipes from the kiddies come in for publication, there seems to be some trouble with vegetable acceptance. I can't think of a vegetarian in the group, yet we are talking about the food that is BEST for you. Let us strive for quality control in our diets and give this chapter of the book deep consideration when planning menus! Because if you don't eat your vegetables, you won't get any dessert!

TOMATO PUDDING _____

Cut crusts off **8 slices of bread** and dice bread to make 2 generous cups of cubes. Put in 1 quart casserole.
Melt **1 stick of butter** and add
1 cup brown sugar   **1 - 6 oz. can tomato paste**
1/4 tsp salt   **1 - 6 oz. can cold water**
Mix together and pour over the bread cubes being sure they are all covered. Bake 35 minutes at 375°, uncovered.

PARTY GREEN BEAN CASSEROLE

1/2 lb fresh sliced mushrooms
1 medium onion, chopped
Sauté mushroom and onions in
1 stick of butter
Then add
1/4 cup flour
2 cups whole milk
1 cup light cream
3/4 lb. sharp cheddar cheese, diced
1/8 tsp Tabasco
1 tsp salt
2 tsp soy sauce
1 tsp MSG
Simmer until cheese melts. Cook **5 packages green beans** and add to sauce along with **1 5 oz. can sliced and drained water chestnuts.** Pour into large casserole and top with **3/4 cup sliced almonds.**
Bake at 375° for 20 minutes
Serves 15

SPINACH STUFFED ZUCCHINI   Henriette Rassekh

3 zucchini
1 10 oz. pkg frozen, chopped spinach, cooked and very well drained
2 Tblsp flour
1/2 cup milk
1/3 cup cheddar cheese
4 slices bacon, fried crisp and crumbled

Trim ends from zucchini, cook whole for 10 to 12 minutes in boiling water. Drain, halve lengthwise and scoop out centers. Chop centers and add to drained spinach.
In saucepan, blend flour and milk, add spinach mixture and cook and stir til thickened. Place zucchini halves in shallow baking dish, sprinkle cavities with salt, spoon spinach mixture into shells. Top with cheese and bacon and bake at 350° for 15 to 20 minutes.

TWICE BAKED POTATOES

Bake **8 large Idaho potatoes** til done. Split in half and scoop out hot potato. Mix with:
1 Tblsp salt
1 tsp fresh ground pepper
1 Tblsp minced dried onion
1 pint carton sour cream
1 1/2 sticks butter
3/4 cup grated cheddar cheese

Blend all seasonings with the potatoes until creamy and smooth. Fill the shell halves and top with grated cheddar cheese. Bake at 400° about 15 minutes til hot and sprinkle with paprika.

The average person has Five Senses:
TOUCH • TASTE • SIGHT • SMELL • HEARING
The successful person has Two More:
HORSE & COMMON

Only ROBINSON CRUSOE had everything done by FRIDAY

IT'S TRUE! All things come to those who wait (on themselves)

❖ ❖ ❖ ❖ ❖ ❖ ❖ ❖ ❖

BAKED CAULIFLOWER

Clean and cook **1 whole head of cauliflower** in a kettle of boiling salted water for about 20 minutes. Drain and put in baking dish. Add in a sauce pan

2 Tblsp butter	**1/2 tsp salt**
2 Tblsp flour	**1/4 tsp pepper**
1 cup milk	

Stir til smooth and thick. Then add
1/2 cup green onions, chopped
2 Tblsp pimento, chopped
Pour over cauliflower and sprinkle with buttered bread crumbs and a little grated cheese. Bake at 375° for 20 minutes til slightly browned.

SPINACH-MUSHROOM
A quick vegetable that even children like

2 pkg. frozen chopped spinach
follow directions on package and press out all water from spinach so that it is almost dry.
Add **1 can Cream of Mushroom soup, undiluted**
Stir together over high heat until hot.

ZUCCHINI WITH SHRIMPS
Jane T. Peters

8 small zucchini
4 med. tomatoes, peeled, seeded and chopped
2 Tblsp butter
1 shallot/scallion, finely chopped
1 tsp paprika, salt, pepper
1/2 lb. cooked, peeled small shrimp
2 Tblsp Parmesan cheese

For Mornay Sauce
2 Tblsp butter
2 Tblsp flour
1 1/4 cup milk
1/4 cup Parmesan cheese
1/2 tsp Dijon style mustard

Trim ends of zucchini. Blanch by boiling whole in salted water for 5 minutes. Drain & refresh in cold water. Cut in half lengthwise, scoop out flesh and chop flesh.
Melt butter in sauce pan, add shallot, cook until brown. Add paprika, chopped zucchini flesh, and tomatoes. Season with salt and pepper. Cook 2 - 3 minutes. Stir in shrimp. Arrange zucchini cases in casserole dish and fill them with tomato and shrimp mixture.

For Mornay Sauce:
Melt butter in sauce pan, stir in flour and when foaming, remove from heat and stir in milk. Bring to boil stirring until sauce thickens. Simmer 2 - 3 minutes. Take from heat, stir in cheese and mustard. Spoon Mornay sauce over zucchini, sprinkle with cheese & bake at 425° for 10 minutes or until brown.

PEPPY LIMA BEANS

Fold **1/4 cup pickle relish** into
2 1/2 cups hot cooked lima beans with
1 Tblsp melted butter and a **dash of salt**
Adds real zest to a good vegetable

Alex in the patch waiting for the GREAT PUMPKIN

FAMOUS CORN CASSEROLE — Jerry Peters

This was generally served with Canadian Bacon accompanied with rings of fried pineapple, broccoli with hollandaise sauce, tomato aspic ring salad, sweet rolls and hot fudge sundae. I always said "yes" when Jerry asked us to come to dinner!

2 cans (2 pounds) of white shoe peg corn, drained
1/2 cup sugar   **4 eggs**
1 tsp salt   **2 cups whole milk**
1/2 tsp baking powder **2 Tblsp flour**
1/2 tsp white pepper   **2 Tblsp melted butter**
1/4 tsp nutmeg, fresh ground

Beat eggs and milk and add corn, flour and seasonings. Place in buttered casserole, set in pan of boiling water and bake at 300° for 1 hour & 20 minutes.

❖ ❖ ❖ ❖ ❖ ❖ ❖ ❖ ❖

COLD GREEN BEANS   Alice Mendenhall

Though the Mendenhalls shift domiciles as the Seasons fluctuate, you can count on finding them either at Okoboji or Fort Myers Beach. In either case, when the door swings open, there is just one wonderful welcome waiting on the other side. They are the ones who invented Picnicking on the Lake, - drifting along in a boat in a state of bliss.

1 can green beans
1 cup or 8 oz. of commercial sour cream
2 Tblsp finely chopped onion
3 Tblsp Miracle Whip Salad Dressing
Salt and Pepper

Mix and CHILL at least 3 hours.

EGG PLANT PARMIGIANA   Jane T. Peters

2 Tblsp olive oil
1/2 cup onion
1 crushed clove garlic
1/2 lb. ground chuck
1 can (2 lb) tomatoes
16 oz. can tomato paste
2 tsp dried oregano
1 tsp dried basil
1/4 tsp pepper

1 Tblsp brown sugar
1 large egg plant
2 eggs, slightly beaten
1/2 cup flour
1 1/4 cup Parmesan cheese
1/3 cup olive oil
1 - 8 oz. pkg Mozzarella cheese
1 1/2 tsp salt

In 2 tablespoons of oil sauté onion, garlic & ground chuck. Add tomatoes, paste, oregano, basil, salt, pepper and sugar. Bring to boil. Reduce heat and simmer. Grease 13 x 9 x 2 inch baking dish. Cut unpeeled eggplant into slices, 1/2 inch thick. In pie plate, combine eggs and 1 tablespoon water. On wax paper combine flour with 1 1/2 cup Parmesan cheese. Dip eggplant into egg mixture and then into flour mixture.
In 1 tablespoon hot oil saute eggplant until crisp. Drain on paper towel. Arrange 1/2 of slices in bottom of prepared dish. Sprinkle with Parmesan cheese. Top with 1/2 Mozzarella cheese. Cover with 1/2 tomato/meat sauce. Repeat.
Bake uncovered 25 minutes at 350°.

MINTED CARROTS _____Ninette Beaver

1 pound carrots, sliced	**pepper**
1/2 cup chicken broth	**2 Tblsp white sugar**
1/2 tsp salt	**1 Tblsp brown sugar**
1/3 cup butter	**6 sprigs of fresh mint, chopped**

Cook carrots covered in chicken broth until tender. Add butter, salt, pepper, brown and white sugar and cook carrots until liquid is almost gone. Sprinkle with chopped mint leaves.

❖ ❖ ❖ ❖ ❖ ❖ ❖ ❖ ❖

VITAMINS

Vitamins are not organic substances contained in food. They do not provide energy, nor do they serve as building material the way proteins do. They are necessary, however, to keep the body's metabolic "equation" balanced. Some vitamins are produced in the body, but we must acquire the major portion from the foods we eat. Essential vitamins and their sources are listed below.

VITAMIN A
Helps resist nose and throat infections (colds). Helps prevent night blindness and other eye diseases. Promotes normal growth.

Apricots (fresh and dried), butter or margarine, cream, egg yolk, liver, milk (whole evaporated), yellow and leafy green vegetables (carrots, beet greens, spinach, sweet potatoes, etc.) whole milk, cheese.

VITAMIN B1 (Thiamin)
Necessary for functioning of nerve tissues. Proper utilization of carbohydrates, fats. Promotes normal growth. Stimulates appetite and good muscle tone.

Brewers' yeast, chicken, dried beans, dried peas, fish, lean meats, lentils, milk (whole, skim, evaporated, nonfat dry), peanuts, variety meats (liver, kidneys, sweetbreads), wheat germ, whole-grain or enriched breads, cereals and flours.

VITAMIN B2 (Riboflavin)
Necessary for healthy skin and hair, good digestion, sound nerves. Increases resistance to infection, general weakness, and some eye conditions.

Brewers' yeast, chicken, dried peas, eggs, fish, green and leafy vegetables (turnip greens, beet greens, kale, green limas, collards, mustard greens, etc.), kidney, lean meats, liver, milk (whole, skim, evaporated, nonfat dry), wheat germ.

VITAMIN C (Ascorbic Acid)
Prevents and cures scurvy. Increases strength of capillary walls, lessening the possibility of hemorrhages. Increases resistance to infection. Necessary for sound teeth and gums.

Cantaloupe, citrus fruits (oranges, grapefruit, lemons, tangerines), green and leafy vegetables (green peppers, mustard greens, brussels sprouts, kale, parsley, etc.), pineapple, potatoes, raw cabbage, strawberries, tomatoes.

VITAMIN D
Aids in utilizing calcium and phosphorus in building bones, teeth. Prevents rickets in children.

Egg yolk, fresh and canned oily fish, liver, sunshine action, vitamin-D-enriched cereals, vitamin-D-enriched milk and evaporated milk.

NIACIN
Factor in cure and prevention of pellagra. Helps maintain a healthy skin condition.

Brewers' yeast, fish, green and leafy vegetables (green beans, broccoli, kale, cabbage, etc.) green peas, heart, kidney, lean meat, liver, milk (whole, skim, evaporated, nonfat dry), wheat germ, whole grain or enriched breads, cereals, and flours.

IRON
Necessary to formation of red blood corpuscles, which carry oxygen in blood. Aids in tissue reparation. Prevents nutritional anemia.

Dried apricots, egg yolk, green and leafy vegetables (green beans, broccoli, kale, cabbage, etc.), liver, molasses, oysters, potatoes, whole-grain or enriched breads, cereals, flours.

CALCIUM*
Builds strong bones and teeth. Necessary for lactation; coagulation of blood; heart, nerve, muscle functions. Helps maintain alkalinity of the blood.

Cheese, cream, green leafy vegetables (green beans, broccoli, kale, cabbage, etc.), milk (whole, skim, evaporated, nonfat dry), sardines.

PHOSPHOROUS*
Builds bones and teeth. Necessary for utilization of fats and carbohydrates by the body.

Brewers' yeast, cereals, cheese, eggs, fish, green and leafy vegetables (green beans, broccoli, kale, cabbage, etc.), liver, meats, milk (whole, skim, evaporated, nonfat dry), shellfish, wheat germ.

* The correct functioning of both calcium & phosphorus depends on sufficient amount & proper proportion of both, as well as vitamin D.